MW01119803

The Pleasure and Pain of
Cult Horror Films

The Pleasure and Pain of Cult Horror Films

An Historical Survey

Bartłomiej Paszylk

McFarland & Company, Inc., Publishers
Jefferson, North Carolina, and London

LIBRARY OF CONGRESS CATALOGUING-IN-PUBLICATION DATA

Paszylk, Bartłomiej, 1975–
The pleasure and pain of cult horror films :
an historical survey / Bartłomiej Paszylk.
p.   cm.
Includes bibliographical references and index.

ISBN 978-0-7864-3695-8
illustrated case binding: 50# alkaline paper ∞

1. Horror films — History and criticism.   I. Title
PN1995.9.H6P33   2009
791.43'6164 — dc22   2009000734

British Library cataloguing data are available

On the cover: Poster art for the 1973 film *Flesh for Frankenstein*,
a.k.a. *Andy Warhol's Frankenstein* (Bryanston Distributing
Company/Photofest)

Manufactured in the United States of America

McFarland & Company, Inc., Publishers
Box 611, Jefferson, North Carolina 28640
www.mcfarlandpub.com

Contents

PART III: TO SCARE THE WORLD

PART IV: THE NASTY EIGHTIES

PART V: THE NEW WEIRDNESS

Introduction

"Ah, believe me, you don't want to watch this — it's *too weird*!" Whenever we hear something like that, we become intrigued rather than discouraged from seeing the film in question. What's so weird about it? Can a movie even *be* too weird? And who is this guy to be telling me what I'd rather not watch? That's the appeal of cult films, too: They're all, in a way, too weird for the general public and therefore temptingly forbidden and challenging.

Definitions of a cult movie may vary from book to book as far as certain details are concerned, but some of its features are inarguable. For one, they cannot be a part of mainstream cinema. According to the editors of *Defining Cult Movies*, a cult film "is not defined according to some single, unifying feature shared by all cult movies," but rather through "a 'subcultural ideology'" that marks it as "existing in opposition to the 'mainstream,'" where "mainstream" is an "amalgam of corporate power, lower-middle-class conformity and prudishness, academic elitism and political conspiracy." A definition presented in J. Hoberman and Jonathan Rosenbaum's *Midnight Movies* completes the above view: "A cult film is a movie that has developed a following outside of the mainstream of popular films. The plots usually require a sustained suspension of disbelief. These films contain a sense of irrationality and nonconformity." And then there's this enticing warning mentioned at the beginning: "It's too weird for you." Aaron Hillis, Michelle Orange, Matt Singer, R. Emmet Sweeney and Alison Willmore, the authors of *Gagging on the Kool-Aid: Cult Films We Just Don't Get*, describe cult films as being produced "outside the Hollywood studio system and catered to an audience not satisfied with the tame product of said system." But however thrilling these movies are for a particular group of people, "they're confusing, even frustrating, on the outside looking in." In effect, cult films attract us because most viewers rejected them: "'*They* don't get it,' the cultist says, 'but *I* do.'"

James Morrison explains in his book *Passport to Hollywood: Hollywood Films, European Directors* the ways in which cult films isolate themselves from wide audiences. "A 'cult' film is one that divides its audiences in terms of the kinds of pleasures it affords them," he writes. "Refusing to produce the usual cinematic pleasure of mastery, the 'cult' film typically excludes viewers whose responses are limited to that pleasure, 'punishing' those viewers for such limitation by reveling in its own vulgarity or badness, or by systematically refusing the imperatives of classical narration, denying narrative cli-

maxes, or heightening them to such a frantic degree that they cease to function as climaxes or closing with an anti–'happy ending.' The target viewer of the 'cult film' is
one who delights in such punishment, surrenders the typical cinematic pleasures in favor
of a kind of ecstatic, knowing *un*pleasure, discovers the novel pleasures occulted in the
film, or identifies with the film's sadistic relation to the mass audience."

Umberto Eco, in his essay "*Casablanca*: Cult movies and intertextual collage,"
writes that "in order to transform a work into a cult object one must be able to break,
dislocate, unhinge it so that one can remember only parts of it, irrespective of their
original relationship with the whole. In the case of a book one can unhinge it, so to
speak, physically, reducing it to a series of excerpts. A movie, on the contrary, must be
already ramshackle, rickety, unhinged in itself. It should display not one central idea
but many. It should not reveal a coherent philosophy of composition. It must live on,
and because of, its glorious ricketiness." Eco also values the use of stereotypes and
banality in cult films: "Two clichés make us laugh," he writes, "but a hundred clichés
move us because we sense dimly that the clichés are talking among themselves, celebrating a reunion. Just as the extreme of pain meets sensual pleasure, and the extreme
of perversion borders on mystical energy, so too the extreme of Banality allows us to
catch a glimpse of the Sublime."

One final addition to the above definitions comes from Bruce Austin's *Immediate
Seating: A Look at Movie Audiences*— and it's essential in understanding the whole phenomenon. "Cult films are not *made* as much as they *happen* or *become*," writes Austin,
who further explains that "it is the audience that turns a film into a cult film"— not
the filmmakers.

Considering all this, it's easy to see that the term "cult film"— and in consequence
also "cult horror"— is very often abused, by fans, reviewers and film historians alike.
Movies like *The Exorcist*, *Jaws* and even recent box office hits like *The Ring* are often
thoughtlessly labeled as "cult favorites" or worse yet, "cult classics." *The Exorcist* and
Jaws are no doubt genre classics that have influenced many horror directors and reshaped
the horror niche; *The Ring*, on the other hand, is an effective version of a story that
had already been told, and is largely responsible for the trend of remaking successful
Asian films. None of the three movies can be called cult, though, because they are all
readily available. Even viewers not particularly interested in the horror genre are usually familiar with them, while the word "cult" implies a movie that does not belong to
the mainstream and is not an easily recognizable genre icon. (*Jaws* and *The Ring* were
made to become crowd-pleasers, so it's impossible to argue they don't belong to the
mainstream, while *The Exorcist* is one of the most popular horror icons.) Cult is, in a
way, a genre within a genre: The viewer is first introduced to a certain type of movie
by watching the most popular examples of these, and then gradually discovers gems
that hold much value despite being infinitely less known than the genre icons. Horror
movie neophytes usually start with films like *The Exorcist* (or *Friday the 13th*, *A Nightmare on Elm Street*, *Carrie* and so on) and then, as they become familiar with the genre,
move to more obscure, genuinely cult titles like *Freaks*, *I Bury the Living*, *At Midnight
I'll Take Your Soul*, *Dr. Terror's House of Horrors*, *The House with Laughing Windows*
and *I Spit on Your Grave*.

Films that owe their success to good advertising and that were put together by big studios don't tend to become cult movies. However, it may happen that, as the years pass by, a movie that once enjoyed box office success changes its status to that of a cult movie; it ceases to be fashionable and is no longer heavily advertised, but it is still remembered by a narrow group of fans who recognize it for its true values. This is what happened to several films described in this book. For example, *The Body Snatcher* and *House of Wax* were quite popular in, respectively, the 1940s and 1950s; the popularity of *The Body Snatcher* was due to the pairing of Boris Karloff and Bela Lugosi, and to the aura of controversy surrounding the movie, while the main reason for the success of *House of Wax* was the 3-D gimmick — a pioneering technique at the time (Vincent Price, who played the main role in the movie, wasn't yet a star back then). Today, however, these two movies are unknown to large audiences; most moviegoers only recognize Karloff for his most iconic roles in *Frankenstein* and *The Mummy*, and when confronted with the title *House of Wax* they tend to think of the 2005 remake starring Paris Hilton. But both *The Body Snatcher* and the original *House of Wax* are still cherished by genre devotees.

This book presents a selection of cult horror movies in chronological order, so as to emphasize certain trends within the genre and help perceive them as interconnected with socio-historical background throughout the decades. Starting with silent films influenced by German Expressionism, we'll move on to so-called haunted house spoofs, Gothic cinema, different takes on famous monsters, mad scientist movies, Poverty Row cheapies, Hammer horrors, video nasties, *gialli*, slashers, gore comedies and modern arthouse shockers. We'll take a look at cult films made in the United States, Canada, Australia, New Zealand, Brazil, Japan, Great Britain, France, Belgium, Luxembourg, Denmark, Sweden, Iceland, Italy, Spain, Germany, Austria, Poland, Czechoslovakia (as well as the Czech Republic and Slovakia) and the Soviet Union (as well as Russia). We'll examine the wonderfully offbeat, non-mainstream films made by the now-famous directors at the outset of their careers — for example, Roman Polanski's *The Fearless Vampire Killers*, Oliver Stone's *Seizure*, David Cronenberg's *Shivers* and Peter Jackson's *Bad Taste*. And since some directors made almost nothing but cult movies throughout their careers (please look at the lengthy list of movies by Herschell Gordon Lewis or Jean Rollin), there were choices to be made as to which of these works should be included in the book; in some cases I opted for the more obscure titles, provided they were good enough and actually had a cult following (hence, for instance, I included Lucio Fulci's *A Lizard in a Woman's Skin* and had to leave out his more famous *Zombi 2* and *The Beyond*).

Cult horror makes for a whole new dimension of cinematic experience and I can only hope that this book will be an invitation to it, as well as a guide to its most memorable, boldest and weirdest representatives. The world of oversized insects, corpse-stealing men, reptilian women, laughing windows and murderous alien clowns is now opening wide — just for you.

PART I:
THE ROOT OF ALL HORROR

The Phantom Carriage (Körkarlen)

aka *The Phantom Chariot; The Stroke of Midnight*
DIRECTOR: Victor Sjöström
CAST: Victor Sjöström, Hilda Borgström, Astrid Holm, Tore Svennberg,
Lisa Lundholm, Concordia Selander, Tor Weijden
Sweden, 1921.

The question of when and where the horror genre was brought to life has been, and will perhaps always be, a subject of many heated debates. Some film historians like to look for it near the end of the 19th century, in the early works of Georges Méliès (whose 1896 shorts *Une Nuit Terrible* and *Le Manoir du Diable* showed, respectively, a man being attacked by a giant spider, and a bat metamorphosing into Mephistopheles); some are quite certain that it was Stellan Rye and Paul Wegener's *The Student of Prague* (1913) that brought all the necessary elements together; others claim that proper horrors weren't brought to the screen until after World War I, when they were disguised as masterpieces of German Expressionism (for example, 1920's *The Cabinet of Dr. Caligari* and 1922's *Nosferatu*); and yet others argue that no movie before 1931's *Dracula* can really be labeled a genuine horror movie. All the aforementioned films were, however, highly inspiring for the future directors, and helped shape the genre as we know it today. Next to these early works that have been long time ago recognized as groundbreaking and influential, there are still some very important but underappreciated titles. Victor Sjöström's *The Phantom Carriage*, an atmospheric depiction of the Grim Reaper's burden, is certainly one of these.

Sjöström himself plays unlikable drunkard David Holm, who treats his two drunkard friends to a ghastly story. His friend, he says, used to believe that whoever dies at the stroke of midnight on New Year's Eve, will be cursed to drive "the Phantom Carriage" and collect the souls of the dead throughout the following twelve months; as bad luck would have it, the superstitious man passed away the previous year, exactly at the dreaded hour. Holm doesn't think there's any truth to the legend of the Carriage, but he savors the cruel irony of the situation. His attitude changes only after he has to deal with the irony of fate himself: not long after having told the grim anecdote, the man is accidentally killed — at the stroke of midnight on New Year's Eve, no less — and his dead friend promptly approaches him and offers him the reins of the Phantom Carriage. Suddenly, as he sees his own lifeless body lying on the ground, Holm decides that he wants to live again, and promises that this time he will live a decent life, and will try and make amends for all the things he did wrong. The dead Carriage driver refuses to help him, and Holm panics, as fragments of his past deeds come back to haunt him in chaotic flashbacks. We see how monstrous he was towards his wife, how careless he was about his children and how ungrateful towards a beautiful nurse who tried to help him on a number of occasions. Among the flashbacks are also interwoven pieces of information on the present state of Holm's wife (who's now suicidal) and the kind-hearted nurse (who's now on her deathbed), which constitutes a very complex and demanding structure for the early 1920s, but also mirrors the state of mind of a person who desperately tries to put his or her whole life in order just when it is announced to be over.

The realistic parts of the movie — that is, the scenes that precede Holm's death as well as the past events revealed via flashbacks — are compelling because of Sjöström's directorial talent for creating passages that are not overly exaggerated for effect (for the standards of the silent cinema, at least), but aim to imitate life. Also, Sjöström's convincingly menacing role gives the movie an edge and an aura of authenticity. The fantastic parts, on the other hand, are impressive because of cinematographer Julius Jaenzon's masterful handling of the trick photography. Double exposure, also referred to as "spirit photography" because it involves superimposition of images, so that one of them looks "ghostly," had already been used in cinema before 1921 (it was pioneered by George Albert Smith as early as in 1898's *The Corsican Brothers*), but never to quite such an extent, or with similar skillfulness, as in *The Phantom Carriage*. Sjöström's movie literally depended on the trick; after all, double exposure was used whenever the two dead men or their carriage appeared on screen. Even from today's point of view, Jaenzon's job is nothing short of stunning, with the "real" and "ghostly" images always matched perfectly, and always in convincing interaction, so that the viewers can actually feel as if they were caught in another dimension, somewhere in between two worlds — that of humans and that of spirits.

A year before *The Phantom Carriage* was released, Sjöström directed another film that might be of interest to fans of horror, 1920's powerful gothic tale *The Monastery of Sendomir*; it was, however, Sjöström's inventive tale of life, death and redemption that attracted the attention of film lovers from all over the world. This soon brought about Sjöström's emigration to the United States where, under the Americanized name of Victor Seastrom, he made several less structurally complex, but nevertheless impressive pictures; the most important of these were the Lon Chaney drama *He Who Gets Slapped* (1924), *The Scarlet Letter* (1926), and the unforgettable study of madness *The Wind* (1928), the latter two starring Lillian Gish. When the era of silent movies ended, Sjöström briefly tried his hand at talkies, but didn't manage to equal his masterpieces and his career as a director came to a halt with the swashbuckling adventure movie *Under the Red Robe* (1937), with Conrad Veidt in the leading role. Sjöström didn't quit acting, though, and from the 1930s to the late 1950s appeared in many Swedish films. Ingmar Bergman's *Wild Strawberries* (1957) gave him his last and greatest role, and was also a tribute to *The Phantom Carriage* (it deals with the familiar themes of mortality, loneliness, emotional coldness and forgiveness; and here, just like in the movie he directed over three decades earlier, Sjöström plays a man who refuses to evaluate his life until the nightmarish moment when he comes face to face with his own corpse).

The Phantom Carriage is a rare example proving that in the early years of cinema, German filmmakers weren't the only ones who could handle dark themes masterfully. The movie has now inspired several generations of artists, genre and otherwise (most notably, Ingmar Bergman), and allowed director Victor Sjöström with cinematographer Julius Jaenzon to perfect the "spirit photography" to a striking effect.

Between Two Worlds
(Der Müde Tod)

aka *Destiny; The Weary Death*
DIRECTOR: Fritz Lang
CAST: Lil Dagover, Bernhard Goetzke, Walter Janssen, Rudolf Klein-Rogge,
Hans Sternberg, Erich Pabst
Germany, 1921

After Victor Sjöström perfected the trick of double exposure in *The Phantom Carriage*, it continued to be used by other directors who wanted to conjure up worlds beyond our own, ones inhabited by ghosts and demons. An early Fritz Lang film, and his first widely recognized success, *Between Two Worlds* is an exquisite example of an exhilarating cinematic experience that ended up inspiring future filmmakers, Luis Buñuel, Douglas Fairbanks, Alfred Hitchcock and Dario Argento among them. It also drew inspiration from past works (the effective use of double exposure is one thing; another is the movie's episodical structure — an echo of D.W. Griffith's *Intolerance*, parts of which were set in different times and places).

The opening scenes of *Between Two Worlds* are as spine-chilling as anything seen in cinema by that time. A young couple (Lil Dagover and Walter Janssen) set out to celebrate their honeymoon in a peaceful hamlet, but their cheerfulness and optimism are dispelled when a pale, black-clad man (Bernard Goetzke) first hops their coach and later insists on sitting at their table at the inn. When the stranger no longer resorts to just casting serious, deathly looks at the newlyweds, but also performs a trick of turning a chalice of wine into an ominous hourglass, it becomes clear that either the young man or the girl is doomed to die. Therefore, when in the morning the girl wakes up and her husband is nowhere around, she realizes that the only chance to get him back is to visit the uninviting, walled house of the grim stranger who, rather obviously by then, appears to be Death impersonated. Fortunately for the girl, Death is tired enough of its monotonous and unrewarding profession that it/he agrees to gamble with her for the life of the husband: she is given three chances to save people destined to die, and if she succeeds at least once, her loved one will be returned to her. The girl then travels to Ancient Persia, 17th century Venice and Imperial China to see whether love actually is, as the Bible says, stronger than death.

The wraparound story is consistently dark and serious, but Lang isn't afraid to cheer the atmosphere up in the three episodes that constitute the main portion of the movie. The part set in China is an all-out comedy, in which even special effects are employed for humorous effect (though the scene where one of the characters is transformed into a cactus with human features is at the same time funny and quite gruesome). This is perhaps why *Between Two Worlds* has never been as lauded by genre fans as *The Cabinet of Dr. Caligari* (1920) or *Nosferatu* (1922), which may have included minor comedic elements, but always kept them in check, so that the worlds they depicted never brightened too much. Then again, when Lang returns to the somber mood in the last reel, he does so with the touch of a genuine horror director, and is greatly helped by Goetzke, who gives here one of the best cinematic portrayals of Death — and he doesn't need tones of makeup to make it work. Even though a large portion of the movie's running time is focused on adventure and comedy, there is still room for a handful of scary moments: the first meeting with Death on the road to the hamlet; the aforementioned hourglass prophecy of death; a queue of spirits passing through the wall to where Death dwells; human lives being represented by numerous candles of various lengths that can be blown out at any moment; the death of a newborn child when one of the candles does get blown out; Dagover's character being chased by a flying horse; and the suspenseful climax in a burning house.

In the end, *Between Two Worlds* emerges as much more than yet another movie about the inevitability of death, a subject that filmmakers from the post–World War I Germany were obsessed with. From the technical point of view, it was a template for many future works of German Expressionism, while plot-wise it was, surprisingly, more like an appraisal of life than an ode to death. There is a telling scene near the end of the movie, in which several characters complain about their lives and admit that they would love to die as soon as possible, but when such an opportunity arises, they all suddenly panic and choose to hold on to the existence they so ostensibly despise.

"All through his life, Lang adjusted his talent to meet the changes in his environment, and in so doing produced a body of creative work of unquestionable importance in the development of the history of cinema," wrote Charles L.P. Silet, suggesting that Lang's works should be analyzed as a whole, without being divided into the "early German period" and the "mature American period" (an approach also preferred by Robin Wood). And indeed, all movies made by Lang display some common themes and features, and prove that he was constantly improving as a director, even though he didn't always work under perfect conditions. After *Between Two Worlds*, Lang never helmed a project with so many horror elements, but some of his subsequent films dealt with very dark themes, for example *Dr. Mabuse* (1922), *Siegfried* (1923), *Kriemhild's Revenge* (1924), *The Niebelungen* (1924), *M* (1931), and *The Testament of Dr. Mabuse* (1932). The groundbreaking sci-fi epic *Metropolis* (1927) was to become the director's most famous movie and even led to Goebbels offering Lang the position of the Third Reich's appointed filmmaker; the proposal was promptly rejected and Lang soon left Germany, first for France and then for the United States, where he continued to make powerful and poignant films (like 1936's *Fury*, 1942's openly anti–Nazist *Hangmen Also Die!*, 1944's *Ministry of Fear*, 1956's *Beyond a Reasonable Doubt*, and classy remakes of works by Jean Renoir: 1945's *Scarlet Street* and 1954's *Human Desire*). In 1958 Lang returned to Germany to make *The Thousand Eyes of Dr. Mabuse* (1960), his last movie and a great finale for the character he brought to life in 1922.

Today overshadowed by Fritz Lang's later masterpieces and largely undervalued, *Between Two Worlds* is a highly inventive and influential piece of work that gives Death one of the most intriguing cinematic faces ever.

Witchcraft Through the Ages (Häxan)

DIRECTOR: Benjamin Christensen
CAST: Maren Pedersen, Clara Pontoppidan, Elith Pio, Oscar Stribolt, John
Andersen, Benjamin Christensen, Tora Teje
Denmark-Sweden, 1922

Benjamin Christensen's *Witchcraft Through the Ages* is perhaps the most striking example of a movie ahead of its time. Even from today's point of view, the themes it deals with
seem bold, its tone is quite unique (there are even some clever and very funny metatex-
tual passages to be found), and the wicked makeup effects are amazing for the times.

It didn't all come about smoothly, though. In 1919 Christensen, who by that time
had done some work as an actor and directed two movies (the thriller *The Mysterious
X* in 1914 and the drama *Night of Revenge* in 1916), was asked by a Swedish film company to helm a documentary on witchcraft. He eagerly agreed to do it, but probably
didn't realize what a challenging and time-consuming task it would eventually become.
It took Christensen about two years to do the necessary research, and the movie wasn't
released until September 1922; three years in the making was definitely much more
than the studio had expected for a simple "educational project." And it wouldn't be
that much of a problem had Christensen's movie at least met the company's expecta-

Maren Pederson (left) and Elith Pio in Benjamin Christensen's funny and shocking *Witchcraft Through the Ages* (1922).

tions as far as its content was concerned; it turned out, however, that the painstakingly researched and carefully put-together piece of work was completely inappropriate. It featured nudity, infanticide, mutilation, urination, tortures, masochism, sacrilege and — most shockingly, according to some — one scene showing witches passionately kissing the Devil's bottom. Also, and this must have been especially puzzling for the studio that ordered the movie, it seemed to be mocking the stiff documentary format it was supposed to fit (even though it was to be one of the first full-length documentaries in the history of cinema, as Robert Flaherty's pioneering *Nanook of the North* was released the same year).

This not-quite-serious approach towards the grim themes is visible from the beginning of the movie — it's just that at first it is hard to believe that such a tone was Christensen's intention. *Witchcraft Through the Ages* is divided into seven parts, and the first ones are almost like academic lectures, complete with a shaky little pointer directing our eyes to certain details in various drawings or models representing early beliefs concerning witchcraft, satanism and sorcery. Relying a bit too much on lengthy intertitles, these introductory bits later give way to a full-blown spectacle (as some of the witches' customs and wrongdoings are being "reconstructed" onscreen), and yet later to the deconstruction of the documentary format (clearly interested in exploring the subject of witchcraft as deeply as possible, Christensen occasionally interrogates — or even tortures!— his actresses), and in the end, to comparing witch hunts and "modern-day" medicine. There is a sketchy plot here (of an old woman accused of witchcraft by a superstitious girl, which then leads to the girl and her family being put on trial as well), but generally *Witchcraft Through the Ages* is exactly what the title suggests: a collection of funny, funereal or fantastic scenes depicting various paradoxes and phenomena of witchcraft. At one point, for example, we learn that this superstition-ridden period of time was very tough for women who were "old and ugly" — but that they weren't any bit kinder for those who were "young and beautiful," either.

Typically for a movie ahead of its time, *Witchcraft Through the Ages* failed at the box office on its original release. The controversial content aside, it was also very difficult to classify, and therefore baffling for both the viewers who wanted to see a documentary and those who expected a "real" movie, with clear storyline and characters at no point revealing that they are actors. Critic James Kendrick writes in an essay "A Witches' Brew of Fact, Fiction and Spectacle" that Christensen's movie "is, in many ways, the cinematic epitome of Freud's uncanny: we recognize elements of it as belonging to known and familiar categories, yet its overall formulation is bizarre and frustrating. To call it a horror film, a documentary, a horror-documentary or even a midnight movie is an easy way out, blithely falling back on the use of dominant genre categories to encapsulate a film that is all and none." Today's viewers and critics regard this as an asset, but for the unsuspecting 1920s audiences, this was no doubt too confusing. The only portion of the movie often criticized by modern film historians is the final, allegedly misogynistic explanation of witchery as female neurosis; Kendrick writes elsewhere in the essay that some parts of *Witchcraft* "feel overly pedantic, particularly when it moves into a then-revolutionary explanation of medieval witch scares through the lens of Sigmund Freud's theories about female hysteria." But can we really say for sure that Christensen was being serious in that closing chapter of his movie, and not ironic like in all the preceding ones? After all, the scene of a woman being examined by a Freud-influenced doctor is staged similarly as the earlier one, in which the state of one character was determined by pouring molten lead into water and "reading" the resulting shape.

Allegedly, Christensen's original idea was to make a trilogy of movies dealing with superstitions, *Witchcraft Through the Ages* being the first installment. Unfortunately, the other two movies — *The Saint* and *The Spirits* — were never made, which doesn't come as much of a surprise considering the many problems and controversies surrounding film number one. In the mid–1920s, like many other talented European directors, Christensen moved to the United States where he kept on making movies until the end of the silent era. Some of his works from this period are now lost, but out of the ones that survived, the most interesting are *Mockery* (1927, starring Lon Chaney) and the wicked, energetic *Seven Footprints to Satan* (1929), the closest reminder of *Witchcraft Through the Ages* in the director's subsequent filmography. Upon his return to Denmark in the 1930s, Christensen focused on working in the theater and didn't make another film until the end of the decade (1939's social drama *Children of Divorce*). He directed three more movies that met with mixed reviews, which prompted him to quit the filmmaking business in 1942. A year before that, however, he managed to re-release *Witchcraft Through the Ages* with an added prologue (which was, essentially, yet another lecture on the history of witchcraft).

Christensen died in 1959, and couldn't witness the second resurrection of *Witchcraft Through the Ages* during the following decade. In 1968 the movie resurfaced in a trimmed version (76 minutes instead of the original's 104), with narration by beat icon William S. Burroughs and jazz score by Jean-Luc Ponty. This new edition prepared by British distributor Antony Balch could hardly be regarded as superior to the lengthier cut, but it introduced the movie to a new generation, and established its reputation as a cult classic that cannot get old.

It may rely too heavily on the intertitles and be a bit too long, but the general impression after having watched *Witchcraft Through the Ages* is that of awe and shock that such a bold, clever and ironic movie could have been made back in the early days of cinema. Some of the special effects and makeup are also quite mind-blowing, with the creation of the wicked, towering Devil (played by the director himself) being a highlight.

The Phantom of the Opera

DIRECTOR: Rupert Julian
CAST: Lon Chaney, Mary Philbin, Norman Kerry, Gibson Gowland,
Arthur Edmund Carewe, John St. Polis
USA, 1925

American filmmakers first took to horror themes via numerous adaptations of Robert Louis Stevenson's novel *The Strange Case of Dr. Jekyll and Mr. Hyde* — starting with Otis Turner's 16-minute movie made in 1908, followed by many other short films based on the story, and culminating with John S. Robertson's effective feature-length version from 1920, with John Barrymore playing the two characters of the title. Other popular works from this early period were J. Searle Dawley's short *Frankenstein* (1910) with James Ogle as the Monster, D.W. Griffith's adaptation of several Edgar Allan Poe texts called *The Avenging Conscience: or "Thou Shall Not Kill"* (1914), several takes on Oscar Wilde's *The Picture of Dorian Gray*, and Wallace Worsley's *The Hunchback of Notre*

Lon Chaney's monster unmasked in *The Phantom of the Opera* (1925).

Dame (1923), starring Lon Chaney in the title role. But it wasn't until 1925 and Rupert Julian's *The Phantom of the Opera* that America's first iconic monster was brought to life: it was another nightmarish creation of Chaney, and its figure of a caped ghoul with a skull-face and crooked teeth was to become an imprint for many horror movies to come.

The Phantom of the Opera was a relatively faithful adaptation of Gaston Leroux's novel, a Gothic romance influenced by the works of Jules Verne, Edgar Allan Poe, and — most notably — George Du Maurier's *Trilby* (a story of a poor girl transformed into a diva by a hypnotist named Svengali). In Julian's movie, grotesquely disfigured Erik (Chaney) lives in the chambers beneath the Paris Opera House, and tries to persuade the owners of the Opera that young and talented Christine Daae (Mary Philbin) should replace the current main singer during the upcoming performance. This works for a while and the Phantom's protégé gets a standing ovation for her debut as a prima donna, but when the previous singer later returns to reclaim her part, Erik interrupts the show by bringing down a huge chandelier onto the audience, and then abducts Christine to his underground lair. The girl, so far fascinated with the mysterious person who wants to boost her career, is petrified when she unmasks him and sees the face of a monster. The only hope of rescue will be Raoul (Norman Kerry), a man whom Christine recently rejected for the sake of professional success, and Inspector Ledoux (Arthur Edmund Carewe), who apparently has been trying to hunt the Phantom down for some time.

On the most obvious level, the movie is a heartbreaking variation on the concept of the Beauty and the Beast, but even more interesting is the way in which the main female character is presented here. Christine not only has her mind set on pursuing the career as an opera singer, but she is also able to bluntly tell Raoul that she doesn't care for him enough to resign her ambitions. Such behavior was much in concordance with the ideals of women's suffrage movement (gaining popularity in the United States since 1920), and perhaps even modern feminists could be proud of Christine for being able to express her needs in such a self-assertive way. Of course, as soon as the girl faces the ugly side to her success (embodied by the Phantom), she realizes she has made a terrible mistake risking everything and everyone she loved in order to achieve her professional goals.

Contrarily, in his book *The Monster Show*, film historian David J. Skal focuses on the post–World War I imagery of Julian's movie — the face of Erik being disfigured in a way reminiscent of war veterans coming home scarred, blinded, or without limbs. "War wasn't mentioned explicitly in *The Phantom of the Opera*," writes Skal, "but since no explanation of any kind was given for the Opera Ghost's hideous appearance, Chaney's skull-like face could pluck at the culture's rawest nerves, unbridled by rationale." It could and it certainly did thanks to the actor's unforgettable performance, and his own ideas for how to make Erik look like death incarnated. Chaney wore makeup so intrusive it would often cause bleeding from the nose. The effect, however, was striking; when during the most suspenseful scene in the movie, Christine reaches for the Phantom's mask and takes it off, the monstrous features are not simply revealed — they literally *come alive*, as Chaney widens his deadman's eyes in surprise and opens the mouth like a shark waiting to be fed. This quick moment — lasting no more than seconds — is one of the most chilling pieces in the history of cinema.

Leroux's novel was no literary masterpiece, but it was engaging and had all the important elements in the right places, so the filmmakers came to love it, and in consequence almost every decade after the first adaptation had its own *Phantom of the Opera.* Arthur Lubin's Technicolor version of the story — made in 1943 for Universal, and starring Claude Rains in the title role — was often criticized at the time of the original release, but from today's point of view it has a lot of old-fashioned charm and makes for an entertaining viewing. Terence Fisher's stylish 1962 take is mainly memorable for Michael Gough's frantic role as Lord Ambrose d'Arcy (although Herbert Lom as the Phantom was good, too), but this Hammer horror remained overshadowed by the company's more groundbreaking works from these years. In 1974 Brian De Palma loosely adapted the novel in his odd horror-comedy-musical *Phantom of the Paradise,* with great turns from William Finley (as the Phantom), Paul Williams and Jessica Harper. Most later versions of the story were rather disappointing — like the ones made by Robert Markowitz (in 1983, with Maximilian Schell and Michael York), Dwight H. Little (1989, starring Robert Englund and Jill Schoelen), Tony Richardson (1990's TV epic, with Burt Lancaster and Teri Polo), and Dario Argento (1998, with Asia Argento and Julian Sands). The latest big-budget adaptation by Joel Schumacher (2004, starring Gerard Butler and Emy Rossum) proved a box office hit, but was in fact a lush version of Andrew Lloyd Weber's stage musical that didn't even try to evoke the atmosphere of the novel or Rupert Julian's film. And even though throughout the years so many Phantoms haunted the opera, none of them managed to be quite as mysterious and scary as the one played by Chaney.

The famous actor himself, with the help of director Tod Browning, gave the audiences many more thrills following *The Phantom of the Opera,* either wearing elaborate makeup or playing freaks of nature. *The Unholy Three* (1925), *The Blackbird* (1926), *The Road to Mandalay* (1926), and the especially macabre *The Unknown* (1927), in which Chaney's character joins a circus pretending he's armless, all play on Freud's fear of castration — and do so in most evocative and shocking ways. Also *London After Midnight* (1927), with Chaney in the role of a fake vampire, appears to have been quite a Freudian nightmare, but sadly the film was lost. (In 1935, Browning remade it with Bela Lugosi as *Mark of the Vampire.*) A man of gestures and masks, Chaney understandably wasn't happy about the end of the silent cinema; he refused to take part in a sound version of *The Phantom of the Opera* (made in 1929), and his only talkie was the new version of *The Unholy Three* (1930). Judging by this effective performance, he could have successfully continued his career as an actor, but soon after making his sound movie debut, throat cancer took first Chaney's voice and then his life. Joseph Pevney's biographical movie *Man of a Thousand Faces* (1957) is an interesting, though not always accurate, account of Chaney's life, with James Cagney in the main role; ironically, though, the makeup effects here are far less impressive than the ones Chaney applied himself over three decades earlier — which is particularly noticeable when Cagney appears in the cumbersome mask of Erik the Phantom.

This atmospheric adaptation of Gaston Leroux's classic novel gave Universal its first iconic monster and highlighted Lon Chaney's talent as an actor and makeup artist. In the mid–1920s, people used to faint during the unmasking scene, and none of the many later movie versions of the story managed to capture this moment better.

Faust (Faust—Eine Deutsche Volkssage)

DIRECTOR: F.W. Murnau

CAST: Gösta Ekman, Emil Jannings, Camilla Horn, Yvette Guilbert, Wilhelm
Dieterle, Frieda Richard, Werner Fuetterer, Eric Barclay, Hanna Ralph
Germany, 1926

Having previously made such masterpieces as *Nosferatu* (1922), *The Last Laugh* (1924)
and *Tartuffe* (1926), director Friedrich Wilhelm Murnau was packing his bags to leave
Germany and start a more financially rewarding career in Hollywood. His last job in his
home country was to be a retelling of a folk legend about Faust, an old doctor who supposedly sold his soul to the devil in order to get back his youth and gain the knowledge
of how to cure people infected with the plague. Murnau was joined by another prominent figure of German cinema, actor Emil Jannings, famous for his roles in Paul Leni's
Waxworks (1924) and the two aforementioned films by Murnau: *The Last Laugh* and
Tartuffe; Jannings was also preparing to move to Hollywood at the time. It was hoped
that Murnau and Jannings' farewell picture would become a worthy competitor to the
already existing takes on the *Faust* legend: the tragedies of Christopher Marlowe and
Johann Wolfgang von Goethe, the opera by Charles Gounod, and the films by Georges
Méliès, the Lumiere Brothers, George Albert Smith, Edwin S. Porter and D.W. Griffith.

"A visual symphony of wind, flames, and smoke, conceived with the artistry that
German film-makers had developed, quite remarkably, amid the chaos and uncertainty
of the years immediately following their country's defeat in World War One," wrote
Peter Spooner of Murnau's *Faust*. The movie indeed was both a visual feast and an anti-
dote to the understandably depressing time in Germany, but it's also interesting to
think of all the things it was supposed to be and never was. Most importantly, it wasn't
another brilliant piece of German Expressionism, something many admirers of the
groundbreaking *Nosferatu* had been expecting. Murnau decided to go back in time and
deliver a work deeply rooted in medievalism, with only occasional touches of the more
modern approach he was famous for. Quite probably, it was a conscious decision of the
director to make the movie more popular with the public, who wanted to be detached
from the present and travel back to a better, purer era. *Faust* was, after all, from the
beginning envisioned as a crowd pleaser; together with Fritz Lang's *Metropolis* (1927),
it was to bring UFA, the company behind it, both money and international fame. While
Lang's movie went on to become a landmark in the history of cinema, *Faust* fell short
of expectations on its original release and apparently wasn't meant to be a "rediscovered classic," either; compared to *Nosferatu* or *Metropolis*, *Faust* still remains underappreciated, and the reasons for it may be two other things the movie was expected to be
and failed: it wasn't a world-famous star vehicle (Lillian Gish was offered the main
female part but she rejected it as soon as she learned that she can't bring an entrusted
American cameraman with her), and it wasn't a deeply philosophical, Goethe-inspired
work. (Ironically, it might have been the pressure to please crowds that drove the
scriptwriter Hans Kyser away from the seriousness of Goethe's take on the legend.)

The movie starts with a curiously cynical wager between the Archangel (Werner
Fuetterer) and Mephisto (Jannings): if Satan manages to capture the soul of an old

Gretchen (Camilla Horn) strikes a zombie pose in F.W. Murnau's *Faust* (1926).

scholar named Faust (Gösta Ekman), then he will be welcome to collect the souls of all other humans. Initially, the mission of Mephisto is surprisingly successful, as the youth *and* knowledge he offers Faust are a package too tempting to refuse, but things become less predictable with the appearance of the young and innocent Gretchen (Camilla Horn). Will Faust use dirty, devilish tricks to seduce the girl or will he choose to let the love bloom naturally, without the involvement of Mephisto? And, yet more importantly, is there any chance of canceling the contract with the devil? Murnau takes his time before answering the questions, and in the meantime provides us with some awe-inspiring horror set pieces (for example, the one with Mephisto, in his winged, beastly form, towering over the town, or another one, with the human-shaped Mephisto, portraying his uncanny reappearances just after he is summoned by Faust). The dark mood is from time to time brightened up by the use of innovative fantasy scenes (Faust and Mephisto's flight over the town and the countryside) and the introduction of pure comedy (courtesy of Jannings and Yvette Guilbert, who plays Gretchen's lovesick aunt).

Those who were expecting another *Nosferatu* were usually disappointed with *Faust* because Murnau wasn't interested in keeping the horror mood throughout the whole movie, while those who wanted another *Tartuffe* must have been put off by *Faust*'s occasional moments of comedic silliness. But if you do not compare Murnau's last German movie to his earlier works, it comes out as gorgeous, bold, sophisticated and innovative. It might have been less visible in the American version of the film that has been in circulation for several decades (it was made of "second best takes" and not as well edited as the original), but now that the German cut is available after being presumed lost, *Faust* again has the power to astonish the horror-loving public with Jannings' bewitching performance, the thoroughly convincing makeup for Faust (those not in the know usually think that young and old Faust were played by two different actors), the chilling imagery, sets and decorations, as well as Carl Hoffmann's clever cinematography. (Hoffmann, in fact, invented a camera dolly after Murnau asked him to think of the best way to show Faust and Mephisto flying.)

Faust was, in many ways, a forewarning picture for both Murnau and Jannings, who have already signed their own contracts with the devil: they were promised more money and exposure to wider audiences but their lives and souls were to be the price. Like Faust himself, however, the two men had some days of glory ahead of them before the ultimate fall. Murnau made four movies in America, of which the most praised were *Sunrise: A Song of Two Humans* (1927, an Academy Award winner for Best Picture — Unique and Artistic Production, Best Cinematography and Best Actress) and *Tabu: A Story of the South Seas* (1931, an Academy Award winner for Best Cinematography), but he didn't even attend the official premiere of the latter as he died in an automobile accident shortly before it. Jannings was a bit luckier than Murnau, as apart from being awarded an Oscar the same year that Murnau was (during the historic, first-ever Academy Awards banquet), he starred in many more movies after *Faust*. But his American career, too, soon came to a halt and then turned sour upon his return to Germany. Jannings' greatest Stateside successes were Victor Fleming's *The Way of All Flesh* (1927) and Josef von Sternberg's *The Last Command* (1928), the two titles that brought him the Oscar. Another collaboration with von Sternberg, *The Blue Angel* (1930, also starring Marlene Dietrich), marked the actor's departure from Hollywood since at the dawn of sound cinema Jannings' thick accent appeared to be a problem: *The Blue Angel* was made in two language versions, English and German, and it's the German one that is now considered a classic. The final Faustian twist to Jannings' biography was yet to come, though, as after his return to Germany the actor decided to devote his skills to the Nazi propaganda, one of his most infamous works being the viciously anti–British *Uncle Kruger* (1941).

A great-looking version of a well-known story, this *Faust* also boasts an unforgettable turn from Emil Jannings in the role of Mephisto and several stunning horror moments. A genre classic in need of being rediscovered and reevaluated, especially now that the original German print has been found.

Vampyr (Vampyr, Der Traum des Allan Grey)

DIRECTOR: Carl Theodor Dreyer
CAST: Julian West, Rena Mandel, Sybille Schmitz, Maurice Schutz,
Jan Hieronimko, Henriette Gérard, Albert Bras
France-Germany, 1932

"This is the story about strange events that happened to the young Allan Gray. His studies into earlier centuries' superstitious ideas on devil-worship and on the activities of Vampyrs have transformed him into a dreamer and fanatic for whom the border between what is reality and what is fantasy has become blurred." This introduction to the plot of Carl Theodor Dreyer's *Vampyr* (taken from the first intertitles, as translated by Trond Trondsen) sets the mood for the movie. Allan (producer Baron Nicolas de Gunzberg, billed as Julian West) arrives in a small town and indeed observes very mysterious happenings right from his first night at the local inn. A stranger (Maurice Schutz) visits him in his room and leaves him a package that should be opened "in the event of his death." Later, after Allan experiences some more eerie moments while walking through the town, it turns out that his nighttime visitor was the lord of the manor, whose daughter, Léone (Sybille Schmitz), was struck by an unknown illness. The symptoms are similar to these of anemia, but it's quite clear that the illness is something much less typical, as the girl's neck bears suspicious bite marks. When Léone's father dies, the young man opens the package and finds out it's a book depicting the history and habits of the vampires. Now, to save Léone, her sister Gisèle (Rena Mandel) and himself from fates worse than death, Allan has to turn into a vampire hunter — and he needs to start by determining the true identity of the village doctor (Jan Hieronimko).

The order of events presented in *Vampyr* is not to be trusted, though, and the viewers can never be sure whether what they see is supposed to be real or dreamed/imagined. According to Michael Grant, author of the essay "Cinema, horror and the abominations of hell" (from *The Couch and the Silver Screen: Psychoanalytic Reflections on European Cinema*), *Vampyr* takes place "in a world which is that neither of life nor of death." "Self-interrogation is ... central to the project of Dreyer's *Vampyr*," writes Grant. "For instance, Gray's first walk to the mill is both a narrative event and at the same time a disruption of the logical sequence of that narrative event. We are first presented with a disruption of the intelligibility of the relations between body and reflection, as Gray sees a figure, in reverse motion, reflected in the river, digging a grave. There is then a further fracturing of normal physical relations, when we see a man's shadow separate itself from his body. At the same time, the usual structure of narrative and temporal order is broken by a sudden, unmotivated irruption of music occurring when Gray enters the mill, an irruption that immediately calls forth what look like cut-out figures, dancing or circling around each other. These different elements of cinematic device, combined with the sudden intrusion of the commanding voice of the vampire, compromise the meaning of the narrative at this point, rendering the presentation of events suspect." The vague nature of the plot is yet emphasized via a masterfully handled sequence in which the main character leaves his body and witnesses his own burial — we can never be quite sure what triggered this vision. And this is what Dreyer wanted to achieve with his bleary, oneiric film, which forces viewers to constantly question the "reality" of the depicted world: "Imagine that we are sitting in an ordinary room," the director said at the time of filming *Vampyr*. "Suddenly we are told that there is a corpse behind the door. In an instant, the room we are sitting in, is completely altered; everything has taken on another look: the light, the reality has changed, though they are physically the same. This is because *we* have changed, and the objects are as we conceive them. That is the effect I want to get in my film."

Vampyr is "officially" an adaptation of Sheridan Le Fanu's novel *In a Glass Darkly*, but apart from the fact that both works feature the figure of a female vampire they are quite dissimilar. Dreyer, who had earlier made the successful *Thou Shalt Honor Thy Wife* (1925) and the critically acclaimed *The Passion of Joan of Arc* (1928), was much less interested in following Le Fanu's plot than he was in creating a unique dreamlike mood and experimenting with various filmmaking techniques. (The camera in *Vampyr* is unbelievably dynamic for the time, the combination of sound and intertitles is quite unusual, some trick photography still impresses today, and the movie's "hazy" look was achieved by using unorthodox lighting.) Borrowing visually from both surrealism and German Expressionism, and touching upon themes like disease, death, insanity and the value of science, *Vampyr* is a stunning, one-of-a-kind achievement that grabs the viewer by the soul with its cold, ethereal fingers.

The movie wasn't received very well upon its release in 1932. As a consequence, Dreyer had trouble financing his next project and decided to focus on his work as a journalist. At the beginning of the next decade, Danish filmmaker Mogens Skot-Hansen managed to convince Dreyer to return to directing. The first step in this direction was the short documentary *Good Mothers* (1942), which encouraged Dreyer to start thinking of another feature-length effort. *Day of Wrath* (1943), a tale of witchcraft set in 17th century Denmark, was a powerful drama with some analogies to the contemporary situation in Europe (i.e., the Nazi terror during World War II). After the movie's premiere, Dreyer left occupied Denmark and settled in Sweden where he made *Two People* (1945), a chamber drama that flopped so badly that the director decided to disown it. As the war ended, Dreyer came back to Denmark and limited his work to documentaries. In 1954 he shot *The Word*, a poignant drama dealing with the notion of faith, based on a play by Dutch World War II martyr Kaj Munk. This movie finally was an international success, getting praise from the critics and winning many awards (the Golden Globe and

Golden Lion at the Venice Film Festival among others). Dreyer's last film, the somber drama *Gertrud* (1964), based on a play by Hjalmar Söderberg, wasn't as unanimously applauded as *The Word* (though it won the FIPRESCI prize in Venice), but it should nevertheless be recognized as a slow-burning masterpiece crowning the director's career.

To watch *Vampyr* is to take a path winding around your dreams and fears, and leading to the depths of your soul. Dreyer's visionary movie could never beat *Dracula* at the box office, but in point of fact, it gives us a much more fearful breed of vampire.

The Old Dark House

DIRECTOR: James Whale
CAST: Raymond Massey, Gloria Stuart, Melvyn Douglas, Lillian Bond,
Charles Laughton, Boris Karloff, Ernest Thesiger, Eva Moore,
Brember Wills, Elspeth Dudgeon
USA, 1932

"Horror cinema began in the early 1930s in the American film industry," writes Peter Hutchings in his engaging and enlightening collection of essays *The Horror Film*. He goes on to explain that "the early 1930s marked the point where the term 'horror'

Eva Moore (right) doesn't want to cheer up her uninvited guest (Gloria Stuart) in James Whale's *The Old Dark House* (1932).

became understood ... as designating a particular type ... of film, with the recognition of this term apparent not just in America but in other countries where American films were distributed." Therefore, such movies as *The Cabinet of Dr. Caligari* (1920), *The Phantom Carriage* (1921) and *The Phantom of the Opera* (1925) were not initially labeled as belonging to the horror genre, even though they certainly fit most definitions of "horror" that were subsequently formed (i.e., they do include supernatural elements and feature scenes that aim to scare the viewers). But while by today's standards all the abovementioned films, as well as such Universal classics as *Dracula* (1931) or *Frankenstein* (1931), are indisputably good examples of horror cinema, there is a group of dark and scary movies made around the same time that didn't adopt the genre moniker quite as easily. *One Exciting Night* (1922), *The Bat* (1926), *The Cat and the Canary* (1927), *The Terror* (1928) and *The Last Warning* (1929) were usually called "haunted house spoofs" (or, alternatively, "old dark house thrillers"), and James Whale's follow-up to *Frankenstein*—*The Old Dark House*—is certainly one of the highlights of this peculiar genre. Unnerving, infused with the atmosphere of dread, full of weird or menacing characters, and clearly influenced by gothic literature and German Expressionism, *The Old Dark House* also proves that it is often impossible to separate a haunted house spoof from a horror movie, and it emerges as a perfect cross between these two genres.

Essentially, a haunted house spoof is a film in which a group of people wind up in a spooky residence that seems to be cursed and somewhat threatening, but in the end turns out to be totally innocuous — unlike its residents who are usually driven to madness, murder or both. In Whale's movie, set in Wales, the accidental visitors to the old dark house of the title are: a handsome couple, Philip and Margaret Waverton (Raymond Massey and Gloria Stuart), their devil-may-care friend Penderel (Melvyn Douglas) and two mismatched companions, Sir William Porterhouse and Gladys Perkins (Charles Laughton and Lillian Bond). They are first introduced to towering, mute and scarred Morgan the butler (Boris Karloff), and then, gradually, to the owners of the house — members of the Femm family, of whom cowardly Horace (Ernest Thesiger) and grouchy Rebecca (Eva Moore) appear to be the sanest ones. Despite the outward unfriendliness of the Femms, the guests decide to stay the night, as the terrible rain outside won't let them travel much further. And so they sign in for an evening full of surprises, thrills and shocks, as hulky Morgan gets aggressive after drinking too much alcohol, 102-year old Sir Roderick (Elspeth Dudgeon) reveals certain secrets of the Femm family, and the house's most dangerous monster — a supposed madman, Saul (Brember Wills) — is eventually unlocked.

The admittedly sketchy plot of *The Old Dark House* is based on the novel *Benighted* by J.B. Priestley, a British author whose works were very often adapted to screen in later years. But the real value of the movie is in the colorful characters Whale brought to life. Gloria Stuart and Lillian Bond are both equally alluring, though their heroines are almost complete opposites (Stuart is a calm, stern blonde, and Bond a cheerful brunette); Eva Moore manages to be funny and sinister at the same time; Brember Wills attempts to steal the movie when he finally appears onscreen; Boris Karloff once again proves he makes a very good "monster"; and Ernest Thesiger, apart from being able to pull out all the stops in the comedy scenes, is so convincingly frail here that it is hard to believe he is the same man who later played the spirited Dr. Pretorius in *Bride of Frankenstein* (1935, which was Thesiger's second and final collaboration with Whale). The only dispensable character seems to be Raymond Massey's Philip, a typically bland horror movie hero. Many critics argue that *The Old Dark House* is not a horror movie or a haunted house spoof, but rather a dark comedy. But however effective all the funny bits are (for example, Thesiger's shameless lying when he for some reason refuses to go to a room upstairs), the whole movie is thick with horror atmosphere and includes too many great scares to be labeled a comedy. One of the horror highlights is the scene in which Eva Moore reminds Gloria Stuart that her young body is "going to rot" (which is accompanied by the distorted images of the two women, as if reflected in a particularly wicked mirror, and climaxes in a wonderfully expressionistic picture when a window opens and gusts of wind start tearing at Stuart's dress, making her figure a helpless white spot amidst the predatory darkness), or the one in which we see Stuart's shadow on the wall and suddenly another, more malevolent shadow jumps out from within it. Equally powerful horror moments cannot be found even in Whale's genre masterpieces *Frankenstein* and *Bride of Frankenstein*.

Soon after *The Old Dark House* was made, Whale made two hugely popular movies, *The Invisible Man* (1933) and *Bride of Frankenstein*, but even his less appreciated efforts were always very good-looking pieces with the director's trademark weird streak (good examples are 1933's drama *The Kiss Before the Mirror* with cinematography by Karl Freund, 1935's oddball mystery *Remember Last Night?* and 1940's adventure movie *Green Hell* starring Vincent Price). In 1941 Whale abandoned the filmmaking business to focus on painting. His death by drowning in 1957 was a mystery until years later when his lover, David Lewis, disclosed Whale's suicide note in which the artist explained that he needed to escape from "old age and illness and pain."

In 1963, William Castle directed a campy remake of *The Old Dark House*, but despite being quite amusing at times, the new version didn't achieve the original's perfect balance between horror, grotesque and comedy.

A defining example of a haunted house spoof, *The Old Dark House* is also a transition movie for James Whale: it's no longer a pure gothic horror like his earlier *Frankenstein*, and it's already a promise of the quirkiness to come in the form of his cross-genre masterpiece *Bride of Frankenstein*.

Doctor X

DIRECTOR: Michael Curtiz
CAST: Lionel Atwill, Lee Tracy, Fay Wray, Preston Foster, John Wray,
Harry Beresford, Leila Bennett, George Rosener
USA, 1932

Michael Curtiz's *Doctor X* is usually remembered as the first horror movie to be shot in Technicolor. However, a closer look at the film reveals many other qualities that make it important, unique and enjoyable — especially for those interested in the development of certain horror themes throughout the decades. After all, *Doctor X* is

A pre–*King Kong* Fay Wray, here as Dr. Xavier's daughter, with reporter Lee Taylor (Lee Tracy) in *Doctor X* (1932).

essentially a very interesting twist on a concept of a mad scientist; a concept, one would think, fresh enough back at the beginning of the 1930s not to yield to innovation.

The movie's script was based on a play called *The Terror* by Howard W. Comstock and Allen C. Miller, and the major change made by the scriptwriters was the replacement of the play's down-to-earth killer with a grotesque monster (still dubbed the Moon Killer, though). The change was an effective one, as despite retaining all the comedy-mystery elements from the original play, Curtiz's adaptation unexpectedly sneaked into the realm of horror as well. The movie's main characters are: Dr. Xavier (Lionel Atwill), his daughter Joanne (Fay Wray) and reporter Lee Taylor (Lee Tracy). When an unidentified killer cannibalizes one victim too many, Taylor decides it is up to him to unmask the psycho and bring safety back to the streets of New York. A very uncommon type of knife used to cut the victims puts the suspicion on the doctors from the Academy of Surgical Research. Dr. Xavier, the head of the Academy, is granted 24 hours to find the killer among his employees. To do this, he invites all the suspects to his old, ominous-looking house and decides to make use of a futuristic, self-made lie detector; at the same time, the reporter secretly gets in the doctor's house and soon finds himself unsure whether his priority should be helping to track the monstrous killer or seducing Dr. X's beautiful and vulnerable daughter.

Peter Hutchings argues in his book *The Horror Film* that there are several reasons for *Doctor X*'s uniqueness. First of all, it seems to be lacking the "moral dimension" of other 1930s takes on the theme of a mad scientist; unlike *Frankenstein* (1931) and *Island of Lost Souls* (1933), Curtiz's film actually employs some scientific inventions (the unlikely prototype of a lie detector) to catch the killer rather than to threaten mankind. Secondly, the movie is set in urban America and therefore much more realistic than the likes of *Dracula* (1931) or *Frankenstein*. And finally, unlike other movies made in that period, *Doctor X* "invites an audience to think about its own relations to scenes of fear and horror" (Hutchings, p. 24). To illustrate this, Hutchings describes the movie's most suspenseful scene, in which characters are chained to their chairs and then witness an attack of the Moon Killer on an unsuspecting woman. Unable to do anything to help the potential victim, the chained characters mirror the members of the movie's audience — people wishing that they could somehow influence onscreen events, often loudly advising the characters what they should or shouldn't do.

The uniqueness of Curtiz's movie doesn't end with all the features mentioned by Hutchings. Apart from being an atypically realistic horror movie, a twist on the mad scientist formula and a re-enactment of the cinema-going experience itself, *Doctor X* is also a controversy magnet, as it deals (albeit marginally) with such gruesome themes as cannibalism and the use of synthetic flesh, and gives us a glimpse of such unsettling sights as a heart in a jar and a limb removed from the body. By today's standards these things are far from shocking but for some people who saw the movie soon after the milder *Frankenstein* this was decidedly a step too far. (The scene where one of the characters is using synthetic flesh was censored in Great Britain.)

And then there is the most easily recognizably unique feature of *Doctor X*— the effect of utilizing two-strip Technicolor, a technique never before used in a horror movie. Apparently, the greenish tint with occasional splashes of brighter colors is not a drawback of the pioneering technique in question, but a conscious decision of Technicolor's Natalie Kalmus, made to give the film a more mysterious look; a decision that is difficult to judge by a contemporary viewer (the remastered DVD version of the movie is said to be quite different color-wise from the original print), but one that no doubt helped increase *Doctor X*'s overall distinctiveness.

Interestingly, even though Curtiz's movie has so many features that make it stand out from other horror movies of the time, it also has many ties with more typical — or more popular — horror titles. Soon after finishing *Doctor X*, Hungarian director Curtiz made the very successful *Mystery of the Wax Museum* (1933) and based the movie on themes and characters that were similar to those employed for *Doctor X*: actress Fay Wray, here uttering her first onscreen scream, went on to star in *King Kong* (1933) and soon became the world's favorite scream queen; and actor Lionel Atwill continued to star as a doctor, scientist, killer or some other suspicious character in movies like *Mystery of the Wax Museum*, *Son of Frankenstein* (1939) or *The Mad Doctor of Market Street* (1942).

In 1939, Vincent Sherman directed a quasi-sequel to *Doctor X* titled *The Return of Doctor X*, and even though it was not quite as interesting or well-made as the original (Sherman admits he had been learning how to direct on the set of *The Return of Doctor X*, using pieces of advice from his cameraman, Sid Hickox), it was also quite daring and innovative. Distancing itself from the story told in *Doctor X*, Sherman's movie presented the titular doctor as a scientist who sacrificed himself for what he must have considered "the greater good": he was executed for experimenting with children (and to even mention such experiments in a 1939 movie was no doubt highly controversial), then was brought back to life the Frankenstein way, and in effect started craving human blood — the only thing that could keep him alive. *The Return of Doctor X* managed to marry the concept of a mad scientist with the idea of vampirism (a combination that was to be further developed in later horror movies), and at the same time express some doubts about the morality of science (something the late–1930s audiences could certainly connect to). It's a pity then that the movie is now usually recognized as "the one with an uneasy early performance from Humphrey Bogart," who starred as the resurrected Dr. X.

The first-ever horror movie in color. And even if what we see are mainly hues of green, the movie still looks remarkably handsome after all these years. Also here: director Michael Curtiz makes an early attempt at refreshing the mad scientist formula, and pre–*King Kong* Fay Wray treats us to her debut onscreen scream.

Freaks

DIRECTOR: Tod Browning
CAST: Olga Baclanova, Harry Earles, Wallace Ford, Daisy Earles,
Johnny Eck, Leila Hyams, Roscoe Ates, Daisy and Violet Hilton,
Angelo Rossitto, Prince Randian
USA, 1932

In his book *The Monster Show — A Cultural History of Horror*, David J. Skal calls the modern horror film "the most lasting and influential invention of 1931," as it was only with the arrival of Universal's *Dracula* and *Frankenstein* (both made that year) that the term "horror movies" started to be commonly used. Skal explains the need for such an invention at that particular time in the following way: "Cataclysmic junctures in history usually stir up strong imagery in the collective mind, and the years following the 1929 economic crash were no exception.... Horror films served as a kind of populist surrealism, rearranging the human body and its processes, blurring the boundaries between Homo sapiens and other species, responding uneasily to new and almost incomprehensible developments in science and the anxious challenges they posed to the familiar structures of society, religion, psychology, and perception." *Freaks*, director Tod Browning's follow-up to the genre-defining *Dracula*, was all this — and more. As it later turned out, the movie was too much even for the audiences in bad need of cinematic shocks.

The idea for *Freaks* came from the short story "Spurs," written by a popular author of mysteries, Tod Robbins. It was a tale of a circus dwarf taking revenge on his beautiful wife after she had humiliated him during their wedding feast. Although the commercial value of the story seemed poor (there were no likable characters in it), Metro-Goldwyn-Mayer bought the adaptation rights in 1928, hoping it would be good material for another Lon Chaney movie. Chaney died in 1930, but after the huge success of *Dracula*, MGM's Irving Thalberg was eager to produce a horror of his own, so

Where the terror starts: the infamous wedding feast scene in Tod Browning's *Freaks* (1932).

he contacted Browning, summoned scriptwriter Willis Goldbeck, and started the casting process. The main roles of the unlikely married couple were given to the normal-sized Olga Baclanova and midget Harry Earles; it was not their first weird and controversial movie. Baclanova had previously starred in Paul Leni's *The Man Who Laughs* (1928; with Conrad Veidt), a strange story of a permanently grinning jester, and Earles, a 30-year-old midget with the face of a cute child, had already worked with Browning on *The Unholy Three* (1925) in which he played one of the title trio of crooks (Lon Chaney and Victor McLaglen completed the team). (Earles was also in the 1930 talkie remake.) Baclanova met Earles before the shooting, and got on with him very well, but when Browning introduced her to the rest of the cast — the Siamese twins (Daisy and Violet Hilton), a half-boy (John Eck), a human worm (Prince Randian), a skeleton man (Peter Robinson), a hermaphrodite (Josephine Joseph), a bearded woman (Olga Roderick), a group of pinheads, midgets and otherwise deformed people — the actress "wanted to cry," as she later said in an interview.

The plot of *Freaks* essentially remained similar to that outlined in "Spurs," but major changes were made as far as the motivation of some characters was concerned. A trapeze artist, Cleopatra (Baclanova) seduces and marries a midget named Hans (Earles), and then, together with her lover, Hercules (Henry Victor), plots to kill Hans in order to inherit his fortune. Hans' sideshow friends — especially the midget he rejected, Frieda (Daisy Earles), and Hercules' ex-lover Venus (Leila Hyams) — are getting suspicious of Cleopatra's intentions, and when they finally spot her adding drops of poison to her husband's medicine, they decide something has to be done about it.

The main problem the audiences (and the performers, too, apparently) have always had with *Freaks* was that the initially sympathetic sideshow attractions get to show their "dark side" at some point in the movie. The introductory text informs us that "the love of beauty is a deep seated urge that dates back to the beginning of civilization" and that the "revulsion with which we view the abnormal, the malformed and the mutilated is the result of long conditioning of our forefathers." However, it doesn't seem that Browning really wanted to change that, or at least he didn't proceed to do that in an overtly self-evident way. After all, the director set out to *shock* the viewers by casting the real sideshow attractions in the first place, and this is the effect he no doubt achieved. However, the test screenings were disastrous and the movie had to be drastically cut (from the original 90 minutes to about 60), and a marginally more uplifting ending had to replace the previous one.

When *Freaks* was released in February 1932, it turned out to be a huge success as a horror movie: one so frightening that not too many people dared see it. Additionally, its controversial subject matter posed a problem for the studio: a lot of explaining would need to be done as to why such a script was ever accepted; with the slim chances of hitting it big at the box office, the studio decided that it would be much safer to withdraw *Freaks* from theaters than to try to defend it. Just weeks later the movie ended its short theatrical run — after getting a handful of positive reviews and a whole bag of others that expressed utter shock or were fiery critiques — and was not to be widely seen until the 1960s, when it was rediscovered owing to that period's fashion for "being different." Horror movie expert Andrzej Kołodyński argued in his book *Kino grozy* that "the audiences of the 1930s readily accepted even the most terrible masks, on the condition that they were made by make-up artists"; had Browning or Thalberg known this, *Freaks* either would have never been made, or it would have been made the traditional way, with the use of elaborate costumes and rubber masks. As it was, Browning's willingness to push the boundaries of horror resulted in a movie that transcends the genre; it was certainly more unsettling than *Dracula* and *Frankenstein*, and superior to both of them in some ways (it looked better, and had a more interesting and more daring script). But yet it could never compete with them at the box office, just because it was "something else," not "one of them"— the innocuous horror pictures.

Uncompromising and uncommercial, *Freaks* almost ruined Browning's career but also remained his unrivalled masterpiece and — in the opinion of many critics — the most shocking horror picture in history. Most actors playing the freaks of the title may have ultimately disliked or even despised the movie (Olga Roderick often repeated that she regretted having appeared in *Freaks*), but it was a career highlight for most of them, or at least a movie that put them in the spotlight — after all, it elevated them from being sideshow attractions to being Hollywood stars, even if it didn't necessarily last for too long. Harry and Daisy Earles' only notable film roles after *Freaks* were these of Munchkins in 1939's *The Wizard of Oz* (although Harry also appeared in Laurel and Hardy's 1938 comedy *Block-Heads*, and Daisy could be glimpsed in 1952's *The Greatest Show on Earth*); the twins, Daisy and Violet Hilton, were talented vaudeville performers, had the short-lived Broadway musical *Sideshow* based on their lives, and starred in *Chained for Life* (1951), a movie that teasingly raised the question of jailing (or even executing) two Siamese twins after one of them had murdered her husband. Angelo Rossitto, who in later years also founded Little People of America, had the most impressive post–*Freaks* career of all the cast members: he appeared in several movies alongside Bela Lugosi (like 1941's *Spooks Run Wild*, 1942's *The Corpse Vanishes*, and 1947's *Scared to Death*), and acted in various other films — *Doomed to Die* (1940; with Boris Karloff), *The Spider Woman* (1944; a Sherlock Holmes mystery with Basil Rathbone), *Dracula vs. Frankenstein* (1971; with Lon Chaney Jr.), the crime TV-series *Baretta* (1975–78), the film adaptation of Ray Bradbury's novel *Something Wicked This Way Comes* (1983), *Mad Max Beyond Thunderdome* (1985; with Mel Gibson and Tina Turner) and the horror anthology *The Offspring* (1987; aka *From a Whisper to a Scream*, with Vincent Price, Martine Beswick and Clu Gulager). Olga Baclanova, on the other hand, didn't get another leading role after *Freaks* (her strong Russian accent was an obstacle), but she continued her career performing on Broadway, then on stages in London, and got supporting parts in several dramas (1932's *Downstairs*, 1933's *Billion Dollar Scandal*, 1943's *Claudia*).

The "ultimate horror film" indeed. And still a very controversial one, especially for the viewers aware of how some of the actors employed to play the freaks reacted to the finished movie, and how badly most of them fell off with director Tod Browning.

White Zombie

DIRECTOR: Victor Halperin
CAST: Bela Lugosi, Madge Bellamy, Joseph Cawthorn, John Harron,
Robert Frazer, Frederick Peters, Brandon Hurst, Clarence Muse
USA, 1932

In *White Zombie: Anatomy of a Horror Film*, the most informative book wholly devoted to Victor Halperin's classic, author Gary Don Rhodes explains that the early American horror movies were drawing from the xenophobia that developed during the 1920s (the controversial trial and execution of Sacco and Vanzetti, two Italians accused of robbery and murder; blaming the Europeans for U.S. involvement in World War I and for causing the Great Depression; the First Red Scare during World War I). "If perceived villains in real life were foreigners," writes Rhodes, "so were those in the horror film of the thirties ... [which] saw fit to place Americans in Europe or some other unfamiliar locale to confront trouble outside the U.S. Troubles are faced by Renfield in *Dracula* on his journey ... as they are faced by Neil and Madeleine in *White Zombie*."

And indeed they are. Neil Parker (John Harron) and Madeleine Short (Madge Bellamy) arrive at a plantation in Haiti in order to have a wedding ceremony. However, the owner of the plantation, Charles Beaumont (Robert Frazer), is smitten with pretty Madeleine and hopes he can convince the girl to let him replace Neil at the altar. When he finds out that she is actually in love with her fiancé, there is only one thing left for Beaumont to do: have the local voodoo master, "Murder" Legendre (Bela Lugosi), turn Madeleine into a zombie so that the wedding will be canceled. Then, reckons Beaumont, he'll have plenty of time to persuade his zombiefied sweetheart that no other man loves her as much as he does. But "Murder" Legendre needn't be played by Lugosi if he didn't have his own mischievous plans concerning Madeleine, while the girl's fiancé is apparently willing to fight to get her back.

Lugosi, with the hypnotic stare inherited from Dracula and a surprising little beard, easily outdoes all other cast members, and breathes life into another distinguished villain in his career. Nevertheless, Madge Bellamy is quite effective, too, as the most fragile of all undead, and the supporting turns from Joseph Cawthorn (as a missionary who doesn't approve of Legendre's tactics) and Clarence Muse (as an apprehensive coach driver) are also noteworthy. The attractive sets, apparently recycled from the shoot of *Dracula* (1931) and several other films, add to the overall unearthly atmosphere, as does Jack Pierce's minimalistic makeup and, most notably, full musical score—something other early horrors lacked. Plus, whatever problems director Halperin might have had with controlling some of the actors, he made up for it with the ability to control the sound and dialogue (the scene in which we are invited to Legendre's sugar mill is filled with all kinds of unnerving noises), which was rare in this early age of sound cinema. George E. Turner, the movie's famous enthusiast, remarks in the foreword to Rhodes's *White Zombie: Anatomy of a Horror Film* that Halperin "shows ... a surer instinct than any of his contemporaries for dramatically marrying images to sound," and that "not until the advent of Val Lewton in the mid-forties do we encounter his equal at using sound to create audience suspense and terror." The fact that *White Zombie* looks and sounds so good is all the more commendable since it was an independent movie, made for a fraction of the standard Universal horror budget.

Some things are never clear in the movie's plot—is it, for example, possible to turn all the zombies back into humans?—but whether this is a disadvantage or not would depend on each viewer's personal taste. After all, the many unanswered questions do make *White Zombie* yet more mysterious and intriguing. The uncertainty whether supernatural forces are involved or not, on the other hand, makes the movie remarkably different from most other horrors and haunted house spoofs from that period, as the traditional approach was to have all the strange events explained either as cunning human tricks or as the effect of employing advanced science. Here, even as the end credits start to roll, the viewer can only make educated guesses about the range of Legendre's powers or the interdependence between the zombies and their master.

White Zombie wasn't Halperin's only horror movie, but it was definitely his best, as well as the most influential one. Still, the tale of a young woman being possessed by a spirit of a murderer told in *Supernatural* (1933; with Carole Lombard) and the story of a mad doctor who carries out experiments on criminals in *Torture Ship* (1939; based on Jack London's *A Thousand Deaths*, starring Lyle Talbot) are entertaining enough and have some moments of greatness; especially admirable is the atmospheric cinematography in *Supernatural* by Arthur Martinelli, who also worked on *White Zombie*. Stock footage of Bela Lugosi's hypnotic eyes from *White Zombie* (but not the actor himself) returned in Halperin's next take on the theme, *Revolt of the Zombies* (1936). This time the plot involved a group of expeditionists in Cambodia trying to get hold of a secret formula for turning people into the living dead. Unfortunately, the movie was widely regarded as a disappointment, and it's not hard to see why: in comparison with Halperin's zombie classic, *Revolt* lacks an intriguing story and a memorable villain.

White Zombie introduced the living dead into the horror oeuvre, and several interesting movies featuring the creatures followed, like George Terwilliger's *Ouanga* (1936), George Marshall's comedic horror *The Ghost Breakers* (1940), and Jean Yarbrough's *King of the Zombies* (1941). These were always set in some exotic location (usually on an island in the Caribbean); as Peter Dendle states in *The Zombie Movie Encyclopedia*, it was Wallace Fox's *Bowery at Midnight* (1942; with Bela Lugosi in the main role) that first showed the living dead residing in the United States. However, there are two reasons why Dendle's theory may turn out debatable: first of all, some may claim that the reanimated dead in *Bowery at Midnight* are not zombies in the traditional sense, and secondly, if we apply a looser definition of the notion, why not claim that Dr. Maurice Xavier (as portrayed by Humphrey Bogart in 1939's *The Return of Doctor X*)—a reanimated corpse feeding on human blood—was the first-ever onscreen zombie on U.S. soil?

In the subsequent years, Jacques Tourneur would make the most gorgeous zombie movie ever, *I Walked with a Zombie* (1943), Ed Wood was to present the theme at its silliest in *Plan 9 from Outer Space* (1959), and George A. Romero would be responsible for transforming the creatures into brutal cannibals in *Night of the Living Dead* (1968).

This isn't just the first-ever horror movie to feature the living dead, but one of the best ones, too. Bela Lugosi, who plays a zombie master with mesmerizing eyes and a devilish little beard, is in his element here, and the plot is thoroughly entertaining, if also full of conundrums that are never explained.

WereWolf of London

DIRECTOR: Stuart Walker
CAST: Henry Hull, Warner Oland, Valerie Hobson, Lester Matthews,
Spring Byington, Lawrence Grant, Charlotte Granville
USA, 1935

After several silent wolf-man films were made (for example, 1913's *The Werewolf* and 1914's *The White Wolf*), director Stuart Walker set out to make the first-ever sound movie about a man transforming into the fearsome beast when the moon is full. And even though Walker's *WereWolf of London* is hardly ever referred to as one of the most important movies on the subject, it does have some irresistible charm and sense of mystery that many other werewolf movies clearly lack.

To provide us with a welcome amount of exoticism, the movie opens in Tibet where an adventurous botanist, Dr. Glendon (Henry Hull), is looking for a rare flower that only blooms on full moon nights. He is lucky enough to find the flower but when he is about to pick it up, a werewolf suddenly attacks him. And even though the doctor

**Dr. Glendon (Henry Hull, left) and Dr. Yogami (Warner Oland) in *WereWolf of London*
(1935).**

chases the hairy beast away without too much effort, it still manages to bite the man's arm, so that we know he's now a werewolf, too. Next we are invited to Dr. Glendon's English house where we meet other important characters: there's his lovely wife Lisa (Valerie Hobson), Lisa's childhood boyfriend Paul (Lester Matthews) and mysterious Dr. Yogami (Warner Oland). All these people have something important to tell us, so before we witness any real horror we learn that Lisa is disappointed in her husband's coldness and constant preoccupation with his work, that Paul is still in love with Lisa, and that Dr. Yogami is the daytime body of the werewolf that attacked Dr. Glendon in Tibet. Another important piece of information is that the rare Tibetan flower Dr. Glendon took to England is the only known cure for lycanthropy; anyone afflicted with the curse can use it to immediately stop the beastly metamorphosis. Naturally, Dr. Yogami will try to snatch the flower from his colleague's laboratory, and Dr. Glendon will have to cope with the murder instinct that takes control over him at certain nights. When we are also informed that a man changed into a werewolf usually first kills people dear to him, it becomes obvious that the doctor's wife will soon be in peril.

The person most often blamed for the movie's lack of success is Henry Hull, and although he plays his role with confidence, it is true that his character is neither as sympathetic nor as memorable as those created by Bela Lugosi, Boris Karloff or Lon Chaney Jr. in Universal's more famous monster movies. But even with the main character being a bit of a bore, there's enough good acting in *Were Wolf of London* to keep us interested in what's happening onscreen. Valerie Hobson is great as the main character's sensitive wife (she played a very similar character in the same year's *Bride of Frankenstein*, and these are two equally great roles that radiate sympathy and suppressed eroticism). Warner Oland hams it up in the role of the villain, and Spring Byington's Aunt Ettie injects some mild humor into the story. The truly hilarious addition is that of Ethel Griffies and Zeffie Tilbury who play old ladies with a weakness for drinking, and therefore convinced that whatever man-to-wolf transformations they witness, they're nothing more than alcohol-induced visions.

The movie's other virtues are Albert D'Agostino's wonderful art direction (please note Dr. Glendon's bizarre laboratory, full of flesh-eating plants and futuristic gadgets), Charles J. Stumar's inspired photography (Stumar previously worked on Karl Freund's *The Mummy* and some of the magic of this legendary movie returns here), and Jack Pierce's disturbing makeup. Famously, when Hull wouldn't agree to wear the makeup Pierce originally wanted to use for the film, the acclaimed monster-maker had to come up with a toned-down version of it, one that gives the beast more humanly features, and consequently makes the movie more like Robert Louis Stevenson's *Dr. Jekyll and Mr. Hyde* than any other werewolf film. (Pierce eventually got to use some of the ideas rejected by Hull when he was preparing the werewolf makeup for Lon Chaney Jr. in *The Wolf Man*, now known as the beast's most popular image: definitely much hairier and more beastly than Hull's, but therefore also less realistic and not quite as unsettling.) The scenes where the main character morphs into a wolf are nicely done, too, showing the transformation in subtle yet very effective ways (for example, when we see a man disappearing behind a pillar and then — only seconds later — a beast appearing on the other side).

Another interesting thing about *WereWolf of London* is that it has a completely different subtext than all werewolf movies made afterwards. If *The Wolf Man* was a metaphor for Nazism (as writer Curt Siodmak claims it to be), and *An American Werewolf in London* a metaphor for puberty (director John Landis says that this is what he was aiming at), *WereWolf of London* uses the theme to speak of the main character's difficulty in expressing his emotions, and it may eventually be viewed as a critique of Britain's upper class.

Often regarded as *The Wolf Man*'s less handsome older brother, *WereWolf of London* has plenty of charm and is the more sophisticated of the two siblings. Henry Hull may not be as sympathetic as *The Wolf Man*'s Lon Chaney Jr. but good supporting actors easily make up for the lack of a more charismatic leading man.

Mad Love

aka *The Hands of Orlac*
DIRECTOR: Karl Freund
CAST: Peter Lorre, Frances Drake, Colin Clive, Ted Healy,
Sara Haden, Edward Brophy, May Beatty, Keye Luke
USA, 1935

Having worked with such influential directors as Paul Wegener (1920's *The Golem*), F.W. Murnau (1924's *The Last Laugh*, 1926's *Tartuffe*) and Fritz Lang (1927's *Metropolis*), the talented and inventive cinematographer Karl Freund moved from Germany to the United States and soon contributed his skills to Lewis Milestone's intense war drama *All Quiet on the Western Front* (1930) and Tod Browning's *Dracula* (1931). Afterwards, Freund started working as a director as well, and even though it didn't last very long, he made several interesting movies, two of them being undisputed horror masterpieces: *The Mummy* (1932) with Boris Karloff's haunting performance in the title role, and his final effort as a director with an equally good role by Peter Lorre —*Mad Love*.

Lorre's character is a genius surgeon, Dr. Gogol, who falls in love with an actress of the Grand Guignol theater, Yvonne Orlac (Frances Drake). Since he has already "conquered science," Dr. Gogol wants to "conquer love," too, and therefore he tries to win Yvonne's heart even after he learns that she is married. In a wicked twist of fate, the woman's husband, famous pianist Stephen Orlac (Colin Clive), is soon seriously injured in a train accident, and Dr. Gogol is asked to help him. Orlac's hands cannot be saved, so the doctor amputates them and in a bold surgery replaces them with the hands of a recently executed murderer, Rollo the Knife-Thrower (Edward Brophy). Naturally, when the bandages are taken off, Orlac finds out that his new fingers would rather play with knives than play the piano.

Mad Love was the first sound adaptation of the novel *Les Mains d'Orlac* written by Maurice Renard and published in 1920 (four years later it was made into a movie by one of the masters of the silent cinema, Robert Wiene, as *The Hands of Orlac*). His 1908 novel *Le Docteur Lerne — Sous-Dieu* being a clever tribute to H.G. Wells's *The Island of Doctor Moreau*, Renard quickly became one of the greatest authors of the early "mad

Scary eyes and scary hands in Karl Freund's *Mad Love* (1935): Dr. Gogol (Peter Lorre) with Yvonne Orlac (Frances Drake).

scientist novel," and Freund in his take on *Les Mains d'Orlac* emphasized Renard's reputation by choosing the lunatic doctor to be the main character. (Wiene and the directors who got to adapt the novel later [Edmond T. Gréville in 1960's *The Hands of Orlac* and Newt Arnold in 1962's *Hands of a Stranger*] were focusing on the doctor's victim.)

Typically for movies made by Freund, either as a cinematographer or director, *Mad Love* is visually phenomenal and very effectively evokes the spirit of German Expressionism (to help him achieve this, Freund hired another genius cinematographer, Gregg Toland — who later provided striking photography for Orson Welles' 1941 masterpiece *Citizen Kane*). Many other components of *Mad Love* are quite remarkable as well (Dimitri Tiomkin's disquieting score, Frances Drake's morally ambiguous role, the perverse representation of Le Grand Guignol), but it is Peter Lorre's Dr. Gogol that owns the movie from the moment we see him. This was Lorre's first performance in an American movie and it understandably made quite an impact on the critics; after the movie's premiere, Andre Sennwald of *The New York Times* introduced the actor to the U.S. audiences with the following words:

> Perhaps you have not yet made the acquaintance of Mr. Lorre: squat, moon-faced, with gross lips, serrated teeth and enormous round eyes which seem to hang out on his cheeks like eggs when he is gripped in his characteristic mood of wistful frustration. As if these striking natural endowments were not enough, his head has been shaved clean ... for the occasion, and his skull becomes an additional omen of evil in the morose shadows which Karl Freund has evoked for the photo-play.

Content-wise, *Mad Love* is an exceptionally complex horror movie, too: it brings to mind the legend of Pygmalion (as at one point Gogol buys a statue of the beloved actress, which then "comes to life"), and the story of Frankenstein's monster (Colin Clive — Henry Frankenstein in James Whale's two movies — here plays Dr. Gogol's monster), as well as many psychoanalytical theories of Sigmund Freud's (the Oedipus complex and the concept of sublimation, among others). However, as film historian Ruth Goldberg observes in the essay "Of Mad Love, Alien Hands and the Film Under Your Skin," it all boils down to the "exploration of *how we become monstrous to ourselves*: how the ambiguous self is revealed to be more monstrous than any external horror, and how true horror is rooted in the vulnerability of our physical form."

Mad Love was the final film directed by Freund. Although it did receive some rave reviews, it wasn't a financial success, and since Freund's skills as a cinematographer were still in demand, he went back to lensing films. And perhaps it was a fair enough deal, as soon afterwards Freund won an Oscar for his work on Sidney Franklin's *The Good Earth* (1937), and then continued working with legendary directors, for example James Whale (1940's *Green Hell*) and John Huston (1948's *Key Largo*).

On its original release, *Mad Love* bombed almost as spectacularly as Tod Browning's *Freaks*, and in this case, too, the box office results poorly reflect the quality of the movie. The collaboration of director Karl Freund and cinematographer Gregg Toland renders impressive visuals, Peter Lorre's shaven-headed mad doctor is unnervingly convincing, and the story of transplanted killer hands is effectively creepy on its own.

Mark of the Vampire

DIRECTOR: Tod Browning
CAST: Lionel Barrymore, Elizabeth Allan, Lionel Atwill, Bela Lugosi,
Carroll Borland, Henry Wadsworth, Holmes Herbert
USA, 1935

Several years after making the unsettling horror drama *Freaks*, director Tod Browning decided to revisit his two more audience-friendly movies—*London After Midnight* (1927, starring Lon Chaney) and *Dracula* (1931, starring Bela Lugosi). The idea for this new film, first called *The Vampires of Prague* and then *Mark of the Vampire*, was simple: Browning attempted to make more or less a traditional haunted house spoof, but one that would borrow a large portion of the *London After Midnight* plot and would also—in a way—allow Bela Lugosi to reprise his most famous role.

Lugosi's new vampire is called Count Mora but we still recognize this character as a reincarnation of the most iconic vampire in the history of cinema, and the actor does everything to reassure us that Mora is indeed Dracula re-named; he gives us the typical haunted stares and half-smiles, avoids speaking, wears the trademark cape, and even re-enacts some scenes straight from the 1931 movie, like the slow descent from the stairs, or the walk through the cobweb without touching it. The main difference is the fact that this time the vampire has an accomplice, the pale and mesmerizing Luna (Carroll Borland), and the two undead creatures have the tendency to pop up in a village near Prague and scare the wits of the people living there. It's no surprise then, that when noble Sir Karell Borodin (Holmes Herbert) dies with suspicious marks on his neck, most villagers believe that the vampires are to blame. The arrival of Professor Zelen (Lionel Barrymore), a specialist in the occult, will hopefully help solve the mystery and convince Inspector Neumann (Lionel Atwill) that Sir Borodin's daughter, Irena (Elizabeth Allan), may become the next victim.

The plot soon becomes much more twisty, as Browning is clearly not interested in making yet another clichéd vampire tale. The results are mixed since some twists are completely illogical and unconvincing, but it's a joy to see both Browning and Lugosi having so much fun with this tongue-in-cheek riff on their past glories. Obviously, for some viewers *Mark of the Vampire* will be a huge disappointment, as it shies away from Browning's trademark grittiness, and it seemingly forces Lugosi to do nothing but repeat his old vampire schtick; if, however, one chooses to look at the movie from a different angle, it emerges not as less gutsy than expected but as fresh and experimental, and Lugosi's role turns out to be not a mere repetition of an old routine but a more powerful interpretation of it. (If the actor's performance in *Dracula* strikes us as a bit too unnatural for its own good, similar artificiality in *Mark of the Vampire* fits this particular character perfectly.) The addition of a female vampire, wonderfully portrayed by pale and unblinking Borland, is another advantage; her character doesn't just add to the attractiveness of certain set pieces (the short scene in which Borland flies on batwings is particularly memorable), but it also injects some perverseness into the otherwise timid plot (the moment when she approaches Elizabeth Allan's defenseless Irena and threatens to bite her may be a suggestion of a lesbian affair—an impressively bold

Mark of the Vampire (1935) sees Bela Lugosi as a vampire again —now with a lovely accomplice, Luna (Carroll Borland).

move at the time, something to be further explored in Lambert Hillyer's 1936 film, *Dracula's Daughter*). Admittedly, the original idea for *Mark of the Vampire* included some more controversial elements, like the incest between Count Mora and Luna, but they were all excised from the final version as MGM wanted to avoid the censorship problems that the rival company Universal has just experienced with *Bride of Frankenstein* (1935). The studio's interference didn't just reduce the movie's ability to shock the viewer, but it also destroyed the coherence of the original plot (Browning wanted to present vampirism as stemming from incest guilt), and deemed some parts of it incomprehensible (Count Mora has a visible bullet wound in his temple; initially it was intended to be seen as the remainder of the character's suicide caused by the consuming guilt, but it has no justification in the final version of the film).

We cannot compare *Mark of the Vampire* with the lost *London After Midnight*, but the comparison between *Mark ...* and *Dracula* shows many advantages of Browning's second take on the subject of vampires. Of course, the newer movie wasn't nearly as groundbreaking or influential as *Dracula*, but James Wong Howe's striking photography made it the more handsome and more "gothic" of the two, the talented actors pushed the somehow one-dimensional characters taken from *Dracula* to another level (Lionel Barrymore's wild interpretation of the Van Helsing character is especially delightful), and the final twist, however contrived, was an evidence to the director's sense of humor and playfulness which his more famous effort lacked. And honestly, can a single male vampire really beat an equally fiendish bloodsucker *and* his female companion, especially one as alluring as Luna?

Sadly, *Mark of the Vampire* was Browning's next-to-last horror movie. The studios were not willing to risk money and reputation by letting the director delve any deeper into his grim fascinations, so they first prevented him from adapting Horace McCoy's dark novel *They Shoot Horses, Don't They?* (written in 1935 and eventually brought to the big screen by Sydney Pollack in 1969), and then ordered cruel censorship for his project *The Witch of Timbuctoo* (which was to become 1936's *The Devil-Doll*, an enthralling tale starring Lionel Barrymore and touching upon such themes as wrongful accusation, revenge and the art of shrinking people). Afterwards Browning made one final movie, the engaging murder mystery *Miracles for Sale* (1939), and quit the filmmaking business to spend the rest of his life in a Malibu house.

By turns silly and ingenuous, *Mark of the Vampire* is more than it initially seems to be, as it allows director Tod Browning and star Bela Lugosi to lovingly twist the concept of *Dracula* and combine it with the plot of the lost classic *London After Midnight*.

PART II:
MONSTERS AND MADMEN

Dr. Cyclops

DIRECTOR: Ernest B. Schoedsack
CAST: Albert Dekker, Janice Logan, Thomas Coley,
Charles Halton, Victor Kilian, Frank Yaconelli, Paul Fix
USA, 1940

Scenes with miniaturized people were the highlights of James Whale's *Bride of Frankenstein* (1935) and Tod Browning's *The Devil-Doll* (1936), so it doesn't come as a surprise that several years later someone decided to devote most of the running time to the small, helpless characters that have to face the dangers of the gigantic world around them. That someone was Ernest B. Schoedsack, already a famous director back then thanks to the success of 1933's *King Kong* (co-helmed by Merian C. Cooper), and the movie in question was called *Dr. Cyclops*, named after the nickname of the central character, Dr. Alexander Thorkel — a mad scientist who finds a way to reduce living entities to toy size.

As portrayed by Albert Dekker, the mad doctor looks like a foreshadowing of Marlon Brando's Colonel Kurtz: bald, hulking and with sparks of fanaticism in the eyes. There appears to be even more to the similarity between these two characters when we learn that the titular scientist has withdrawn from the modern world and is now secluded in the Amazon jungle in order to continue experimenting with miniaturization with the use of radium. He honestly hates having guests for too long, so when fellow scientist Dr. Rupert Bulfinch (Charles Halton) and his team refuse to leave immediately after having helped him identify certain crystals, Dr. Thorkel locks them all in his atomic chamber and shrinks them to approximately 12 inches. From then on, the five minute characters — Dr. Bulfinch, attractive biologist Dr. Mary Robinson (Janice Logan), handsome mineralogist Bill Stockton (Thomas Coley), mule herder Steve (Victor Kilian) and likable assistant Pedro (Frank Yaconelli) — will have to find a way to escape from their oppressor, avoid being eaten by one of the now-huge animals, and — perhaps? — prepare for living the rest of their lives as sad Lilliputians. Luckily for them, the psycho doctor has very poor eyesight, so snatching or destroying his glasses may be the ticket to freedom for the tiny prisoners.

The movie's script is not always logical and too often resorts to silly comedy when suspense would be much more welcome, but the core idea is intriguing enough and it allows Schoedsack and the special effects team of Gordon Jennings and Farciot Edouart to create some spectacular visuals. The scene in which Dr. Thorkel catches the miniaturized, panicking Dr. Bulfinch and holds him close to his face for a careful inspection is not only very well done and full of tension, but it's also a nice echo of a similar shot in *King Kong*, with Kong grasping Ann Darrow and observing her with great attention. There are several more such beautifully rendered moments in *Dr. Cyclops*, like the one in which we see a very convincing miniature horse or that in which the tiny Dr. Bulfinch is caught in a net. (Not surprisingly, Jennings and Edouart got an Oscar nomination for the movie.) It all looks yet more impressive because the film was shot in three-strip Technicolor — something rare for a genre movie in the early 1940s. Add to this a truly mesmerizing turn from Dekker and fine art direction that sets the mood for the picture, and *Dr. Cyclops* emerges as one of the most interesting — and certainly one of the most innovative — mad scientist films of the era.

Another movie that successfully employed the idea of miniaturization was Jack Arnold's *The Incredible Shrinking Man* (1957). Based on Richard Matheson's novel, it tells the story of a man exposed to a mysterious substance and starting to get gradually smaller and smaller, so that at some point he lives in a doll house, has to escape from the claws of a cat and defend himself against a spider. *The Incredible Shrinking Man* is much more unsettling than *Dr. Cyclops*, and its special effects are even more impressive, but considering that it was made as many as 17 years after Schoedsack's take on the subject, the latter must be nevertheless regarded as a great pioneering work. Both movies are discussed by Thomas C. Renzi in his book *H.G. Wells: Six Scientific Romances Adapted for Film*, as ones that effectively conveyed Wells' message included in his 1904 novel *The Food of the Gods and How It Came to Earth* (about animals and then humans being fed on the title foodstuff and growing to giant sizes). "Wells uses increased size allegorically," writes Renzi, "to indicate how a few specially gifted individuals, by their exceptional contributions to humanity, represent the potential for progress and a greater society. Ironically, although these mighty giants offer benefits to the world, they must struggle against ridicule and alienation from the common masses who view them as a threat to tradition and convention." At the same time, the author seems to disapprove of the presentation of giants in movies like *The Beast from 20,000 Fathoms* (1953; directed by Eugène Lourié) and *The Amazing Colossal Man* (1957; by Bert I. Gordon), as they "reverse Wells's intent and use the giant as an evil threat to society, not as a benefactor." According to Renzi, *Dr. Cyclops* and *The Incredible Shrinking Man* work much better than the aforementioned oversized monster films because "humans made small, like humans made gigantic, are eccentric to the world of common people and must struggle to survive on their own terms, by their own grit and determination"; plus, "the miniaturized human relates to the audience personally and empathetically in a way similar to that suggested by Wells's innocent giants."

Instead of having the characters confront an oversized monster like in his earlier *King Kong*, here director Ernest B. Schoedsack miniaturizes a group of people, so that to them the whole world turns into a monstrous enemy. Good special effects and the genuinely evil presence of Albert Dekker as Dr. Cyclops make the movie a memorable achievement, and a pioneering effort almost entirely focused on the miniature protagonists.

The Mad Monster

DIRECTOR: Sam Newfield
CAST: George Zucco, Glenn Strange, Anne Nagel, Johnny Downs,
Gordon De Main, Reginald Barlow, Robert Strange, Mae Busch
USA, 1942

Meet the Wolf Man, Dracula, Dr. Frankenstein and Frankenstein's creature — all in one cheap movie by Sam Newfield: *The Mad Monster*.

The comparisons to George Waggner's *The Wolf Man* (1941) are the most obvious ones: *The Mad Monster*'s main character, Dr. Lorenzo Cameron (George Zucco), is trying to find a way to change humans into ravaging beasts by experimenting on his half-wit gardener Petro (Glenn Strange); he is day by day injecting the poor man with the blood of a wolf. The effects are quite surprising. Petro conveniently falls asleep and quickly transforms into a werewolf, ready to tear apart everything in his sight — except for the doctor himself who, apparently, learned how to control the beast. The character played by Strange is similar to Lon Chaney Jr.'s Larry Talbot — a huge, handsome, likable male cursed with lycanthropy; there are scenes, however, in which he looks more like Boris Karloff's Monster from *Frankenstein* (and just like that monster, he is controlled by the scientist who created him). Then there is Zucco's Dr. Cameron: clearly a riff on the character of Dr. Frankenstein, but with a mean streak and often with the look borrowed directly from Bela Lugosi's Count Dracula. Another similarity to the latter character is the fact that instead of fancy formulas and mixtures, Dr. Cameron chooses to use blood for his experiments.

The movie is a fun horror ride with high camp factor (don't miss the scene in which the werewolf is finally unleashed on the neighborhood — and walks through the garden with a crazy look on his face, but still wearing the funny-looking dungarees); however, there seems to be a surprisingly serious undertone to it, too. It's no coincidence, after all, that the fanatical Dr. Cameron reminds the viewers of Adolf Hitler: he's interested in amending nature's mistakes and creating a perfect soldier. Before *The Mad Monster*, director Sam Newfield had already made one openly anti–Nazi movie —1939's *Hitler — Beast of Berlin*, which was initially banned by pro–German censors — but he must have reasoned that it would be easier to disguise a similar message in a horror movie; or maybe he wanted to remind the Americans how easily a man can change into a violent beast, but how difficult it is then for him to regain humanity. (When the movie premiered, U.S. troops were already involved in World War II.) Newfield also pointed out certain pitfalls of fiddling with science (even the scientists who seem thoughtful and practical are sometimes tempted to do crazy things, seemed to be his warning), promoted the image of a strong, modern woman through the character played by Anne Nagel (which could be read as another criticism of Nazi Germany where women were subordinate to men), and tried to mask it all as an homage to 1931's *Dracula* and *Frankenstein*. It didn't all work perfectly, though, as *The Mad Monster* was an ultra-cheap movie that couldn't come close to the attractiveness and technical value of the Universal horrors. But it was nevertheless an interesting and in a way quite ambitious piece of work.

Although slow-paced and lacking suspense, *The Mad Monster* is one of the better "Poverty Row horrors" that had been quite popular in the States since the 1930s. They were produced by small independent studios (usually located around Hollywood's Gower Street and Sunset Boulevard) that wanted to exploit the popularity of the horror genre initiated by Universal's two 1931 classics. Companies like Grand National, Republic, Mascot, Monogram, Supreme Pictures and Syndicate Pictures were all doing their best to emulate what the big studios were producing at the time, but on a fraction of their budgets. Producers Releasing Corporation (or PRC, often dubbed "Pretty Rotten Crap") — the Poverty Row company that produced *The Mad Monster* — was founded in the late 1930s and soon became one of the most prolific independent studios of that time. Newfield's aforementioned *Hitler — Beast of Berlin* was their first release (after being renamed *Beasts of Berlin* in order to appease the censors), but after that, PRC started specializing in horrors and thrillers. Apart from *The Mad Monster*, PRC's most noteworthy efforts were: *The Devil Bat* (1940; with Bela Lugosi as a master of murderous bats), *Bluebeard* (1944; directed by Edgar G. Ulmer, with John Carradine as a painter who likes to kill his models), and *Strangler of the Swamp* (1946; about a series of mysterious murders committed by a vengeful ghost).

Newfield continued working for PRC and was an astonishingly prolific director: he made around 300 movies throughout his whole career. His output in the horror genre was uneven, but he had a way of casting actors who could save even the most dreadful scripts — for example, *The Mad Monster*'s George Zucco who also appeared in *The Black Raven* (1943), *Dead Men Walk* (1943) and *The Flying Serpent* (1946), and J. Carrol Naish, who was great as a mad doctor in *The Monster Maker* (1944). In the late 1940s, as television was gaining popularity, many Poverty Row studios went into decline; in 1947, PRC morphed into Eagle-Lion Films, another company strictly interested in making B-movies.

The Mad Monster is a cornucopia of the genre's most famous monstrosities from the 1930s and early 1940s — and one that echoes the real-life monstrosities of that time. It is not a particularly scary movie, but it does possess a lot of charm, sports a werewolf in dungarees, and stars George Zucco in one of his best mad scientist roles (this time portraying a cross between Dr. Frankenstein and Adolf Hitler).

I Walked with a Zombie

DIRECTOR: Jacques Tourneur
CAST: Frances Dee, Tom Conway, James Ellison, Edith Barrett,
Christine Gordon, James Bell, Theresa Harris, Sir Lancelot, Darby Jones
USA, 1943

In 1995's documentary *A Personal Journey with Martin Scorsese Through American Movies*, the famous director cites *I Walked with a Zombie* as one of the movies that hugely influenced his work, and even if you're not really into zombies or horror movies, Scorsese's passion for the film may turn out to be contagious. He admires Jacques Tourneur's skill for creating suspense by the use of light and shadow, as well as the beauty of J. Roy Hunt's black-and-white photography; as an example, Scorsese shows us the scene with delicate Frances Dee and deathly pale Christine Gordon walking at night through the sugar cane field to meet the tall, bug-eyed zombie Darby Jones. This short piece — tense, curious and unbelievably attractive — is effective enough to make any cinema lover start searching madly for a copy of the film. And even if the sugar cane walk is its most easily recognizable scene, *I Walked with a Zombie* is just as good-looking and intriguing from the mysterious start to the dramatic finish.

Tourneur's horror career commenced with *Cat People* (1942), the first movie produced by the legendary Val Lewton. It was a success that established the director as a

From left to right, Jieno Moxzer, Jeni Le Gonr and Martin Wilkins in Jacques Tourneur's *I Walked with a Zombie* (1943).

filmmaker with a gift for horror and suspense, but one that would rather suggest the presence of a monster than show it. Tourneur and Lewton must have got on rather well, as they soon started working together on another project — a horror take on Charlotte Bronte's classic *Jane Eyre*.

Like *Jane Eyre*, *I Walked with a Zombie* is a tale of love that can't be fulfilled because of the dark secret of one of the persons involved. In this case the secret-keeper is sugar planter Paul Holland (Tom Conway), whose wife Jessica (Christine Gordon) has mentally withdrawn from the outside world; the woman can still walk but she never reacts to whatever is happening around her. Of course, there are some attempts at explaining her condition — a tropical fever is mentioned at one point — but since the events take place in the Caribbean and there is a "zombie" in the title, we expect Paul's wife to be a victim of voodoo rituals. When a beautiful nurse named Betsy Connell (Frances Dee) arrives on the island to take care of the woman, she soon falls in love with the patient's husband. Still she is determined to bring Jessica back to the world, even if this means taking her to a voodoo priest. In the meantime, Paul's half-brother Wesley Rand (James Ellison) tells Betsy that it may be Paul himself who is responsible for his wife's sorry state and warns her against becoming Paul's new victim. The warning is backed up by a random calypso singer (Sir Lancelot) whom the woman meets during her walk in the town, and who unexpectedly starts singing about "shame and sorrow" in the family of a certain sugar planter.

The calypso-singing scene is one of many memorable moments in the movie, and it reveals Tourneur's gentle ways for creating suspense. First we hear the song in the broad daylight and the main heroine is accompanied by the newly met Wesley. As the lyrics unwind we realize that Jessica's disease has already become one of the island's legends, but the singer falls silent as soon as he finds out that Wesley and Betsy are listening. Then, when the night comes and Wesley drinks himself unconscious, the calypso singer comes back to finish his tale of a sugar planter and his undead wife. Now looking Betsy straight in the eyes and slowly moving towards her, the man seems a completely different person, either haunted or mad. The emphasis put on this contrast between the world of daylight and the world of night — and how the veil of darkness can change people — is all Tourneur needs to unnerve the viewers.

I Walked with a Zombie also looks much more expensive than it actually was. As usual with Tourneur's movies, the photography is impeccably beautiful and even though the film wasn't shot on location it strikes us with its exoticism. To evoke the atmosphere of the Caribbean, Tourneur often cuts the screen with horizontal shadows that make us think the characters are constantly surrounded by half-drawn Venetian blinds; and this clever deception also helps to create the feeling of claustrophobia whenever the action takes place within the sugar planter's house. This feeling is then contrasted with that of overwhelming freedom when the characters stray away from the house — even if it is to end up walking through the sugar cane fields and face the ghoulish zombie.

The famous scene of Betsy leading Jessica through the sugar cane to the voodoo priest marks many more contrasts than the one between freedom and claustrophobia. It's just as importantly the contraposition of medicine and magic, the rational and the superstitious, and it all boils down to the conflict between the two cultures in the Caribbean: this of the white land owners and that of their black slaves. *I Walked with a Zombie* suggests that even if at first glance white people seem to have an advantage in places such as the movie's colony, in reality they will always be helpless strangers there, with their medicine and religion ceasing to work on foreign soil — much as they want to believe they are the ones in control.

Typically for Tourneur, *I Walked with a Zombie* is also a very ambiguous movie, one that constantly forces the viewers to question both the rationalistic and the supernatural explanation of the presented incidents. And even though the director chose to base his film on the much-exploited theme of voodoo, he wisely refused to follow the horror movie trend of showing it as something at the same time ridiculous and threatening. Tourneur's idea was to present voodoo rituals as alien and perplexing in the eyes of the main characters in order to emphasize their isolation and displacement. To achieve this effect, he had to have a serious approach towards the subject, and that's why he had to get rid of some hackneyed horror scares included in Curt Siodmak's original script. It was certainly worth the effort, as I *Walked with a Zombie* to this day remains a rare zombie movie that is gorgeous, thrilling and intelligent.

Tourneur's next movie after the successful *Cat People* manages to be even more unsettling and better looking than its predecessor. Darby Jones still makes one of the creepiest onscreen zombies ever.

The Body Snatcher

DIRECTOR: Robert Wise
CAST: Boris Karloff, Henry Daniell, Russell Wade, Edith Atwater,
Rita Corday, Sharyn Moffett, Bela Lugosi
USA, 1945

Robert Louis Stevenson's short story "The Body Snatcher" was written in 1881 but because of the gruesome subject matter it wasn't published until three years later. The story starts with a drunk and jaded old man named Fettes unexpectedly meeting an old acquaintance, Dr. MacFarlane. The short reunion ends in a row between the two men and prompts a lengthy flashback to the good old times of Fettes and MacFarlane's youth. It turns out they were both studying medicine in Edinburgh under one Professor K.— apparently a very famous and respectable figure. However, for his scientific research Professor K. needed regular deliveries of dead bodies and his young students inevitably got involved in the grim trade. At first, Fettes only had to pay the grave robbers for the corpses, and even though he was not exactly happy about the task, he never refused to perform it. Everything changed when one day Fettes discovered that the men who were delivering the bodies were most probably also killing people to then sell their fresh corpses. Fettes decided to stop following Professor K.'s orders but when he confessed this to Mac-Farlane, his friend advised him against it. "You can't begin and then stop," he said. "If you begin, you must keep on beginning; that's the truth. No rest for the wicked."

In Robert Wise's adaptation, the present-day intro is taken out and the relationship between Fettes and MacFarlane switches from that of school acquaintances to the two being a mentor and a pupil. Fettes (Russell Wade) learns that the renowned anatomy teacher Dr. MacFarlane (Henry Daniell) is involved in the shady business of buying exhumed bodies. The doctor then uses obtained body parts for research prior to perform miraculous surgeries, which poses a great problem for Fettes: should he expose the body-dealing scandal or should he keep quiet about it, so that more lives can be saved? While the young man is still deep in thought, things suddenly get out of hand: MacFarlane's favorite body snatcher John Gray (Boris Karloff) reasons that it will be much easier for him to kill people than to exhume them. When MacFarlane tells Gray that he doesn't want to do any more business with him, the murderer threatens him to reveal their cooperation so far.

The character of John Gray was also present in Stevenson's short story but he wasn't the main villain there. As soon as the studio decided that Karloff should play the part, Gray's character in the script started to evolve and eventually became a figure equal to MacFarlane and Fettes. And as soon as Karloff's participation was secured, the producers thought it might be a good idea to find a supporting role for Bela Lugosi, so that the movie could be advertised as another pairing of the two legendary actors.

This is how Lugosi got the part of Joseph, a simpleton servant to MacFarlane, who at some point visits John Gray and tries to blackmail him without realizing how dangerous this can be for him. The blackmailing scene is among the best in the movie, Karloff's Gray towering over Lugosi's Joseph, smiling devilishly and continually pouring him alcohol while listening to the visitor's lame plan of earning some extra money. During the shoot of *The Body Snatcher*, Karloff was suffering from severe back problems and Lugosi was addicted to morphine but this single scene between them is so powerful and well-acted that one could never guess they were both having such a tough time; it also somehow makes up for the lack of other good Boris-Bela scenes, which must have been disappointing for all the viewers who went to see *The Body Snatcher* because the trailers were calling it "the unholiest partnership of Karloff and Lugosi this side of the grave."

Director Wise once said that in order to get good performances in his movies he always made sure that he had "the right parts for the right people." Here it paid off wonderfully with Karloff and Lugosi but a bit less so with Russell Wade, whose character is too common and uptight to carry a large portion of the movie. Much better is Henry Daniell as the ambiguous doctor: as cold as Vincent Price in his best roles (and sometimes even speaking in a manner similar to Price's), he totally owns the role of a self-confident genius who suddenly starts feeling unnerved and insecure. Another great scene is when Daniell's character, accompanied by Fettes, meets Gray in a tavern and is, unexpectedly to the viewer, intimidated by him. This is when Dr. MacFarlane's self-assuredness starts to crumble and the actor pulls it off perfectly—his voice remains steady as always but the eyes fill with fear.

Unlike some other Stevenson's works (*The Strange Case of Dr. Jekyll and Mr. Hyde* and *Treasure Island*), *The Body Snatcher* wasn't an often adapted story but the British version of it that was aired in 1966 as part of the TV series *Mystery and Imagination* is certainly worth mentioning. It was directed by Toby Robertson and starred young Ian Holm in the role of MacFarlane. The show, later renamed *Tales of Mystery and Imagination*, spanned five seasons (1966–1970) and covered important works of horror from the likes of Edgar Allan Poe, M.R. James, Bram Stoker, Algernon Blackwood and Sheridan Le Fanu.

A movie directed by Robert Wise, produced by Val Lewton, starring the duo of Boris Karloff and Bela Lugosi, and based on a story by Robert Louis Stevenson should perhaps be even more impressive than *The Body Snatcher* is, but you will still find a lot of good acting and many creepy moments here.

Dead of Night

DIRECTORS: Alberto Cavalcanti, Charles Crichton, Basil Dearden, Robert Hamer
CAST: Mervyn Johns, Roland Culver, Barbara Leake, Mary Merrall, Renee Gadd, Frederick Valk, Googie Withers, Anthony Baird, Judy Kelly, Sally Ann Howes, Basil Radford, Naunton Wayne, Michael Redgrave
UK, 1945

The period of World War II, with the daily reports of real-life horrors, wasn't the most appropriate time for filmmakers to indulge in onscreen violence. As soon as the war ended, however, both the audiences and the artists felt the urge to exorcise the demons of the past few years, and the horror genre was again gaining popularity. Even the famous British Ealing studio, best recognized for its light comedies, decided to give horror a try — and happened to make one of the best genre movies of the 1940s.

Dead of Night is a combination of five separate stories linked with a wraparound narrative. The movie's credits boast some remarkable names: the script was based on the writings of such authors as H.G. Wells, E.F. Benson, John Baines and Angus MacPhail; also, there were as many as four directors involved in the project — Alberto Cavalcanti, Charles Crichton, Basil Dearden and Robert Hamer—each of them responsible for a different portion of the movie.

The linking tale sees Walter Craig (Mervyn Johns) arriving at the house of Eliot Foley (Roland Culver), and immediately recognizing the house as identical to the one where his recurring nightmare takes place. Things get worse when he also recognizes the guests as characters appearing in the same dream, and is even able to occasionally predict what they are going to do — just as if this *was* his nightmare come true. Eliot's memory of the exact chain of events is not clear, but he knows one thing: it will all end in violence. The other guests are in equal measures as frightened as they are fascinated with the perfect stranger claiming he has dreamt about them, and as they try to explain how this could be possible, it turns out they, too, have their own supernatural stories to tell. In *Hearse Driver*, Hugh Grainger (Anthony Baird), a racing driver recovering in a hospital from a serious accident, has an ominous vision that first makes him afraid he's losing his mind, but later saves his life. The second tale, *Christmas Party*, comes from the youngest of the guests, Sally O'Hara (Sally Ann Howes). The girl relates the outcome of one hide 'n' seek game organized during a Christmas Party, and says that she found the ultimate hiding place in the room of a ghost. *Haunted Mirror* is one of the two creepiest and most interesting segments of the movie. In it, Joan Cortland (Googie Withers) buys a large, ornamental mirror for her would-be husband Peter (Ralph Michael), only to see him become more and more mesmerized by the gift. When the woman learns that the mirror was once witness to a murder, she starts worrying it may have a bad influence on Peter. *Golfing Story* is more of a typical Ealing comedy than an out-and-out horror movie (even though this is the episode adapted from a story by H.G. Wells), but it does play with a supernatural theme. Two good pals, George Parratt (Basil Radford) and Larry Potter (Naunton Wayne), play a game of golf in order to decide which one of them is going to marry the cheerful and attractive (albeit a bit silly) Mary Lee (Peggy Bryan). When the winner is finally established, the other man commits suicide and then comes back to haunt his ex-friend, accusing him of having cheated in the game. The final episode is, together with *Haunted Mirror*, a definite highlight here; *Ventriloquist's Dummy* stars a deliciously demented Michael Redgrave as Maxwell Frere, a ventriloquist obsessing that his spooky doll is trying to take control over him.

It was a wise choice to make *Dead of Night* so varied in both the subject matter and the tone (after all, even the comedic golfing episode turns out intriguing enough). Not all stories included here are horror gems (*Hearse Driver* and *Christmas Party* seem to lack the necessary punch), but all are at least interesting and the suspenseful finale stitches them all together in an uncanny way. But perhaps the main reason why *Dead of Night* works so well is that it distorts the image of British society shown in most movies made up to that point. Here these clean, uptight characters have to face occurrences and phenomena that just can't be dealt with on a normal basis; shaken and puzzled, these men and women eventually wake up to real life and realize that there's more to it than safe and lazy day-to-day existence. (It's hard to deny that the memory of World War II changing the lives of most Europeans must have haunted the makers of the movie.) For Hitchcock fans there's one more nice surprise here: Basil Radford and Naunton Wayne reprise their roles from *The Lady Vanishes* (1938) in *Golfing Story*, and some other of his actors can be spotted elsewhere in the movie.

The success of *Dead of Night* didn't convert Ealing into a horror studio, nor did it start a horror craze in Britain, but it certainly was an inspiration for filmmakers during the genre revival in the late 1950s and 1960s. The portmanteau horrors from Amicus in particular bore the unmistakable *Dead of Night* mark (1964's *Dr. Terror's House of Horrors* being a prime example of these). The most influential *Dead of Night* episode was no doubt *Ventriloquist's Dummy*, inspiring everything from *Devil Doll* (1964; about a knife-wielding dummy called Hugo, which is also the name of the dummy in *Dead of Night*) to *Magic* (1978; with a disturbing turn from Anthony Hopkins as a ventriloquist going mad), and even the less similar plot-wise horror movies featuring creepy dolls, like *Child's Play* (1988) and *Dead Silence* (2007). Out of them all, however, only *Magic* comes close to effectively imitating the sheer horror and unnerving atmosphere of *Ventriloquist's Dummy*.

Not a typical output from the Ealing Studio renowned for its comedies, but nevertheless considered one of its best productions. It's also the most coherent horror anthology made so far, and one of its episodes is the freakiest portrayal of a ventriloquist dummy *ever*. Scary, inventive and influential, *Dead of Night* is an unmissable horror experience.

The Beast with Five Fingers

DIRECTOR: Robert Florey
CAST: Peter Lorre, Andrea King, Robert Alda, J. Carrol Naish,
Victor Francen, John Alvin, Charles Dingle, David Hoffman
USA, 1947

Today horror movies featuring a living severed hand are a common thing. Most fans of the genre remember comedic scenes from *Evil Dead II* (1987) or *The Addams Family* (1991), and those who like to dig deeper into horror history must have already encountered such titles as *The Crawling Hand* (1963), *Dr. Terror's House of Horrors* (1965) or *The Hand* (1981). All of them are movies of many values (although Oliver Stone's *The Hand* didn't get many good reviews), but if you want to know where the story of a creepy, cut-off hand begins, you need to get hold of Robert Florey and Curt Siodmak's take on the subject, the aptly and handsomely titled *The Beast with Five Fingers*.

The body part of the title doesn't look like a beast at all, but it does feel a beastly urge to kill, as it untiringly searches for necks to strangle. The hand once belonged to famous pianist Francis Ingram (Victor Francen), who died under strange circumstances soon after a quarrel with his secretary Hilary Cummins (Peter Lorre). When Ingram's last will is opened, it turns out that it's neither the secretary nor the man's family that become the heirs but Ingram's attractive nurse Julie (Andrea King). This is troublesome for everyone concerned: the family members will have to challenge the will, Hilary will have to think of a way to stay in his master's library in order to continue his astrological studies, Julie will have to forget about running away from Ingram's Italian villa with Bruce (Robert Alda), and local law enforcer Commissario Castania (J. Carrol Naish) will be busier than ever keeping his eyes on all people mentioned above. When the dead pianist's hand is severed, it enters the house of its previous owner in order to bring justice amidst the angry crowd.

A legend has it that the sequence with Ingram's severed hand scuttling around the house was invented by none other than Spanish surrealist Luis Buñuel, who was working for Warner Bros. back in the 1940s. The studio never admitted to this being true, perhaps because they initially rejected the idea for the scene and later refused to pay the artist, but Buñuel himself mentioned it in one of his interviews, and the sequence in question does look surreal enough to be considered his invention. (The whole scenario becomes more plausible when you think of the severed hand that could be spotted many years before in *Un Chien Andalou* [1929], an unnerving and influential short movie directed by Buñuel. While watching this scene you almost expect the hand to suddenly jump to life and attack the characters who surround it.) Whatever credit the Spanish artist should be given for *The Beast with Five Fingers*, there are many other people responsible for the movie's success, especially the talented, if a bit unlucky, director Robert Florey, famous scriptwriter Curt Siodmak and actor Peter Lorre, here in one of his best roles.

Florey's career and esteem within the horror genre could have been entirely different had he been chosen, as was originally intended, to direct 1931's *Frankenstein*. Replaced by James Whale, he went on to make his own dark-themed movies, like *Murders in the Rue Morgue* (1932) and *The Face Behind the Mask* (1941, also starring Lorre in a fine role), but it's *The Beast with Five Fingers* that remains Florey's most valued work among those interested in horror and haunted house spoofs. It's no coincidence, either, as apart from setting the killer hand trend, the movie manages to be a very convincing depiction of madness (just look into Lorre's eyes to see how painful it is for his character to keep a grasp on reality), as well as an impressive tribute to German Expressionism (the crooked camera angles and peculiar lightning are similar to those from 1920's *The Cabinet of Dr. Caligari*, though Florey's visuals are never as obviously unrealistic as Robert Wiene's). Siodmak's script, based on a story by William Fryer Harvey, is very involving, with an especially suspenseful middle part, and together with the screenplays for *The Wolf Man* (1941) and *I Walked with a Zombie* (1943), it is one of his best and most original works. One has to wonder, however, if all the abovementioned talent could make a movie half as enjoyable as *The Beast* if it weren't for Peter Lorre's astonishingly quiet performance as the weak and frightened psycho in love. And another neat twist to Florey's movie is the fact that with his sensitivity and the need to safeguard everything and everyone he loves, Lorre's Hilary Cummins is the most humane character here, even though he is clearly pinpointed to act as a villain.

The Beast was about to reach true horror greatness when studio executives stepped in and ruined the mood by adding an unnecessary and totally unfunny coda in which Naish's Commissario Castania (very effective as comedic relief up to this point) has a forced monologue that explains certain parts of the plot. It didn't happen for the first or last time in the history of cinema, of course: similarly anticlimactic codas were added to movies as famous as *The Cabinet of Dr. Caligari* and *Invasion of the Body Snatchers* (1956). The case of *The Beast* is, however, an especially painful one; if the annoying punchline was taken away, the movie could have become Warner Bros.'s classiest horror title, one to finally rival the genre titles from Universal.

Nineteen forty-seven was the year when horror movies about a severed hand were invented. In this pioneering effort, you can already see some very good special effects that bring the killer hand to life, and Peter Lorre's sad main character is one of the most sympathetic villains ever brought to screen.

The Thing from Another World

DIRECTOR: Howard Hawks, Christian Nyby
CAST: Kenneth Tobey, Robert Cornthwaite, Margaret Sheridan,
Douglas Spencer, James Arness, Dewey Martin, James Young, Robert Nichols
USA, 1951

The 1950s began with an unexpected blast from the Space in the form of Howard Hawks and Christian Nyby's *The Thing from Another World*. Apart from being a very entertaining piece of cinema, the film was also an important step in the development of sci-fi–horror (it was the first ever feature-length movie about alien invasion), it raised many questions about putting proper labels on movies (people began to wonder whether it should be categorized as horror or sci-fi), started the tendency of interpreting the 1950s films as metaphors for Cold War conflicts (it's still the most popular interpretation of *The Thing*, albeit not the only one), sparked the society's interest in UFOs (producer-director Howard Hawks wanted to use assistance from the U.S. Air Force but they refused to help him, not wanting to be connected with the subject), and it even made all the fans suddenly discuss the responsibilities of a movie director (Christian Nyby was officially the helmer, but the movie had trademark Hawks touches all over it). Not a bad accomplishment for a movie that is, essentially, a suspenseful, quick-paced story of an intelligent carrot from outer space that comes to Earth and tries to annihilate all humans in sight.

The script was based on the novella *Who Goes There?* by John W. Campbell Jr. (which Hawks bought for adaptation), but scriptwriters Charles Lederer, Ben Hecht and Hawks himself weren't interested in copying the plot too faithfully. In their version, Captain Patrick Hendry (Kenneth Tobey) and journalist Ned Scott (Douglas Spencer) fly to an army base at the North Pole to take a look at something that may be a meteorite that crashed and is now buried under the ice. They muster several other people from the base and head to look for the thing from space. To everyone's surprise, the "meteorite" turns out to be a flying saucer — and so excited are they with the idea of taking the spaceship out of the ice, that they accidentally destroy it with a thermite bomb. At this point, Hendry's expedition could have been written off as another case of humans having blown their chance to face remnants of an unknown race, but it appears that there's something — some*one*— still buried under the ice. Now much more careful than before, Hendry & Co. decide to cut the thing — most probably the saucer's pilot — out of the ice and transport it to the base. They do that, and before the block of ice thaws, thus freeing the not-at-all-friendly pilot (James Arness), we get to know and like all the characters at the base except for Dr. Carrington (Robert Cornthwaite), an uptight and fanatic scientist who claims that there are "no enemies in science, only phenomena to be studied." Naturally, when the showdown between the people and the alien begins, Dr. Carrington chooses to do anything to save the creature (by then defined as an intelligent — but also bloodthirsty!— form of plant life), while Hendry's main aim is to save his people — and his lovely girlfriend Nikki (Margaret Sheridan) — even if it means blowing the walking plant to tiny pieces.

James Arness, an intelligent and dangerous carrot in *The Thing from Another World* (1951).

That Hawks had a huge influence on the final version of *The Thing* is undeniable: the characters, as likable and convincing as in his other movies (a trick that Nyby never pulled off after this debut, when directing on his own), speak Hawks's trademark overlapping dialogue and are led by a tough guy reminiscent of the noir heroes. Also, the movie has the perfect balance between the scenes that flesh out the characters and those that are pure action — and hardly any first-time director in the history of cinema could achieve that (even the later box office charmers like Steven Spielberg or Peter Jackson did have their problems to get it right at the beginning). The most important thing is, however, not the question of how much of the movie was actually directed by Nyby, Hawks' previous editor — the best bet being: just several scenes — but the fact that this collaboration of Hawks and Nyby still is one of the very best alien invasion movies ever. Its effectiveness, on the other hand, can be traced back to the material the two filmmakers collaborated on before, including *The Big Sleep* (1946) and *Red River* (1948). In *The Thing* they approached the subject as seriously as they did all their previous works (instead of deciding that it has the right to be artificial and overblown, as many directors do), and this paid off with tension and atmosphere of dread not typical for science fiction movies. The scares are rare but highly effective: the scene when we first spot the alien, not quite sure what it is yet; the one in which the monster is found behind one of the doors, much to everyone's shock; and the moment when the characters try to set the alien on fire, but it doesn't seem to be stopping him.

As for the Cold War subtext — i.e., seeing the movie as a vote for military action rather than for discussion while dealing with enemies — there's no doubt it makes sense, but perhaps reading *The Thing* as a post–World War II trauma or a fear of the atomic age is just as pertinent. Dr. Carrington, the man willing to risk his life in order to examine the monster, doesn't necessarily have to be seen as a naïve politician; he can be as well an incarnation of Adolf Hitler, a man who wants everyone to share his obsessions, or a scientist happy to tamper with the atomic bomb and put the whole world at risk just to check whether his speculations were correct.

When *The Thing from Another World* turned out to be a box office success (even though it certainly wasn't the favorite of the critics), the 1950s alien invasion craze started for good, and many similar movies were soon hitting the screens like the thickest meteorite rain. Most of them were forgettable trifles (like 1956's *It Conquered the World*, directed by Roger Corman), but some are now considered the landmarks of science fiction or sci-fi–horror cinema. Byron Haskin's solemn adaptation of H.G. Wells' *The War of the Worlds* (released in 1953) wasn't quite as thrilling as *The Thing*, and its preachiness is a bit annoying, but it nevertheless managed to create a palpable otherworldly atmosphere that immediately owned the audience. Even better is Jack Arnold's *It Came from Outer Space* (1953), operating on suspicions and uncertainties rather than special effects; with its plot about aliens controlling humans, the movie was a foreshadowing of *Invasion of the Body Snatchers* (1956) directed by Don Siegel, the decade's second most important sci-fi movie after *The Thing*. Unlike the alien visitors in *It Came from Outer Space*, those in *Invasion* were again sworn enemies of mankind, and — understandably — the Cold War interpretations had to follow, even if Siegel himself wasn't very happy with them, and was repeatedly saying that he hadn't aimed at making a political movie.

Decades later, John Carpenter decided to refresh the plot of Hawks and Nyby's movie for the 1980s viewers in *The Thing* (1982) — not so much a remake of the movie, as another attempt at adapting John W. Campbell Jr.'s novella to the big screen. Carpenter was a bit more faithful to the original story but he, too, opted for having his own kind of monster in the movie — this time a shape-shifting beast that could perfectly imitate its victims (brought to life via the jaw-dropping effects by Rob Bottin and Stan Winston). As is often the case with the early 1980s movies, Carpenter's *The*

Thing was later interpreted by some critics as a metaphor for AIDS (it did feature a suspenseful blood-test scene, after all), but it is quite impossible that the director really planned it that way — before 1982, the disease was hardly known, though already identified, and it didn't become the well-known threat until several years later. (Another 1982 horror movie described in this book, Jean Rollin's *The Living Dead Girl*, also faces the problem of being a potential AIDS metaphor had it only been made a bit later.)

Whether it was directed by Howard Hawks or Christian Nyby, and whether it was really meant as a tip for the American leaders dealing with the Cold War conflict, *The Thing from Another World* is without doubt one of the very best alien invasion films of all time. Sure, John Carpenter's effects-heavy version is a treat, but the original holds its ground, too — even over half a century later.

House of Wax

DIRECTOR: André De Toth
CAST: Vincent Price, Phyllis Kirk, Paul Picerni, Frank Lovejoy,
Carolyn Jones, Paul Cavanagh, Charles Bronson, Roy Roberts
USA, 1953

Vincent Price plays Henry Jarrod, a genius sculptor in love with the wax figures he creates. No surprise then that when his business partner, Burke (Roy Roberts), decides to set the museum on fire to get the insurance money, Henry tries to save his beloved "people" from "death." Unfortunately, the fire spreads too quickly for him to do anything except for running around madly as the whole room turns into a fiery trap. He cannot even help the object of his special affection, the pale and beautiful Marie Antoinette. Henry's work of a lifetime melts down in flames in a grotesque scene, with the camera looking closely at the eyeballs morbidly popping out of the wax heads and the wigs of the exhibits being consumed by the hungry fire. The greedy Burke manages to get out alive and soon receives his insurance money. Now he doesn't even have to split the sum with Henry, as the latter is reported to have died in the fire. But when Burke is then killed by a deformed stranger, we expect this is in fact part of Henry Jarrod's revenge. More people soon disappear and, coincidentally, at the same time Jarrod's House of Wax reopens, now complete with a Chamber of Horrors and the figurines looking even more real than before. When a beautiful brunette, Sue Allen (Phyllis Kirk), notices that one of the exhibits is most probably her dead friend covered in wax, she doesn't realize that she herself may soon face a similar fate. After all, she looks shockingly similar to Jarrod's greatest love — the late Marie Antoinette.

In the 1950s, when television was suddenly gaining huge popularity with the American audiences, the theatre owners and the filmmakers started coming up with ideas on how to improve the experience of seeing movies on the big screen; one of them was 3-D. *House of Wax* is not only one of the first movies to employ it (1952's *Bwana Devil* preceded it) but, most importantly, the best one to do so. Certain scenes are put in it purely for the 3-D effect and may seem overlong or even annoying to modern viewers (like the can-can scene, for example, which in 1953 was undoubtedly bold and

André De Toth's *House of Wax* (1953): a career-making turn for Vincent Price.

putting the 3-D technique to good use). Fortunately, it doesn't happen very often. André De Toth was a gifted filmmaker and *House of Wax* is a good vehicle both for his visual skills (the sets, costumes and colors draw us right into this fictional world) and his ability to direct the actors. Price is perfect in the role of the artist-gone-mad, no less convincing as a sensitive loner at the beginning than as an all-out psycho near the end. And Crane Wilbur's screenplay provides him with enough juicy scenes and sinister lines to properly shine here. It's a great pleasure to watch Price's pained look when saying "I once had hands like these" to a young sculptor in his employ. The only disappointment concerning Price is the introductory fight with the character of Roy Roberts — highly unrealistic and somehow spoiling the impact of the movie's first scenes.

Just as good as Price is Phyllis Kirk, whose character is not that of a typical woman-in-peril but rather of a girl who emanates eroticism and intelligence in equal measures. One of the movie's most memorable moments is when Kirk's Sue is running away from a phantom figure through the dark streets of New York, and the actress manages to make the audience truly feel for her in this scene. She is also great when she then has to play a bold and nosy investigator in the wax museum, or when she eventually becomes a helpless victim. Kirk's character never loses her dignity — not even when she is stripped naked by the mad sculptor and has to wait for somebody to save her from the cruel fate of becoming one of Jarrod's waxworks (please watch her carefully in the movie's very last scene where she jokes about her own helplessness). Other actors don't impress as much as Price and Kirk do, but that's because the script simply didn't call for any more significant characters. Carolyn Jones surely is quite irritating as Burke's giggling girlfriend but this is exactly what was needed for this particular role. Also worth mentioning is an early appearance by Charles Bronson, here playing Jarrod's helper Igor.

House of Wax is a remake of 1933's *Mystery of the Wax Museum*, directed by Michael Curtiz, and starring Lionel Atwill and Fay Wray in the main roles. This first version has an even more mysterious aura to it than *House of Wax*, and the first visit to its museum is arguably more impressive. On the other hand, it is a more typical horror movie, with lots of screaming from the female protagonists, some examples of bad acting (never from Wray or Atwill, though) and lots of stilted dialogue. Also, anyone who first saw De Toth's take on the story and only then Curtiz's will no doubt miss the presence of Vincent Price.

In 2005, Spanish director Jaume Collet-Serra remade *House of Wax*, casting Elisha Cuthbert, Chad Michael Murray, Brian Van Holt and Paris Hilton as characters arriving in a ghost town where a spooky Wax Museum is the sole attraction. The new version is actually much better than one could expect any movie starring Paris Hilton to be; it is surprisingly grisly at times, moves at a brisk pace and sports several well-made set pieces. But it bears no resemblance to the wax-themed films of De Toth and Curtiz — either in atmosphere or script-wise.

Vincent Price's career-maker does not cease to amaze after all the years: it has a fine, complex villain, a likable heroine, interesting supporting characters, and some of the creepiest wax figures in the movie history.

Tarantula

DIRECTOR: Jack Arnold
CAST: John Agar, Mara Corday, Leo G. Carroll, Nestor Paiva, Ross Elliott,
Raymond Bailey, Edwin Rand, Hank Patterson, Clint Eastwood
USA, 1955

The 1950s are, as far as sci-fi–horror movies are concerned, very often dubbed "the age of atomic monsters" or "the age of invasions from outer space." Quite appropriately so, of course, since classics such as *The Thing from Another World* (1951), *Invaders from Mars* (1953) and *Them!* (1954) were hitting the screens from the very beginning of the decade. But imagine how much charm and class the 1950s would lose if it weren't for Jack Arnold, a man who tackled the most exciting subjects of that time, and always with the most impressive results. His vision of aliens visiting Earth —*It Came from Outer Space* (1953)— still belongs to the most enthralling encounters of the third kind ever; his attempts at adding a new monster to Universal's gallery of monsters — in *Creature from the Black Lagoon* (1954) and *Revenge of the Creature* (1955)— proved hugely successful; and his reply to the Monster Bug-mania —*Tarantula*— still remains one of the best films of its kind.

"The disease of hunger, like most diseases ... well, it spreads," says Professor Gerald Deemer (Leo G. Carroll) in order to explain to the audience the importance of his

Dr. Matt Hastings (John Agar, second from right) and sheriff Jack Andrews (Nestor Paiva, on right) spot traces of the monster in Jack Arnold's *Tarantula* (1955).

experiments that involve growing animals to giant sizes. "There are two billion people in the world today," he continues. "In 1975 there'll be three billion. In the year 2000, there'll be 3,625,000,000. The world may not be able to produce enough food to feed all these people!" The question viewers may start asking themselves at this point is: would many people feel like eating a giant tarantula? This is, after all, one of the over-grown animals the professor has been experimenting upon; however, instead of allowing billions of hungry people to feed on its huge, hairy legs, the tarantula escapes from the laboratory and turns the scientist's plan upside down by helping itself to the cattle and local people. The professor cannot help hunt the deadly creature because he himself had been experimented upon and is dying of acromegalia — an extreme bone growth that gradually turns him into a hideous monster. Therefore, the future of Desert Rock, and the whole of Arizona — or perhaps even the whole *planet*— depends on the hero-ism and ingenuity of the professor's lovely assistant Stephanie (Mara Corday) and hand-some Dr. Hastings (John Agar). The problem is, the already big tarantula is constantly growing to eventually become "fiercer, more cruel and deadly than anything that ever walked on earth." Thus, even though Stephanie and Dr. Hastings can count on a lit-tle help from the U.S. Air Force (with none other than young Clint Eastwood as a brave pilot), it looks like this may be one tough war to win...

When describing *Tarantula* in his book *Dziedzictwo Wyobraźni* Polish film critic and genre enthusiast Andrzej Kołodyński wrote: "There's a particular sense of poetry in this movie; not the atomic experiments but the desert is the cradle of the unknown — the desert that is mysterious, untamed by the humans." Kołodyński admires Arnold's unquestionable talent for bringing to life concepts that would end up silly or pretentious in the hands of lesser directors, and favorably compares *Tarantula* with some other 1950s monster movies — e.g., Roger Corman's cheap *Attack of the Crab Monsters* (1957) and Eugène Lourié's ambitious but uneven *Behemoth the Sea Monster* (1959). There are several factors that help *Tarantula* stand out from the crowd of the giant monster movies: the unrelenting atmosphere of mystery (created by eerie, omnipresent shots of the beautiful yet forbidding desert), and the ingenious special effects. Unlike the giant ants in the more popular *Them!* and other oversized creatures in many 1950s horror movies, Arnold's tarantula wasn't a puppet but the real thing unleashed on miniature sets or made bigger by trick photography.

Arnold claimed to dislike typical, gruesome horror movies (he was never a fan of *The Exorcist*, for example), and this is perhaps yet another reason why his own output was so different from that of other genre directors. His sci-fi–horrors were always good-looking, suspenseful and clever, and even when Arnold was aiming to shock the audiences — and he undoubtedly did in the finale of *The Incredible Shrinking Man* (1957), one of his best works — he was always able to pull it off in a classy way.

An effort that puts most other giant spider films to shame, *Tarantula* doesn't resort to using hairy puppets of the title bug but opts for utilizing convincing trick photography and miniatures instead. As a bonus, the movie lets us admire the mesmerizing beauty of Mara Corday and gives us a glimpse of an early performance from Clint Eastwood.

The Curse of Frankenstein

DIRECTOR: Terence Fisher
CAST: Peter Cushing, Christopher Lee, Robert Urquhart,
Hazel Court, Valerie Gaunt, Paul Hardtmuth
UK, 1957

Hammer Film Productions was founded in 1934 but it had to wait 20 years, and undergo a management change, before releasing its first hit, *The Quatermass Xperiment* (1954; aka *The Creeping Unknown*, directed by Val Guest). It was an adaptation of Nigel Kneale's science fiction series broadcast on TV in 1953, with the title slightly changed from *The Quatermass Experiment* in order to emphasize the fact that it was Britain's first X-rated film ever. In 1957 Guest followed the successful movie with an equally enjoyable sequel, *Quatermass 2*, but that year the studio had an even bigger hit, one to become a blueprint for British horrors in the late 1950s and throughout the 1960s: *The Curse of Frankenstein*, starring Peter Cushing and Christopher Lee.

The movie's director, Terence Fisher, had made several movies for Hammer earlier (like 1953's sci-fi effort *Four Sided Triangle* and 1954's mystery *Murder by Proxy*), but quality-wise they didn't even come close to *The Curse of Frankenstein*, as they lacked its atmosphere, its overall impact and, obviously, had no lead actors as strong as Cushing and Lee. Fisher's abilities as a director were still far from immaculate back in 1957 (he clearly didn't control all his actors, and didn't seem to care much about the pacing of the movie), but *The Curse of Frankenstein* still remains one of his best works, as well as one of the most consistently enjoyable horrors from Hammer. Plus, *The Curse* didn't resort to simply copying the plot of Mary Shelley's book or James Whale's 1931 classic film *Frankenstein*: the script offered new twists on the story, the monster was much more gruesome than that portrayed by Karloff (Jack Pierce's makeup from Whale's *Frankenstein* was copyrighted, so the Hammer

Hammer gives us a new, shocking Frankenstein's monster: Christopher Lee in *The Curse of Frankenstein* (1957).

people had to come up with something markedly different), and the character of Frankenstein was no longer a well-meaning scientist torn between his beloved work and the loving woman. Genre expert Kim Newman compared the two Frankensteins in the following way: "Whale's Henry Frankenstein might as well be a sorcerer, but Hammer's Baron is a chilly scientist, forerunner of the conscience-free obsessives who pioneered rocketry under the Nazis and the nuclear weapons throughout the Cold War." This re-examination of a familiar character apparently went over very well with the viewers, and sparked a renewed interest in horror in a decade that was slowly growing tired of the genre.

That the new Frankenstein (Cushing) is a mean and dangerous character is clear from the beginning: he is in prison, waiting for the hangman and telling the story of his life to a priest (Alex Gallier). Together with the priest, *we* learn that Frankenstein's childhood tutor was one Paul Krempe (Robert Urquhart), a kind-hearted and God-fearing man, who eventually had to give him a hand in abominable experiments, reviving the dead and creating a perfect creature (Lee). But neither Krempe nor Frankenstein's lovely fiancée (Hazel Court) could predict the lengths to which the fanatic monster-maker would go to achieve his goal.

Showing Frankenstein in a new light from the very first scene immediately hooks the viewer's interest, all the more effectively so because of the charged performance from Cushing. The early stages of the experiments are great visually, and Frankenstein's growing contempt for people around him is a thing to behold; the suspense gradually rises when it is made clear that in order to give life to a dead body, another life has to be taken. The first glance at the monster is an unforgettable horror moment: the grotesque makeup comes as a shock, and Lee perfectly controls his movement and facial expressions, making the monster as convincingly pained as he is threatening. Another asset of *The Curse* were the lush colors that made it look like no other horror before (this was Hammer's first color production, and the sharp, vivid photography was to become the company's trademark from 1957 on). The movie's highly controversial content (the immoral Frankenstein being the greatest offense) augmented by its impressive technical values caused furious critique, especially in Great Britain; *Sight and Sound* critic Derek Hill argued in his article "The Face of Horror" that "only a sick society could bear the hoardings, let alone see [such] films," and many other reviewers backed him depicting *The Curse* as "repulsive" and "meaningless."

Hammer followed *The Curse of Frankenstein* with six other movies featuring Baron Frankenstein, and they were never less than entertaining. The first sequel was *The Revenge of Frankenstein* (1958), a direct continuation of the original that saw the return of Cushing and director Fisher, but not Lee (who chose to explore the character of Dracula instead, and never played the Monster again). Next was *The Evil of Frankenstein* (1964) which, unlike its predecessors, bore some striking similarities to the Universal Frankensteins in the Monster's makeup (it was distributed by Universal and the copyrights were no longer an issue); Fisher was at the time recovering from a car accident and had to be replaced by Freddie Francis. *Frankenstein Created Woman* (1967) and *Frankenstein Must Be Destroyed* (1969) were again helmed by Francis and brought the usual amount of menace and controversy to the screen (the latter movie included an infamous rape scene). *The Horror of Frankenstein* (1970) was the directorial debut of screenwriter Jimmy Sangster (who provided scripts for this, *The Curse* and the first sequel) and the only Frankenstein movie from Hammer that didn't star Cushing as the title character (he was replaced with Ralph Bates). *The Horror* is usually regarded as the weakest of all these films, but even though it is simply a less serious remake of *The Curse*, it has good moments, too, and David Prowse makes an interesting Monster. Cushing and Prowse then starred in Fisher's excellent *Frankenstein and the Monster from Hell* (1974), Hammer's farewell to the character, taking place in an insane asylum.

Obviously, the Frankenstein films were not the only successful horrors from Hammer. *Dracula* (aka *Horror of Dracula*; directed by Fisher, starring Lee, Cushing and Michael Gough in an atypically annoying role) was not quite as good as *The Curse of Frankenstein*, but audiences loved the 1958 shocker, and several more Dracula films followed. Other Hammer highlights throughout the 1960s and 1970s were *The Curse of the Werewolf* (1961; with Oliver Reed turning into a hairy beast), *She* (1965; an expensive thriller-adventure movie with Cushing, Lee and Ursula Andress), *The Reptile* (1966), *The Plague of the Zombies* (1966), *Quatermass and the Pit* (1967; arguably the best movie in the Quatermass trilogy), *The Devil Rides Out* (1968; Lee's own Hammer favorite),

The Vampire Lovers (1970) and *To the Devil a Daughter* (1976; different from any other film from Hammer, and with a great turn from Lee). In the 1980s, a new management decided to focus on TV and the studio produced two memorable series: *Hammer House of Horror* (1980) and *Hammer House of Mystery and Suspense* (1984). Both shows were uneven, but their best episodes (for example, *The Silent Scream* with Cushing, *The Two Faces of Evil*, John Hough's *Black Carrion*, and Val Guest's *In Possession*) were a treat.

The Curse of Frankenstein was not just the beginning of a whole new era in British horror and the introduction of two iconic genre actors (Peter Cushing and Christopher Lee), but it also re-ignited people's interest in genre cinema, and presented a revitalized, very '50s character of Frankenstein, the cold scientist.

The Fly

DIRECTOR: Kurt Neumann
CAST: Patricia Owens, David Hedison, Vincent Price, Herbert Marshall,
Charles Herbert, Kathleen Freeman, Torben Meyer
USA, 1958

Although *The Fly* was director Kurt Neumann's most successful movie, famous writer James Clavell's first screenplay ever, and one of the most impressive sci-fi–horrors of the 1950s, today the movie is usually remembered as "the funny little thing that was then bettered by David Cronenberg." Undoubtedly, Cronenberg's 1986 version of the story is much more shocking and stomach-turning than the original, but there's something about Neumann's effort that makes comparison with the remake quite difficult.

Shortly before making *The Fly*, Neumann proved he had an eye for horror in a story of a terrifying female monster (*She Devil*, 1957) and a tale of a giant alien machine that rises from the sea (*Kronos*, 1957). Both movies involved scientific experiments and human characters metamorphosing into otherworldly entities, but neither of them managed to capture the attention of U.S. audiences quite as well as *The Fly* did. Here, the scientist is Andre Delambre (David Hedison)—a handsome man happily married to attractive Helene (Patricia Owens), and with son Philippe (Charles Herbert) gleefully growing up in a huge, safe, super-clean house. But just as Dr. Frankenstein was once dissatisfied with leading a normal, boring life, so is Andre, and when he invents a machine for "integrating and disintegrating matter," he makes a flash decision to test it on himself. A fly trapped in the machine with the scientist is responsible for the horrors to come: when the experiment ends, the human body is blended with that of an insect, which makes Andre (and probably also the fly) seriously unhappy. The man does have some ideas about how to reverse the process, but we already know that they are of no use, as Neumann decided to open the movie with a scene of the scientist being killed (in a quite brutal way, too) by his wife, who then tells the whole story of her husband's experiments gone wrong to Andre's brother, Francois (Vincent Price).

The decision to show us the death of the main character in the first scene was certainly a bold one, and must have been a really tough one to make. By doing this, Neumann discarded the possibility of building the suspense that would have stemmed from the "will he/won't he survive" scenario (two years earlier, a similar, studio-imposed introduction lessened the impact of Don Siegel's *Invasion of the Body Snatchers*). However, there are also advantages to such a move: not having much space for suspense within the main plot thread, Neumann and Clavell look for it elsewhere, and eventually find it in the characters of Helene and Philippe. Even if we already know the fate of poor Andre, we still care about the mental and emotional shape of his wife and son. As a result, the scene in which Helene is hunting the fly that has her husband's head is tense not because we believe that catching the insect may save the scientist but because it effectively reflects the hopelessness of the situation and emphasizes Helene's near-nervous breakdown state of mind. Likewise, Philippe's vain attempts at helping his mother are truly heartbreaking, as they foretell the boy's guilt to come after the tragedy we know is bound to happen. (It's hard to forget the moment when Philippe brings his mom a bunch of flies he caught in the garden, hoping it will make her happy, but the woman delves back into sadness as soon as the boy says that he didn't manage to catch "the one with the white head.")

The Fly differs from most science-fiction-horror hybrids made in the 1950s not only because it is visibly quite an expensive movie — not many genre movies were shot

Horror just behind the door: Patricia Owens and David Hedison in Kurt Neumann's *The Fly* (1958).

in color back then — but, much more importantly, because it twists the popular formula for a plot where strange entities are attacking humans. In this case, the danger doesn't come from outer space or from some cruel, crazed scientists. It comes from within a dream house, from one of the members of a seemingly perfect family, which makes Neumann's movie a powerful metaphor of the naïveté of the Atomic Age. Neumann appears to be saying that, in the end, it will be our optimism about science that will destroy us, *not* alien predators.

In an ominous turn of events, *The Fly* came to foreshadow the fate of Neumann himself: just like Andre Delambre, though not in comparably grisly circumstances, the director committed suicide soon after the movie's premiere, and was therefore never aware of the movie's huge box office success. But there was still more money to be squeezed out of the already profitable idea, so director Edward Bernds stepped in to replace Neumann for 1959's sequel, *Return of the Fly*. This time, the movie was shot in black-and-white and more screen time was devoted to demonstrating the horrible half-man half-fly, but fortunately Vincent Price returned in the role of Francois Delambre, and the makers retained some of the charm of the original. There's no Price, however, in the second sequel, *Curse of the Fly* (1965), directed by Don Sharp. The mood of *Curse* further departs from that of the first movie, but Sharp's work still contains some unnerving moments, and even though it refuses to focus on a scientist turned into a fly, it closes the trilogy with class.

Too often overshadowed by David Cronenberg's morbid remake, Neumann's *The Fly* is, in fact, a stunningly original movie that allows dark themes to seep through the bright and happy color photography. In a decade of oversized animals, *The Fly* was one of the most interesting species.

I Bury the Living

Director: Albert Band
Cast: Richard Boone, Theodore Bikel, Howard Smith,
Peggy Maurer, Robert Osterloh, Herbert Anderson
USA, 1958

When Robert Kraft (Richard Boone) becomes chairman of a cemetery committee, he discovers that the position allows him to control the lives of all the people who have bought the plots there. On the wall in his office there's a big map of the cemetery and all the plots are marked with pins — black ones for the owners who are already dead and buried, and white ones for those who bought the plots for future use. Accidentally, Robert marks a newly bought plot with a black pin instead of the proper white one, and is soon informed about the young people who owned the plot turning up dead. The man suspects that some paranormal powers may be involved in this strange incident, but just to make sure that the black pins do kill people, he places one in a randomly chosen spot on the map. The spot is marked with the name of W. Isham, and before long poor Mr. Isham drops dead — to Robert's great shock, of course, as he now blames himself for causing three deaths. Still in need of experimenting to prove that the previous cases were no coincidence, Robert terminates the lives of several more people and starts panicking for good. He even calls the police and explains how he is responsible for all the deaths because ... well ... he put wrong pins in the map. Lt. Clayborne (Robert Osterloh) decides against locking Robert in jail — or in a lunatic asylum — and as soon as the man is once again left alone with the ominous map he tests it some more and eventually comes up with one brilliantly mad idea. What if he now chose to replace the black pins with the white ones? Wouldn't that bring all his victims back to life?

There is a moment in *I Bury the Living* where the plot gently balances on the verge of becoming an early version of *Night of the Living Dead* (which premiered ten years later). Director Albert Band either didn't yet have the courage to go that deep into horror with his movie or was persuaded not to do that by the producers, because some sources prove that the original script for *I Bury the Living* was much more gruesome than what the outcome may suggest. Instead of becoming an iconic movie and robbing George Romero of the status of an innovator, Band's film settles for being an enjoyable and unpretentious tale of the paranormal, much similar to those that were to form *The Twilight Zone*, the famous TV series born just a year later.

It's a wasted opportunity then, especially since enough many good ideas, fine acting and visual trickery have already been put into the movie — it just needed this one final push towards greatness, a knock-out conclusion that eventually refused to materialize. Richard Boone (of *Have Gun — Will Travel* fame) is the strongest actor here, and

Robert Kraft (Richard Boone) becomes the Black Pin Killer in *I Bury the Living* (1958).

it's just as well, as his weary character hardly ever leaves the screen. His highlights are the scenes where he doesn't have any other actor to play against—the ones in which he's starting to suspect that there's something very wrong about the map of the cemetery, and later the ones that show him sitting on the floor in the office trying to calm down his conscience and to shake off the visions of his victims leaving their graves. Please note the simple but effective tricks the director and the cinematographer Frederick Gately are using to help us understand the character's state of mind: the map looks completely ordinary and insignificant at the beginning but gradually, as Boone's Kraft is learning more and more about its extraordinary powers, the image of the map gets a much more menacing look—firstly, it becomes dark to emphasize its mysteriousness and the alleged connection with black magic or voodoo, then it starts to blur and flutter, as if to show that it's either an entity with its own will or—perhaps more likely—to suggest that Kraft is going out of his mind; finally, the map becomes a huge rectangle shining brightly in the background of Kraft's dramatic internal struggle. (There's a great image in the final third of the movie: the black shape of the tired man on one side, an unused chair on the other, and the powerful whiteness of the map in the middle—growing larger and overwhelming everything else in the frame.) Considering all the tension the makers extracted from the simple script and all the acting effort invested in the movie, the ending can't be viewed other than as unrewarding and unconvincing. It makes a bold attempt at tying all the movie's loose ends but fails miserably and ultimately feels like a cheap cheat.

Even though *I Bury the Living* is a bit disappointing as a horror movie, it remains Albert Band's best work. The director then went on to make some of the guiltiest pleasures in movie history (for example: *Dracula's Dog*, 1978; *Ghoulies II*, 1987; and *Doctor Mordrid*, 1992), and also helped his son Charles found production company Empire Pictures. Aimed at B-movie audience, Empire Pictures didn't last long but put Albert Band's son on the map of the filmmaking world, and he soon became a master of camp horror and the main man behind the love-or-loathe company Full Moon Pictures, then renamed Shadow Entertainment. Apart from producing some memorable genre films (1985's *Ghoulies*, 1986's *Troll* and 1989's *Puppet Master*, to mention a few), Band Jr. directed such B-horror "classics" as *Parasite* (starring Demi Moore; 1982), *Trancers* (1985), *The Gingerdead Man* (2005) and *Evil Bong* (2006).

An interesting, creepy and memorable little movie that ultimately shies away from becoming the blueprint for George Romero's *Night of the Living Dead*.

Plan 9 from Outer Space

DIRECTOR: Edward D. Wood Jr.
CAST: Gregory Walcott, Mona McKinnon, Dudley Manlove,
Joanna Lee, Duke Moore, Tom Keene, Tor Johnson, Vampira,
Bela Lugosi, Tom Mason, Criswell, John Breckinridge
USA, 1959

Is Ed Wood really the world's worst director and his intended magnum opus, *Plan 9 from Outer Space*, the worst movie ever? The answer may, of course, depend on how we define a bad director and a bad movie, but objectively speaking, unlike some obscure Poverty Row filmmakers, Wood showed at least *some* flashes of talent—even in *Plan 9*—and therefore it would be much more fair to call him "the most famous bad director ever." Because *bad* he certainly was.

Wood served as a Marine in World War II, then joined a carnival (playing a bearded lady in the freak show, among other jobs), and yet later directed—as well as wrote, produced and starred in—a play based on his war experiences, "Casual Company." Despite crushing reviews, Wood was determined to stay in Hollywood and in 1953 he debuted as a movie director. *Glen or Glenda*, initially planned as an exploitation flick about transsexual Christine Jorgensen, in the end became the director's quasi-autobiographical tale of a man who likes to cross-dress and has an angora fetish. The film was made in just four days and most of its sequences were visibly rushed (with such a tight schedule there was usually no time for second takes); if it's nevertheless watchable, it's because of Wood's likable turn as the main character (under the pseudonym Daniel Davis), Bela Lugosi's strange role of a narrator-scientist speaking in riddles, and a long, mind-boggling dream set piece. *Glen or Glenda* was a flop, but Wood pushed on and soon followed it with a bland gangster movie, *Jail Bait* (1954), and a mad scientist horror, *Bride of the Monster* (1955), in which Lugosi's character kidnaps people in order to experiment on them. The latter movie made a small profit at the box office, which encouraged Wood to pursue an even "more ambitious" project: a sci-fi horror first named *Grave Robbers from Outer Space* and then re-titled *Plan 9 from Outer Space*. It was partially funded by the Beverly Hills Baptist Church (Wood and actor Tor Johnson had to be baptized for the privilege), starred the once-famous Vampira, as well as Bela Lugosi in a "posthumous role" (the director included some old footage of the actor and used a double for the rest of the scenes), and it had a ridiculously "elaborate" plot.

"My friends, we cannot keep this a secret any longer. Let us punish the guilty; let us reward the innocent. My friends, can your hearts stand the shocking facts about grave robbers from Outer Space?"—with these words, the super-serious narrator (Criswell, in real life a self-proclaimed prophet) introduces us to the bizarre and illogical tale of alien invasion. Apparently having already tried as many as eight plans to control humans, the aliens decide to apply the devilish Plan 9. *Plan 9?* wonders the extraterrestrial Ruler (John Breckinridge) at this point. "Ah, yes. *Plan 9* deals with the resurrection of the dead. Long distance electrodes shot into the pineal and pituitary gland of the recently dead." It's all *that* banal. A genius plan like this simply has to work and the aliens quickly resurrect three recently deceased people, somehow hoping they will help them control or destroy all humanity. The slow, theoretically very easy to evade zombies are: the Ghoul Man (Lugosi and his double Tom Mason), the Vampire Girl (Vampira) and bulky Inspector Clay (Tor Johnson). The humans who will have to face them are: brave American airliner pilot Jeff Trent (Gregory Walcott), his attractive wife Paula (Mona McKinnon) and a couple of policemen. All of them have to deliver some hilariously inept lines throughout the movie; it's near impossible to choose a favorite excerpt. ("I've never seen you in this mood before," says concerned Paula to her husband, to which he ingeniously replies, "I guess that's because I've never been in this mood before"; an Air Force captain is surprised to hear about the aliens visiting the Earth: "Visits?

Too funny to be the worst movie ever: Vampira and Tor Johnson try hard to look scary in Ed Wood's *Plan 9 from Outer Space* (1959).

That would indicate visitors!" he muses; and Criswell wants to scare us witless when he says, "Perhaps, on your way home, someone will pass you in the dark, and you will never know it — for they will be from outer space!") The two ridiculously uptight aliens — Eros (Dudley Manlove) and Tanna (Joanna Lee) — also have their share of silly speeches and dialogue to deliver, but they at least have something important to say here and then. For example, Eros gets to inform us about the reasons why implementing Plan 9 was necessary: the humans, he says, are nearing self-destruction. "First was your firecracker, a harmless explosive. Then your hand grenade. You began to kill your own people, a few at a time. Then the bomb. Then a larger bomb. Many people are killed at one time. Then your scientists stumbled upon the atom bomb, split the atom. Then the hydrogen bomb, where you actually explode the air itself. Now you can arrange the total destruction of the entire universe served by our sun: the only explosion left is the Solaranite." It is not quite clear then whether the viewers should cheer for the suicidal, Solaranite-holding mankind or the murderous aliens.

Plan 9 fails on many levels as a horror–sci-fi flick, but its shortcomings are so funny that they quickly become the heart and the main advantage of the movie. The Lugosi double who is so unlike him that he has to constantly cover half of his face; the visibly cardboard tombstones during the graveyard scenes; the saucer toy hanging from wires; the confusing changes between day and night; the ultra-cheap sets — it's all a part of horror history, whether we like it or not. Surprisingly, however, Wood also managed to get several moments in *Plan 9* right, and despite all the silliness around they work pretty well as straight-faced genre sequences. These are mostly the moody footage of Vampira wandering through the cemetery and several very good shots of Tor Johnson, especially his rising from the grave (an almost George A. Romero–worthy piece) and the scene in which he carries unconscious Mona McKinnon to the spaceship.

Movie critics and viewers who discovered *Plan 9 from Outer Space* decades after its premiere tend to look for these tiny specks of brilliance in it and cherish its unintentional hilarity (Tim Burton's loving biography *Ed Wood* no doubt inspires such an approach), but those who saw the film around the time of the original release don't always think of it quite so fondly. In his non-fiction book *Danse Macabre*, Stephen King — known for his tolerance towards many bad movies of the 1950s — calls *Plan 9* an "abysmal, exploitative, misbegotten piece of trash" and a "sad and squalid coda to a great career" (Bela Lugosi's). Worse yet, King doesn't see the so-bad-it's-good aspect of the movie, because "there's nothing funny about watching a Bela Lugosi ... wracked with pain, a morphine monkey on his back" (the actor was indeed addicted to morphine at the time). Also Arthur Lennig, the author of *The Immortal Count: The Life and Films of Bela Lugosi*, writes that in the eyes of Lugosi's most faithful fans, *Plan 9* was "the most undeserving of legacies. It was like opening a coffin of a loved one to find only bones and a few decayed wisps of cloth."

Ed Wood's post–*Plan 9* output was just as patchy and amateurish as his earliest movies, and at some point he decided to add porn movies to his résumé, hoping they would be better money spinners than sci-fi–horrors (they were, but not significantly so). Some of *Plan 9*'s charm and ridiculousness can be found in 1959's haunted house adventure *Night of the Ghouls*, 1960's "police thriller" *The Sinister Urge* and 1971's skin flick *Necromania: A Tale of Weird Love*; Stephen King wouldn't be amused with any of them, though.

Forget all the labels that have been put on the movie throughout the years, and just enjoy it for all its true assets: bad acting, mad editing, puzzling dialogue, terrible special effects and occasional flashes of cinematic ingenuity. And, of course, don't forget it should also be treated as a rather serious warning for the stupid-minded mankind perpetually tampering with science.

A Bucket of Blood

DIRECTOR: Roger Corman
CAST: Dick Miller, Barboura Morris, Julian Burton, Antony Carbone,
Ed Nelson, John Brinkley, John Herman Shaner
USA, 1959

Art can be pretentious, boring, hilarious and irritating — often at the same time. Roger Corman reminds us about this in the first scene of his legendary *A Bucket of Blood*: a self-proclaimed neo-poet, Maxwell H. Brock (Julian Burton), is nervously generating chains of bon mots in front of an awed audience, with the sound of a lengthy, brain-bending saxophone solo in the background. "Life is an obscure hobo, bumming a ride on the omnibus of art," says Brock, and no one dares argue with such a vague philosophical statement. The artist's unique talent is, however, to forget his witticisms immediately after speaking them out, and to never ever repeat them again. "Repetition," he claims gravely, "is death." The performance takes place in a fashionable cafe, and one of the people most impressed with Brock's babble is likable halfwit Walter Paisley (Dick Miller), who works there as a busboy. Inspired by the cafe's artistic ambience, Walter dreams of doing something praiseworthy, too, so this very evening he covers a dead cat in clay and presents it as a sculpture during the cafe's next talent night. Initially, people are disgusted with his work but as soon as respected Brock proclaims it art, all the others suddenly start to appreciate it as well. Afraid that his fame may soon fade, and eager to dazzle the beautiful Carla (Barboura Morris), Walter tries to quickly come up with a new sculpture and when he finally does, patrons of the cafe are again as much shocked by the rather somber piece as they are full of respect for its maker. This time the sculpture is the size of an adult person and its name is as simple and straightforward as it was the first time around: next to a "Dead Cat" we can now admire a "Murdered Man."

What starts out as an odd mixture of horror and comedy, gradually becomes an enjoyable treatise on the pitfalls of being an artist. Ironically, Corman — a director who in future would be often criticized for doing hack jobs — here manages to harshly reprimand all those who call themselves artists but lack the necessary talent. He also makes fun of the urge to become an artist, the more compelling the less talented a certain person is (the main character is a good example of a man struggling with the problem), and he effectively ridicules the questionable process of distinguishing of what is and what isn't "art" (in the movie, nothing can become art until an influential figure pronounces it so). Therefore, the main character is not just a caricature of an ambitious Beat artist but also an anticipation of Corman's own fate — a man who once had faith in his abilities as a filmmaker but at some point had to settle for one subgenre (that of "cheap horror"), and started copying his praised past works. If repetition is indeed death, Corman chose to ignore his own movie's message long before he became a legendary producer and decided to finance remakes and re-imaginations of old horror classics.

A year after making *A Bucket of Blood*, Corman achieved true success with another horror-comedy — *The Little Shop of Horrors*, which famously featured Jack Nicholson in one of his earliest roles. But even though the latter movie is much more recognizable as the director's career-making accomplishment, it is *A Bucket of Blood* that squeezes more laughs out of the script and works better as a metaphor. Apart from Corman, the credit for this should mainly go to Charles B. Griffith, the author of the highly quotable script (who, in fact, also wrote *The Little Shop of Horrors*), and to Dick Miller in his juiciest role ever. Miller went on to have a career as a cameo actor in movies like *Piranha*, *Gremlins* and *After Hours*, and even returned several times as Walter Paisley (most notably in Joe Dante's *The Howling* and Jim Wynorski's *Chopping Mall*), but was never offered anything as emotional as the role of a resourceful sculptor in *A Bucket of Blood*. He may occasionally overact here and there (in the scene of the frying pan-kill, for example) but most of the time his acting is the heart of the movie, and it quickly makes us take to his weird character.

Since acting has been mentioned, it would be cruel to dismiss the roles of Barboura Morris (truly adorable as Walter's love interest), Antony Carbone (providing funny set pieces as the cafe's owner), and Julian Burton (priceless as the movie's most distinguished beatnik). Together with Miller's main character they steer the movie away from the position of "yet another funny horror" to that of a "cult favorite." This is also why some fragments of the film are so addictive that you just need to see them over and over again — like the scene with Morris and Carbone seeing the sculpture "Murdered Man" for the first time, or the one in which deadpan Burton provides us with the reasons for his enigmatic stream of consciousness being art. And as much fun as *A Bucket of Blood* is, it also has historical value: Corman says that with this movie he created an altogether new genre of horror-comedy, and it's hard to disprove his claim. Movies mixing horror and black comedy no doubt existed before but the two genres were never mixed in proportions that would result in a dark tale inducing so many hearty laughs.

In 1995, Corman produced a remake of his film (today the remake is known as either *The Death Artist* or simply *A Bucket of Blood*), hiring Michael McDonald as the director. The charm of the original was lost even though the new version closely followed the old script, but at least we got to see some good actors in it: Anthony Michael Hall and Justine Bateman in the lead roles, plus cult movie icon Paul Bartel and future comedy star Will Ferrell playing smaller parts.

While not an example of perfect cinema, *A Bucket of Blood* is a satisfying marriage of horror and comedy that eventually morphs into a clever metaphor for the traps awaiting wannabe artists.

Horrors of the Black Museum

DIRECTOR: Arthur Crabtree
CAST: Michael Gough, Graham Curnow, Shirley Ann Field,
June Cunningham, Geoffrey Keen, Beatrice Varley, Gerald Anderson
UK, 1959

"With the release of *Horrors of the Black Museum* in 1959, British horror films entered a new phase, one in which more explicit violence and gore were allowed on the screen," wrote critic Jeff Stafford in his review of the movie. It was produced by Anglo Amalgamated, a British company helped by an American, Herman Cohen, a producer who had already become infamous in the United States by that time (his were the "outrageous" ideas, as some would call them, for the 1957–58 teen-terror productions *I Was a Teenage Werewolf*, *I Was a Teenage Frankenstein* and *How to Make a Monster*); Cohen was ready to stir British audiences, too, and *Horrors of the Black Museum* was his first attempt to do so. A fairly successful one, apparently, as despite all the bad reviews the movie originally received, the ticket sales allowed Anglo Amalgamated to follow the movie with two other nasty pieces: Sidney Hayers' *Circus of Horrors* (1960) and, more notably, Michael Powell's *Peeping Tom* (1960; now considered a classic, but back in the early 1960s the movie was deemed so shocking that it had to be withdrawn from the theatres and eventually ruined the director's career). *Horrors of the Black Museum* cannot be compared with *Peeping Tom* in terms of artistic values, but it is equally entertaining, includes some shocking set pieces as well, and should be recognized as a movie that paved the way for Powell's unsettling horror gem. Had *Horrors* made no impact on 1950s audiences, *Peeping Tom* might have never been made to open the 1960s with a bang.

Coincidentally, the movie's director, Arthur Crabtree, used to work with Powell at the start of his career in the 1930s: he was a cinematographer on Powell's 1935 comedies *Lazybones* and *The Love Test*. Then Crabtree started slowly but persistently moving up the filmmaking ladder to finally debut as a director in 1945 (with a grim drama, *Madonna of the Seven Moons*). Powell kept on writing and directing more and more distinguished movies — he received Academy Award nominations (Best Original Screenplay for 1942's *One of Our Aircraft Is Missing*), the BAFTA and the Golden Palm, and won the Silver Berlin Bear (Best Musical for 1951's *The Tales of Hoffmann*). These two highly promising careers were cut short soon after Crabtree and Powell delivered the shockers Anglo Amalgamated demanded: *Horrors of the Black Museum* was Crabtree's farewell to directing, while *Peeping Tom* was Powell's last truly impressive work.

Horrors of the Black Museum was inspired by Herman Cohen's visit to Scotland Yard's actual Black Museum that stored various weapons used in the many killings committed throughout Great Britain. Some of these murderous exhibits were so inventive that Cohen decided that a successful movie could be simply based on violent set pieces depicting their use. Therefore, from the opening scene in which an attractive blonde has her eyes pierced with long spikes springing out from binoculars, *Horrors of the Black Museum* sets out to be a marathon of brutality and a test of endurance for the audiences (who were used to much more subtle horrors back when the movie premiered).

The plot is transparently sketchy (it sees a villain using hypnosis in order to transform an innocent young man into a ruthless killer), but it still works quite well thanks to Michael Gough's meaty performance, Gerard Schurmann's atmospheric score and lush cinematography typical of Crabtree's films.

Horrors of the Black Museum came out at the time when William Castle was teasing horror fans with all kinds of gimmicks and hype: during *Macabre* (1958), people were reportedly "dying of fright," so an appropriate insurance was included in the ticket price, and during *House on Haunted Hill* (1959) and *The Tingler* (1959) members of the audience were treated to off-screen shocks. Cohen thought it wise to learn from the master and promptly invented "Hypno-Vista"—a 13-minute introduction by a hypnotist, Dr. Emile Franchel, which was screened before the proper feature in the United States. When watched today, it is an overlong and unconvincing piece but Cohen's recollections of it in Tom Weaver's book *Attack of the Monster Movie Makers* are quite tender: "We tested it in a few theaters and the audience went for it like crazy, hokey as it was. It helped make the picture a success, I guess, 'cause people were looking for gimmicks at that time. But when the picture was released on television in this country, we had to take it off because it *does* hypnotize some people."

Most critics weren't enamored either with the movie or with the gimmick, the opinion of Richard W. Nason from *The New York Times* summarizing the general feeling towards it rather well: "The film's main impact is wrung from the suggestion of sharp objects penetrating human flesh. Its arrival was emblazoned with a broad advertising campaign. It is decked out in wide screen and florid color. It flamboyantly claims for itself the introduction of a new film technique called Hypno-Vista." To make matters worse, some reviewers deemed *Horrors* misogynistic, which might have been a serious problem at the time when the second wave of feminism (from the early 1960s until the 1980s) was about to come. And it's indeed difficult to argue that Cohen and Crabtree's movie shows women in a bad light: from the first scene to the last one, female characters are presented as naïve, mindless or annoying, and when the hypnotized ghoul disposes of them one by one, the audience is relieved rather than sympathetic toward the victims (the opening shock is an exception). In fact, Cohen, who also wrote the script, so exaggerated the male-female tensions presented in *Horrors* that instead of being interpreted as misogynistic, the movie could just as well be viewed as dealing with the fear of women gaining power and controlling their men. "A woman can't begin training her husband too soon," says one of the female characters and then claims that her fiancé "tells her everything"; to this, the villain reacts furiously, afraid that his accomplice reveals too much of their wrongdoings to his wife-to-be: "No woman can hold her tongue! They're a vicious, unreliable breed!" he shouts at the man, at the same time enraging the critics who set their minds to treating this as the movie's key statement. But much more interesting in this scene is the fact that being hypnotized into a murderous frenzy seems to be juxtaposed with being "trained" into marital obedience—and it is suggested that they are both equally effective and frightening.

Crabtree and Powell's careers may have ended with their respective films made for Anglo Amalgamated, but at least Herman Cohen did pursue producing horror movies after he crossed paths with the company. To get a double-bill companion piece for

Horrors of the Black Museum, Cohen produced a rushed horror-comedy, *The Headless Ghost* (1959), a movie he was never very fond of. He didn't receive credit as a producer for the upcoming Anglo Amalgamated project *Circus of Horrors*, even though he worked on the movie during the early stages, but at that time his mind was already on his pet project *Konga* (1961; with Michael Gough in the leading role). This turned out to be a cheap-looking riff on 1933's *King Kong* and 1949's *Mighty Joe Young*, but Cohen seemed quite satisfied with it. A string of hits and misses followed: a fun horror on an animal-worshipping cult, *Black Zoo* (1963; starring Gough again); the atmospheric Sherlock Holmes mystery *A Study in Terror* (1965; starring John Neville as Holmes and young Judi Dench in a small part); the patchy psycho-in-a-circus horror-thriller *Berserk!* (1967; starring Joan Crawford and Gough); an eerie mixture of western and horror, *Stranger's Gundown* (1969; aka *Django the Bastard*); and two ridiculous horror movies helmed by Freddie Francis, *Trog* (1970; with Crawford and Gough) and *Craze* (1974; with Jack Palance). In 1977 he co-produced his last movie, the brutal but somewhat involving giallo *The Cat with the Jade Eyes* (aka *Watch Me When I Kill*).

Arthur Crabtree's last feature film is also one of his best and most shocking pieces: it opens with an astonishingly cruel scene that the viewer just can't shake off throughout the rest of the running time, but there are many more inventive set pieces to follow, and Michael Gough's acting is a riot. Back in the day, *Horrors of the Black Museum* also gave 1950s audiences the impression that they would have to be much tougher to stomach what genre cinema was about to offer them in the 1960s.

Eyes Without a Face (Les Yeux Sans Visage)

aka *The Horror Chamber of Dr. Faustus*
DIRECTOR: Georges Franju
CAST: Pierre Brasseur, Edith Scob, Alida Valli, Juliette Mayniel,
Alexandre Lignault, François Guérin, Béatrice Altariba
France-Italy, 1959

It was only appropriate for the era of the mad scientist-mad doctor movies — the decades of the '40s and '50s — to close with the most beautiful and at the same time the creepiest addition to the subgenre — Georges Franju's *Eyes Without a Face* (in the United States inappropriately renamed *The Horror Chamber of Dr. Faustus*). Today the film is most often labeled as "poetic" and "poignant," but at the time of its original release it was usually regarded as "shocking" and "exploitative," and seemed to attract horror rather than arthouse audiences. As a genre movie it was unanimously praised, though, and together with Henri-Georges Clouzot's *Diabolique* (1955) it was later seen as a very rare classic horror movie made in France.

In fact, Franju hired the writers of *Diabolique*, Pierre Boileau and Thomas Narcejac (who also worked on Alfred Hitchcock's *Vertigo* [1958]), to adapt Jean Redon's novel into the script of *Eyes Without a Face*. This hardly meant that Franju wanted to copy Clouzot's style, though. "The trouble with Clouzot," he once said, "is that he tries to knock the audience's head off. That's wrong; you should twist it off." And that's the technique Franju is using in *Eyes Without a Face*: he takes his time to deliver the shocks, but when they do come, they catch the viewers at their most vulnerable.

The process of "twisting our heads off" begins with the opening scene. We see a stern blonde woman (Alida Valli) driving a car at night. She seems to be apprehensive about something and the feeling is contagious — we, too, very quickly start expecting bad things to happen, the tension coming virtually out of nowhere and immediately seeping through these introductory frames. The suspense rises yet further when we see a vague figure sitting awkwardly on the backseat, the face covered by the brim of a hat. But instead of capping the sequence with the climax we've been waiting for, Franju decides to temporarily vent the tension: the woman stops the car near the bank of a river, then takes the motionless backseat passenger — who appears to be a girl — and drags her to the water. The next day, the girl is brought to a morgue and identified as the daughter of Doctor Génessier (Pierre Brasseur), who's been missing for some time. Actually, Génessier's *real* daughter, Christiane (Edith Scob), is alive and hidden in a house near the doctor's private clinic: she'd been disfigured in a car accident and since then her father has been trying to restore her face. To do that, he and his assistant — the blonde from the opening scene — have been abducting young women to surgically remove their faces and graft them onto Christiane's. It hasn't worked so far, but now it seems that the doctor has finally developed a technique to do everything right.

There are many memorable horror moments in *Eyes Without a Face*: the sight of the mysterious backseat figure in the introductory sequence; the scene when we first meet Génessier's daughter, her face constantly beyond our field of vision; the cold, detailed depiction of a girl's face being removed; and, finally, the frightening seconds when we finally have to face Christiane, looking at her through blurred lenses, from the point of view of a tied-down girl who's going to be another face donor. It is, however, the uneasy blend of these elements of pure horror with Franju's arthouse ambitions that truly distinguishes the movie. Brilliant critic Pauline Kael recollects the day when she saw *Eyes Without a Face* in her essay "Zeitgeist and Poltergeist; Or, Are Movies Going to Pieces?" (published in *I Lost It at the Movies*):

> [The movie is] both bizarrely sophisticated (with Alida Valli ... doing the kidnapping in a black leather coat, recalling the death images from Cocteau's *Orpheus*) and absurdly naive. Franju's style is almost as purified as Robert Bresson's, and although I dislike the mixture of austerity and mysticism with blood and gore, it produced its effect — a vague, floating, almost lyric sense of horror, an almost abstract atmosphere, impersonal and humorless. It has nothing like the fun of a good old horror satire like *The Bride of Frankenstein* with Elsa Lanchester's hair curling electrically instead of just frizzing as usual, and Ernest Thesiger toying with mandrake roots and tiny ladies and gentlemen in glass jars. It's a horror film that takes itself very seriously, and even though I thought its intellectual pretensions silly, I couldn't shake off the exquisite, dread images.

Apparently, Kael merely *tolerates* Franju's arthouse ambitions, but is impressed with the horror values of the movie. An opposite approach is presented by Adam Lowenstein in *Shocking Representation: Historical Trauma, National Cinema, and the Modern Horror Film*; Lowenstein sees *Eyes Without a Face*, as well as Franju's previous film, the documentary *Blood of the Beasts* (1949), mainly as a means to express the director's thoughts on contemporary socio-political situation of France and Europe in general. *Blood of the Beasts*, an emotionless report from the slaughterhouse, "forces a reckoning with the disturbing historical events...: the long shadows of World War II, specifically the German Occupation and the Holocaust." Similarly, Lowenstein argues that in the case of *Eyes Without a Face*, "Christiane and the other horribly mutilated young women clearly evoke the victims of Nazi medical experiments conducted in concentration camps, just as Génessier's practices portray him as a Joseph Mengele–like figure." And even though it's not easy to agree with all the parallels Lowenstein presents in his book, it becomes clear that Franju's movie is one of those rare horrors that is as rewarding for viewers like Kael, who simply enjoy it for its thrills, as it is for viewers like Lowenstein, who like to explore them and interpret all their tiniest details.

A horror director who most often borrowed from Franju's classic was no doubt Jesus Franco. First he made *The Awful Dr. Orloff* (1962), a cheap thriller about a mad doctor and his assistant Morpho kidnapping attractive females in vain attempts to transplant skin from their faces to that of the doctor's scarred daughter. The character of Dr. Orloff reappeared in several sequels that either had little to do with the plot of the original, or were its blatant re-imaginings (for example, 1984's *The Sinister Dr. Orloff* sees the doctor's son abducting women and using their body parts in order to bring his mother back to life). The motif of kidnapping girls to restore the face of a loved one returns in Franco's *Faceless* (1988, starring Telly Savalas), a relatively good work from this director, about a doctor who will stop at nothing to make his sister beautiful again. According to Joan Hawkins ("The Anxiety of Influence" in *Cutting Edge: Art-Horror and the Horrific Avant-Garde*), Franco used Franju's ideas "to push Eurohorror into a new, more overtly sexual arena, and in so doing, he changed the face of European horror."

Eyes Without a Face—one of a few French horror masterpieces — is a missing link between arthouse cinema and exploitation movies. And, most importantly, the film's visceral shocks are as effective as its cerebral scares, leaving the viewer doubly drained.

PART III:
TO SCARE THE WORLD

Black Sunday (La maschera del demonio)

aka *Mask of the Demon; The Mask of Satan; Revenge of the Vampire*
DIRECTOR: Mario Bava
CAST: Barbara Steele, John Richardson, Andrea Checchi, Ivo Garrani,
Enrico Olivieri, Antonio Pierfederici, Tino Bianchi
Italy, 1960

Hammer Films reintroduced Gothic horror to contemporary audiences with *The Curse of Frankenstein* (1957) and *Dracula* (1958), but if the trend was to last, other filmmakers had to join in and help develop it. Luckily, just then — at the turn of the 1960s — a very talented Italian cinematographer, Mario Bava, was looking for a subject that would fit his official directorial debut. (He had already been the uncredited co-director of 1956's *Lust of the Vampire* and 1959's *Caltiki, the Immortal Monster*, among others.) He eventually chose to adapt "The Viy," a short story by a brilliant Ukrainian writer, Nikolai Gogol. It's difficult to tell what was so appealing about "The Viy" to Bava, as his adaptation throws away everything that was original in the story (most importantly, the vicious social criticism), the only Gogol character that made it to the movie being a vengeful old witch. But even though *Black Sunday* is not much of an adaptation of the eponymous story, it surely is an original and great-looking piece of Gothic horror — one to rival the best films of that kind made up to that point, and functioning as a landmark for future genre directors.

Burning witches in Mario Bava's *Black Sunday* (1960).

The choice of British actress Barbara Steele for the leading female role was most fortunate: she is an attractive lady, but also possesses a certain devilish aura, and a delicate contortion of her lips is enough to transform her from a sweet, helpless girl to a voracious creature who only temporarily took on human form. This works well in *Black Sunday*, as Steele plays a double role here — she is the murderous witch Asa Vajda as well as her kind-hearted descendant, Katja. The opening of the movie depicts the grisly fate of Asa after she's been accused of witchcraft: first she is marked with the sign of Satan, then an iron mask with spikes is hammered to her face, and finally her body is placed in a family crypt, in a coffin guarded by a stone cross. Two hundred years after Asa's execution, Dr. Andre Gorobec (John Richardson) and Dr. Thomas Kruvajan (Andrea Checchi) are stranded in the vicinity of the crypt. Kruvajan's panicky reaction to a sudden bat attack causes the guardian cross to smash, and when the man injures his hand, the drops of his blood fall on the witch's coffin and start the process of rejuvenation. But to be fully alive again, Asa will need to drain the energy from the body of her doppelgänger, Katja.

Apart from being a beautiful Gothic horror in an evocative fairy tale setting, *Black Sunday* is also one of the genre's best presentations of "the double," or "the evil twin." "Given that good girl Katja and bad woman Asa are both played by the same actress," we read in the book *The Horror Film* by Peter Hutchings, "[*Black Sunday*] disturbingly seems to imply that lurking behind all women is this otherness, this archaic power." Steele's innocent/evil face becomes, obviously, a perfect means to bring this unsettling dichotomy to life; plus, the implementation of the dichotomy brings *Black Sunday* closer to Fyodor Dostoyevsky's novella "The Double" than it ever was to Gogol's "The Viy" (actually, it is also much closer to Gogol's masterpiece novel *Dead Souls*, which includes passages hinting at the concept of the doppelgänger). On the other hand, the very fact that Asa is a *female* monster (something rare in pre–1960s horror movies) inevitably brings to mind Freud's castration anxiety. In his book, Hutchings claims that the tortures Asa undergoes in the opening scenes, climaxing with the spiked mask being hammered to her face, are "attempts to make her 'castrated,'" while "her resistance ... reveals a non-phallic potency that ... is ultimately the power of the archaic mother."

Black Sunday wasn't Steele's onscreen debut, but it was her first big success, and — in a way — a curse. From 1960 on, Steele was usually invited to play in horror movies, which became tedious for her after some time ("I never want to climb out of another freakin' coffin again!" she famously exclaimed in one interview), and since the early 1980s she hasn't done much acting. But the two decades in the horror business were enough to make Steele a genre icon, and she worked with some of the most popular directors at that time: Bava, Roger Corman (*Pit and the Pendulum*, 1961), Riccardo Freda (*The Horrible Dr. Hichcock*, 1962; *The Ghost*, 1963), Lucio Fulci (*The Maniacs*, 1964), Antonio Margheriti (*Castle of Blood* and *The Long Hair of Death*, both 1964), Mario Caiano (*Nightmare Castle*, 1965), Michael Reeves (*Revenge of the Blood Beast*, 1966), David Cronenberg (*Shivers*, 1975), and Joe Dante (*Piranha*, 1978). Outside the horror genre, she got a memorable role in Federico Fellini's *8½* (1963), and gave a strong performance in Jonathan Demme's guilty pleasure directorial debut *Caged Heat* (1974).

It is often repeated that after *Black Sunday* Bava never again made a movie quite as beautifully demonic. It is, however, hard to measure the greatness of *Black Sunday* against the director's later Gothic horrors like *Black Sabbath* (1963) or *Kill, Baby ... Kill* (1966), and it is yet harder to compare them with his groundbreaking *giallo* movies (*The Girl Who Knew Too Much*, 1963; *Blood and Black Lace*, 1964), an atmospheric vampire tale in space (*Planet of the Vampires*, 1965), or a violent horror that triggered the slasher craze (*Bay of Blood*, 1971). Bava constantly made the effort to escape being labeled as a director of one genre, and among his dark pieces there is also a historical drama (*Esther and the King*, 1960), a fantasy film (*The Wonders of Aladdin*, 1961), adventure pieces (*Erik the Conqueror*, 1961; *Knives of the Avenger*, 1966), a crazy comedy (*Dr. Goldfoot and the Girl Bombs*, 1966), an odd heist flick (*Danger: Diabolik!*, 1968), and several westerns. His last movie — as a second unit director — was Dario Argento's *Inferno* (1980), and he allegedly helped make its most effective scene that took place in a room flooded with water.

In *Black Sunday*, Nikolai Gogol's short story "The Viy" was hardly touched upon, but several years later, its faithful adaptation was made in the Soviet Union (*Viy*, 1967), sporting some haunting special effects and an atmosphere entirely different from that of Bava's film.

Black Sunday was Mario Bava's directorial debut, it introduced Barbara Steele to the world of horror, and there was never a more gorgeous Gothic horror in the history of the genre. It's impossible not to adore it, just as it is impossible not to notice the influence it had on many modern filmmakers.

The Blancheville Monster (Horror)

DIRECTOR: Alberto De Martino
CAST: Gérard Tichy, Joan Hills, Leo Anchóriz, Helga Liné,
Irán Eory, Francisco Morán, Richard Davis
Italy-Spain, 1963

The movies of Italian director Alberto De Martino don't have a good reputation in the celluloid world, and not without a reason: some of them are truly painful to watch, even for the toughest enthusiast of cult cinema (1980's superhero movie *Puma Man*, starring Donald Pleasence, is the ultimate challenge). There were several brighter moments in De Martino's career, though, and *The Blancheville Monster* — a thinly veiled adaptation of Edgar Allan Poe's "The Fall of the House of Usher" — is undoubtedly one of them.

Poe's short story (first published in 1839) is the tale of Roderick Usher grieving after the death of his beloved sister, only to eventually discover that she was entombed alive. In the end, the house of Usher breaks in two, crumbles down and the two characters are buried in the ruins. De Martino's movie may not feature a building that falls apart but it does include a character named Roderick and one of its best scenes is that of his sister's funeral, with none of the mourners noticing desperate attempts of the "deceased" at letting them know that she is, in fact, still alive. De Martino also suggests possible incest between the siblings and hints at some other themes popular in

Poe's short stories and poems. At various stages in the movie the characters have to question their sanity and the true identity of the people around them.

The movie starts with Emily de Blancheville (Joan Hills) returning home after a long absence; accompanying her are siblings John and Alice Taylor (Richard Davis and Irán Eory). We soon learn that Alice is Emily's best friend and John is hoping to win Emily's heart. When they all finally reach the Blancheville castle in Brittany, Emily can't hide her disappointment in how things changed since she last was there: the old servants have been replaced by new ones, and some of them look as if they are not to be trusted. The stern Eleonore (Helga Liné), who is in charge of running the house, seems especially suspect, but the family doctor (Leo Anchóriz) also raises some suspicions, especially since — as Emily discovers by accident — he is much interested in the science of mesmerism and hypnotism. The three visitors are also shocked to learn that Emily's father, allegedly dead, is in fact locked in one of the rooms — insane and with his face terribly burnt in a fire accident some time ago. To add to all this, Emily's brother Roderick (Gérard Tichy) mentions a family curse according to which the line of the Blanchevilles will end when their female child reaches the age of 21. Coincidentally, Emily's 21st birthday is drawing near, so her mad father, obsessed with the curse, may want to kill her one of these days.

The script is bulging with illogicalities, improbable twists and unanswered questions: Why would the killer resort to hypnotism if much quicker ways of getting rid of the victim are at hand? And if the title monster kills to avoid the family curse, then why would he wait until the very last night before Emily's birthday? The acting doesn't help to create the illusion of realism, either, as all the actors involved are guilty of going a little bit over the top in at least some of the scenes. (The one where Eleonore forces Emily to take her medicine can be considered a good example; even Helga Liné, by no means a bad actress, here overdoes her gesturing and spits out her lines in an overly nervous manner.) Somehow neither the overacting nor the many flaws of the script can take away the pleasure of watching *The Blancheville Monster*, and sometimes they even seem fitting for this type of a movie. Apparently, the best method to speak of insanity may be through a movie that is in a way insane itself.

Perhaps, however, we shouldn't disregard *The Blancheville Monster* as nothing more than a guilty pleasure or a cheap and weird version of a classy story. After all, several scenes strike the viewer as surprisingly attractive and suspenseful. The premature entombment has already been mentioned but there's more: the creepy introduction of the monster (during what may or may not be a dream/vision one of the characters is having), and the part where hypnotized Emily is walking at night to the ruins of a chapel followed by the hooded killer. (A huge advantage of the movie is that it was shot on location instead of in a studio, and that is one of the reasons why this particular scene came out so effective.)

The Blancheville Monster doesn't credit Edgar Allan Poe's short story as its basis but the influence was so easily recognizable that the movie was constantly being compared to the earlier adaptations of the tale — most notably Jean Epstein's 1928 version and Roger Corman's 1960 *House of Usher*. De Martino's take on the story wasn't as ingenious or captivating as either of the two but it worked very well as a straightforward and slightly campy horror movie. And if we were to compare it to later adaptation of Poe's story — for example, James L. Conway's TV version (1982; starring Martin Landau) or the recent Hayley Cloake effort (2006) — this odd black-and-white film would be an easy winner.

Whether we view *The Blancheville Monster* as a classic haunted castle story or as yet another take on Poe's "The Fall of the House of Usher," the movie delivers enough thrills and good-looking locales to keep us entertained throughout.

Blood Feast

DIRECTOR: Herschell Gordon Lewis
CAST: Mal Arnold, William Kerwin, Connie Mason, Scott H. Hall,
Lyn Bolton, Christy Foushee, Astrid Olson
USA, 1963

Before making *Blood Feast*, director Herschell Gordon Lewis tried his luck with a string of comedies and dramas that didn't shy away from nudity: *The Prime Time* (1960, starring Karen Black), *Living Venus* (1961), and *Boin-n-g* (1963). None of them became a success, so Lewis decided to go for something more extreme — movies that would be sexy and ludicrously violent. And that's exactly what *Blood Feast* was, shocking everyone who dared see it and encouraging a great number of genre filmmakers to follow a similar gory path. "You may need this when you see *Blood Feast*" read the warning on barf bags that were distributed at the movie's premiere as a promotional stunt. Apparently, most critics had to use them — it was very hard to find a positive review of the movie. But the average horror fans were as much delighted as they were traumatized by the experience, and they kept coming back for more.

Whatever name is put on the horror subgenre *Blood Feast* started — be it *splatter film*, or *gore horror*— it always adheres to one simple rule: there has to be a lot of violence in it, with all the bloody details of the cruel set pieces clearly visible on screen. The plot of this type of movie is usually plain and functional — after all, it just has to get the characters from one bloodbath to another. *Blood Feast* is a model example of this. The plot involves Egyptian caterer Fuad Ramses (Mal Arnold) hunting for young girls because he needs various human organs to prepare the feast of the title; provided everything is done right, the feast should help awaken goddess Ishtar. As time after time Ramses stalks his victims and mutilates them for our viewing pleasure (here a leg is chopped off, there a tongue taken out or brains scooped out), two idiot policemen (William Kerwin and Scott H. Hall) are trying to piece all the clues together and stop the murderous madman before he kills all the sexiest girls in town and summons the mysterious goddess.

Lewis is trying to play the whole story straight, but for a modern viewer it's just impossible to treat *Blood Feast* seriously. Most of the gory scenes don't look very convincing by today's standards, the acting is unbelievably awful (especially by Hall and Connie Mason as Ramses' would-be victim), and the monotonous musical theme is in equal measures laughable and ominous. The strangest thing is, though, that the movie is very entertaining throughout, and its apparent weaknesses often become its strengths. *Blood Feast* may be an awful horror movie, but it's a hilarious and truly unforgettable cult item: the fruitless dialogues between the policemen, and the permanent close-ups on Ramses and his wild eyebrows, are things of bizarre beauty, even more awkward and funny than all the famously bad scenes from Ed Wood's *Plan 9 from Outer Space*.

However similar *Blood Feast* and *Plan 9 from Outer Space* may be from a technical point of view, the ambitions of Lewis and Wood were not quite the same; Wood was simply reassembling what was popular in the genre at the time (i.e., the alien invasion themes), while Lewis was actually trying to change horror cinema. *Blood Feast* became one of the reasons why mad doctors, otherworldly monsters, and menacing aliens were replaced by demented killers. The movie brought Lewis instant fame, but he, too, like Ed Wood, was "rediscovered" decades later, with the invention of the video player in the 1980s. Forbidden fruit for those who grew up in the 1960s, *Blood Feast* suddenly became easily available at the rental stores, and could be relished in its full blood-spattered glory. Of course, the movie soon landed on the list of Video Nasties — horror films prosecuted under the Obscene Publications Act — and had the honor of being the oldest of all the banned titles.

Blood Feast turned out to be quite profitable (after all, its budget was less than $25,000), and Lewis didn't have any problems financing an equally violent follow-up, *Two Thousand Maniacs!* (1964). This time, the director attempted to make a more serious and sophisticated horror movie — albeit without skimping on gore — and he did pretty well in that respect. *Two Thousand Maniacs!* again sports some terrible acting, but the script is much better than that of *Blood Feast*, and several scenes from it could be actually called suspenseful. Lewis's next movie, *Color Me Blood Red* (1965), was apparently not as carefully thought over as *Maniacs!*, and it also lacked the amateurish charm of *Feast*, but for Lewis's die-hard fans it's a must, as it completes the so-called Blood Trilogy. After these gore-drenched pictures, Lewis thought the time had come for ... a musical for kids. The result — *Jimmy, the Boy Wonder* (1966) — is an odd piece that will entertain those who are into Lewis' works not just for the violence, but for their sheer peculiarity. Nineteen sixty-seven was a very busy year for the director: he gave us his version of a vampire story in *A Taste of Blood*, a tale of serial scalpings in *The Gruesome Twosome*, three exercises in cinematic strangeness in *Something Weird*, *The Girl, the Body, and the Pill*, and *Blast-Off Girls*, and he capped it all with another kid-flick, *Santa Visits the Magic Land of Mother Goose*. Lewis kept on making offbeat dramas, erotic comedies and gory horrors, 1970's *The Wizard of Gore* and 1972's *The Gore Gore Girls* being the highlights of the period between 1968 and 1972. The latter movie was Lewis's last before he retired from directing, but in 2002 he came back for one more stint — a long-planned *Blood Feast* sequel. *Blood Feast 2: All U Can Eat* is a surprisingly professional effort, its humor is intentional this time around (there's even an amusing cameo from John Waters), and some of the gory scenes are truly sickening. As a horror movie, *Blood Feast 2* works much better than the original, but as a stunningly awkward cult movie the first *Blood Feast* still remains unbeatable.

By making *Blood Feast*, director Herschell Gordon Lewis proved once and for all that Ed Wood's *Plan 9 from Outer Space* is *not* the worst horror movie in the history of cinema. Despite being as bad as it gets, though, *Blood Feast* is oddly involving and highly amusing (at least from today's point of view), and back in the 1960s it set the trend for gory horror.

At Midnight I'll Take Your Soul
(À Meia-Noite Levarei Sua Alma)

DIRECTOR: José Mojica Marins
CAST: José Mojica Marins, Magda Mei, Nivaldo Lima, Valéria Vasquez,
Ilídio Martins Simões, Eucaris Moraes
Brazil, 1964

Apparently, the sources of inspiration for the horror movies José Mojica Marins would make in the future, were all around him since childhood. From the time when he was five or six years old, he recalls, for example, a disturbing experience concerning his neighbor, a potato seller. The man died and everyone who knew him attended the funeral, deeply saddened, crying and praying for his return; to their shock, amidst all the praying, the man indeed "returned": his body in the coffin started to move and he was then helped out by the few mourners who didn't flee the scene. It turned out he wasn't dead, only cataleptic, but there was no true happy ending to the story. The man's wife filed for divorce claiming that he was no longer the same man; people wouldn't buy potatoes from him anymore; he wanted to move elsewhere, but the gossip followed him and he ended up in a mental institution, where he died two years later. "That made me very interested in the subject of death," says Marins.

Also at a very young age, Marins got interested in films. His father owned a movie theater and the boy used to spend his whole days in it, watching all the science-fiction and horror classics that got there, and in the night he went to sleep behind the screen. At the age of ten he got an 8mm camera from his father and shot his first film, *Last Judgment*. The plot, involving members of an average family who were either suddenly sucked into space or turned into worms, was based on a passage from the Bible, but it wasn't well received by a local priest. "I remember my father was very impressed by my ideas," said Marins in a recent interview with Stefan Rainer Harbach of *Filmmaker Magazine*. "He called a priest to witness this incredible way that a child had imagined Judgement Day. The resulting tragic end was easily predictable: the priest saw those images and said that I should be taken to a sanatorium for treatment. How could a ten-year-old child imagine such terrible things? He must be crazy!"

From the very start, Marins was a very inventive and resourceful filmmaker. When he needed worms for *Last Judgment*, he would tell other kids they could get a matinee ticket to his father's theater for a pound of worms. When he had to buy reels of film, he would pass a hat around to the theater customers, or, to even better effect, he would gather hundreds of kids and instruct them to lie down on the highway, and never let a car pass before someone made a contribution. He wasn't always lucky, though. His unfinished 1958 film *Sentença de Deus* was pronounced cursed when two actresses playing the main role died and the third one lost her leg in a car accident. Then *A Sino do Aventureiro*, also made in 1958, was criticized by the Catholic Church because of its allegedly pornographic content (in fact, it only contained a scene with two hardly visible naked women taking a bath under a waterfall). Marins was a devout Catholic back then, plus he realized what a powerful institution the Church was in Brazil, so he didn't want to aggravate priests and would later make them heroes in *Meu Destino em Tuas Maõs* (1963). He couldn't have expected all the problems his next movie was about to cause, though.

The ideas for *At Midnight I'll Take Your Soul* sprang from one of Marins' nightmares. In it, a faceless figure dressed in black took him to a tombstone on which his date of death was engraved. When the director woke up, he was so overwhelmed with this vision that he terminated production of a movie he was then working on, and focused solely on *At Midnight*, with its anti-hero Zé do Caixão (later renamed Coffin Joe by the American distributor) being the demonic entity in black taken straight from his nightmare. When the actor set for the main role backed away, Marins had no choice but to play Zé himself; and it was a good thing, too, as Marins' performance and his devilish looks are the movie's greatest asset. Wearing a black top hat and black cape, with unnaturally long fingernails and a monobrow, Zé soon became a chief onscreen fiend and a horror icon in Brazil. In *At Midnight* he is a man (not a supernatural entity, apparently) obsessed with the quest for a woman who will give him perfect offspring, and he is ready to kill in order to accomplish the mission. He also despises religion — the "comfort for the weak" — and relishes violence, which allows him to terrorize people in his village. In one powerful scene he combines the penchant for sacrilege and brutality when snatching a crown of thorns from a figure of Jesus and ripping his opponent's face with it.

It wasn't clear what message Marins wanted to deliver through this movie. Since he made it soon after the pro–Catholic *Meu Destino em Tuas Maõs*, it is tempting to theorize that *At Midnight* was an equally religious movie, simply misunderstood by the Church, like once *Judgement Day* was, because of the dark atmosphere and the excessive use of violence. (It was banned in some Brazilian states, while in the others it quickly became a success.) Zé was, after all, a villain, and his evil ways were meant to be eventually discontinued. But the director's fondness for the character — who was to become his alter ego — does not quite support such claims. "He is a character who struggles for innocence and purity," argues Marins. "He protects children. He is always searching for the perfect son through [a] superior woman. And, in reality, he wants to make the world more peaceful. His philosophy is: It doesn't matter if one hundred people die if six billion are safe." This is, of course, hardly a Catholic philosophy, especially since Zé doesn't only kill or mutilate the bad guys, but the innocents as well.

However muddled and mysterious are Zé's priorities, he is certainly a fascinating character, and the fact that he was conceived within one of the most devoutly religious countries in the world makes him all the more of an intriguing conundrum. *At Midnight* was an ultra-cheap movie (the best proof of which is one very crude special effect used near the finale), but Marins managed to collect more money for a 1967 sequel, *This Night I Will Possess Your Corpse*, which was a direct continuation of the original story. From the technical point of view, it was much better than *At Midnight*, and though again shot in black-and-white, it contained a great color insert depicting Zé's journey to the bowels of Hell. Marins' evil protagonist became a genre institution in Brazil — he was an inspiration for comic books and had cameos in several movies (most famously in 1970's *Awakening the Beast* and 1974's *The Bloody Exorcism of Coffin Joe*), but until recently the director couldn't afford to make a proper closer to the trilogy. *Embodiment of Evil* (2008) finally sees the glorious return of Zé/Joe (still played by Marins, now over 70 years old), and though the new movie's amount of gore seems to have been increased to meet 21st century genre standards, the eerie world inhabited by the troubled, long-nailed anti-hero is still like no other and retains its wicked allure.

At Midnight I'll Take Your Soul was Brazil's first horror movie and its caped, top hat-wearing main character, Zé do Caixão (or Coffin Joe), soon became the country's prime boogeyman. Today the movie's main advantage is its old-fashioned charm, but in the early 1960s it was understandably shocking and controversial.

Kwaidan (Kaidan)

aka *Ghost Stories*
DIRECTOR: Masaki Kobayashi
CAST: Rentaro Mikuni, Michiyo Aratama, Tatsuya Nakadai, Keiko Kishi, Katsuo Nakamura, Tetsuro Tamba, Kanemon Nakamura, Osamu Takizawa, Kei Sato
Japan, 1964

In 1904, when Lafcadio Hearn's book *Kwaidan: Stories and Studies of Strange Things* was published, Japan was involved in a war with Russia, and the eyes of the whole world were directed at this conflict, observing Japan's rise to power with the subsequent victory. These first years of the 20th century marked the beginning of a new Japan: successful, modernizing, becoming recognizable by the countries of the West. Hearn, a half-Irish, half-Greek journalist who settled in Japan in 1890, became a spokesman for this "renewed" country. In the introduction to *Kwaidan*, Hearn's most popular collection of stories, there's a reference to the war with Russia and a conclusion stating that "the Russian people have had literary spokesmen.... The Japanese, on the other hand, have possessed no such national and universally recognized figures as Turgenieff or Tolstoy. They need an interpreter." Hearn was a perfect candidate for the position: he was already deeply rooted in the culture, but unlike the Japanese, he was able to pick up on the country's exoticism. Most unfortunately, just when *Kwaidan* and then *Japan: An Attempt at Interpretation* were published, Hearn died of heart failure, leaving behind a body of work that, at least to a certain extent, bridged the gap between Asia and other continents. In the early 1960s, when Japan was still suffering after the World War II defeat and had to sign the controversial 1960 treaty with the U.S., some of Hearn's works were given a second life in Masaki Kobayashi's haunting horror anthology *Kwaidan*.

Despite the title of the movie, not all the stories it's based on are taken from *Kwaidan: Stories and Studies of Strange Things*. The first episode, *Black Hair*, comes from another collection of Hearn's works, "Shadowings" (the short story "The Reconciliation"),

Kwaidan (1964): the priest (Takashi Shimura, left) teaches Hoichi (Katsuo Nakamura) how to become invisible in the eyes of the demons.

and sees a selfish samurai (Rentaro Mikuni) leave his loving wife (Michiyo Aratama) so that he can marry into a wealthier family. When he later has a change of heart and decides to return to his first wife, a nasty surprise awaits him at his old home. In the second episode, *The Woman in the Snow* (the story "Yuki-Onna" from *Kwaidan*), two woodcutters lose their way in a heavy snowstorm and end up in a small wooden hut where they meet the pale lady of the title (Keiko Kishi); she freezes one of the men to death, but spares the other one (Tatsuya Nakadai) on the condition that he never tells anyone what he saw. The longest and most complex of all stories is *Hoichi the Earless* ("The Story of Mimi-Nashi-Hoichi" from *Kwaidan*) which first presents a reenaction of the violent battle between two clans, the Heike and the Genji, and then goes on to tell the story of a talented biwa player, Hoichi (Katsuo Nakamura), who is being bothered by the ghosts of the defeated clan. *In a Cup of Tea* (from "Kottō: Being Japanese Curios, with Sundry Cobwebs") closes the anthology with a tight and spooky tale of a man (Kanemon Nakamura) who sees the reflection of a face of a stranger (Kei Sato) whenever he attempts to drink from a cup.

Just as Hearn was in his works yearning for a Japan that was pure, unaffected by the Western culture (he wasn't an enthusiast of modernization), so Kobayashi in his adaptation of Hearn's stories yearns for traditional values like loyalty and honesty, as well as for the fair judgment of the guilty. *Kwaidan* is, however, not an overtly political movie: Kobayashi perhaps didn't feel like making yet another such statement after his nine-plus-hours long World War II trilogy *The Human Condition* (1959–1961). In fact, as far as the subject matter is concerned, *Kwaidan* is much closer to the director's other masterpiece, *Harakiri* (1962; depicting the samurai crisis in the 17th century), although the theatricality and colorfulness of the anthology makes it the more optimistic of the two, despite the often gruesome twists in its stories. As a horror movie, *Kwaidan* turned out to be a great introduction to the Asian take on the genre: visually stunning, with a very creepy score, telling old-fashioned, moralistic tales. Critic Andrzej Kołodyński claims in his book *Kino grozy* that "the visual beauty of the movie, the masterful use of color, is above anything that European or American horror movies have to offer." This might be polemical, of course — how to compare the beauty of *Kwaidan* with that of *The Phantom Carriage* (1921), *I Walked with a Zombie* (1943) and *Black Sunday* (1960)? But Kobayashi's film definitely opened the eyes of many horror enthusiasts to an entirely new world of horror.

A month before *Kwaidan*, another Japanese horror masterpiece premiered: Kaneto Shindô's *Onibaba*. (Both *Kwaidan* and *Onibaba* were released theatrically in the U.S. in 1965; the former was shortened from the original running time of over three hours to 125 minutes, with *The Woman in the Snow* removed altogether). It was, however, quite different from Kobayashi's anthology: shot in black-and-white, aiming at realism, and telling just one simple story. It takes place in Japan during the 14th century's feudal war, and it sees a wife and a mother of one of the soldiers ambushing samurai warriors and then selling their armor to make a living. The older woman fears that her daughter-in-law may run off with a stranger, so she puts on a demonic mask to scare the girl away from the man's house, but the mask permanently clings to her face and the woman actually *becomes* a demon. Like *Kwaidan*, *Onibaba* was much more than just a spook show (some critics, like Adam Lowenstein, read it as a Hiroshima allegory), and it, too, helped introduce genre fans all over the world to the trademark, carefully composed visuals of Asian horrors. Shindô's later *Kuroneko* (1968), about a samurai fighting a merciless demon, is another fine example of supernatural cinema from Japan.

Modern Asian horror movies still draw heavily from Hearn's scary stories, as well as from Kobayashi's classic adaptation. After all, the "cursed object" theme that constantly reappears in movies like *Ringu* (1998; about a videotape that kills), *Ju-on* (2000; about a murderous house) or *Shutter* (2004; about a possessed camera), comes straight from Hearn's story "Furisode" in which a kimono brings death to anyone who wears it. And, of course, the frightening long hair, another trademark of today's Asian horror, was first seen in *Kwaidan*'s episode *Black Hair*.

In the mid–1960s, the Americans and the Europeans found out how beautifully the Asian filmmakers could scare them. *Kwaidan* still belongs on the list of the most handsome horror movies ever made and its four episodes, although not outright shocking, do crawl under the skin. Just remember you need to reserve a long evening to watch them all in a row.

The Saragossa Manuscript
(*Rękopis Znaleziony w Saragossie*)

DIRECTOR: Wojciech J. Has
CAST: Zbigniew Cybulski, Franciszek Pieczka, Iga Cembrzyńska,
Joanna Jędryka, Gustaw Holoubek, Elżbieta Czyżewska,
Gustaw Lutkiewicz, Zdzisław Maklakiewicz
Poland, 1965

Jan Potocki's book *The Manuscript Found in Saragossa* (completed in 1814) is a breathtaking journey through time and space, in which peculiar new characters pop up on every other page and they all insist on telling us weird, scary and fascinating tales of their lives. Potocki was a Polish adventurer who traveled throughout Europe, Asia and Africa, and his interest in the supernatural and the exotic brought about the variety of themes, places and characters that appear in *The Manuscript Found in Saragossa*. It's as if the author wanted to condense all his obsessions in one stunningly complex story — a story that he would go on to polish and rewrite until the end of his life. Juliusz Kurkiewicz notes in his essay "Rękopis ponownie odnaleziony" (written for the Polish weekly magazine *Polityka*) that the fate of the manuscript in Potocki's story was very similar to that of the novel itself, as it, too, "traveled through centuries, from one trans-

What story are we in now? Captain Alfonse Van Worden (Zbigniew Cybulski, far right) is trying to keep track of the plot in Wojciech J. Has' *The Saragossa Manuscript* (1965).

lator and researcher to another" and it is "inexhaustible, growing in all possible directions through the net of intertextual connections that is being permanently expanded by the readers." Kurkiewicz also sees Potocki's novel as ironically autobiographical, since one of its characters — scientist Hervas — commits suicide because the work of his life was underappreciated; Potocki, too, committed suicide soon after one of the versions of *The Manuscript* was published. But his death was much more mysterious than that of Hervas: he shot himself with a self-made silver bullet, raising suspicions that he believed he was turning into a werewolf (a theory some modern enthusiasts of Potocki's writing, like Neil Gaiman, choose to trust).

Could a book like *The Manuscript Found in Saragossa*— depicting in detail as many as 66 days in the life of the main character, each day unraveling some new colorful stories — be successfully made into a movie? And wouldn't such an adaptation destroy the magic of the original by having to assign images to Potocki's often hallucinatory visions? Virginie Sélavy claims in her review that the novel is "a work of such magnitude, richness and encyclopedic reach that only a very brave man or a lunatic could ever have thought of adapting it for the cinema." This brave man/lunatic was Wojciech J. Has, a Polish director who debuted with an original and painful study of alcoholism (1957's *The Noose*; based on a story by Marek Hłasko), but afterwards made several much more traditional dramas. *The Saragossa Manuscript* was to become one of the greatest challenges in Has' career.

Scriptwriter Tadeusz Kwiatkowski obviously had to cut many tales from Potocki's novel, so that Has could make a three-hour movie out of it, but the plot nevertheless remained complex and perplexing, complete with the Chinese box structure. In 18th century Saragossa, a Spanish officer (Gustaw Lutkiewicz) arrives at an inn where he finds a curious manuscript and starts reading it. Events described on its pages initially focus on Captain Alfonse Van Worden (Zbigniew Cybulski) traveling to Madrid through the Sierra Morena mountains, but soon the main story disintegrates into a series of flashbacks and flashbacks-within-flashbacks narrated by people Van Worden meets on his way, and the characters of their stories: two seductive Moorish princesses (Iga Cembrzyńska, Joanna Jędryka), a hermit (Kazimierz Opaliński) and his strange servant Pacheco (Franciszek Pieczka), a cabbalist (Adam Pawlikowski) and his beautiful sister (Beata Tyszkiewicz), a gypsy (Leon Niemczyk), a knight (Bogumił Kobiela) and many others. The stories pile up so quickly that Van Worden himself— just like the Spanish officer who reads the manuscript and the audience watching the movie — sometimes has trouble distinguishing what has actually *happened* and what was a dream, a vision, or a part of a story he'd been told.

"In Has' film, Potocki's sprawling and polyphonic novel is broken down into two contrasting parts," writes Michael Goddard in the book *The Cinema of Central Europe*. "[I]n the first, the supernatural is presented in terms of inexplicable experiences, accompanied by a highly Baroque and 'Orientalist' aesthetics, in the second part numerous overlapping stories, of a much more urbane nature, serve to demystify the apparently mysterious as merely the result of false perceptions and misguided beliefs. [But] there still remain gaps and inconsistencies that elude any complete rationalization." The fact that it is so difficult to pin down *The Saragossa Manuscript* as either appraisal of rationalism or the triumph of the mysterious and the inexplicable, makes the movie all the more intriguing and open to various interpretations. For example, film historian Małgorzata Hendrykowska writes in *Kronika Kinematografii Polskiej 1895–1997* that, "like Potocki's novel, the movie is a rationalistic satire on human foolishness and superstition," while critic Jan Słodowski argues in *Leksykon Polskich Filmów Fabularnych* that the film is "a vision of world in chaos..., a metaphor of fortuitousness of human life, for which no rational key is to be found."

The most notable deviation of Has' movie from the literary source is a somewhat darker finale, and this is the one issue the adaptation has been criticized for. Overall, however, *The Saragossa Manuscript* is a very faithful presentation of the world Potocki described in his novel: all the movie's characters are just as alive and strange as Potocki intended them to be (even though the rather chubby Cybulski, an icon of Polish cinema that he certainly is, must have seemed a dubious choice for the role of sprightly Van Worden), the most important motifs were nicely fleshed out (with the same actors occasionally appearing in different roles to emphasize the idea of "the double"), Mieczysław Jahoda's cinematography effectively transformed Polish highlands into the 18th century Spain, and Krzysztof Penderecki's score emphasized the otherworldly atmosphere of it all. Characteristically for Polish cinema of the era, the movie deals with the theme of escape (the communist, censorship-heavy People's Republic of Poland wasn't a friendly place for ambitious filmmakers, after all), but Has also managed to sneak some of Potocki's raunchiness into the story. Iga Cembrzyńska, who played one of the sexy princesses, was surprised to realize how perverse her role was: "Imagine socialist Poland, the early sixties," she said in an interview, "and the three of us [Cembrzyńska, Jędryka and Cybulski] are in this bisexual relationship, making out on a bed in that big cave."

No other movie directed by Has has become as popular worldwide as *The Saragossa Manuscript*, but in Poland one of his later features, *The Doll* (1968), has drawn more attention from the critics and viewers. Most probably, the reason was that the book *The Doll* was based on — by one of greatest Polish writers, Bolesław Prus — was itself much better known in Poland than Potocki's novel, originally written in French. Controversially, however, Has chose to present the 19th century Warsaw as a quixotic rather than a realistic place, which stood in stark contrast to its depiction in Prus' novel (labeled as belonging to literary realism and famous for presenting the city with great attention to detail). *The Doll*, about a successful businessman obsessed with the idea of marrying a cold-hearted girl, was seemingly a completely different movie than *The Saragossa Manuscript*, but it, too, dealt with the themes of alter egos/doubles and, in a way, a descent into madness.

Has' next feature film *The Hour-Glass Sanatorium* (1973) was much more similar to *The Saragossa Manuscript*, both in the subject matter and the overall mood. Based on several stories by Bruno Schulz, it tells the story of a man trapped in a dreamlike world, where the notions of time and logic hardly ever apply; he's supposedly traveling to visit his dying father, but at one point it appears as if it is him who's about to face death, and the whole journey is just a chain of flashbacks and hallucinations. Interestingly, according to some critics, *The Saragossa Manuscript*, *The Doll* and *The Hour-*

Glass Sanatorium form Has' "oneiric trilogy": they all feature some unearthly visuals, all are adaptations of books that used to be deemed unfilmable, and all aim to add something new to the source stories (the different ending in *The Saragossa Manuscript*; the departure from realism in *The Doll*; and the vision of Holocaust attached to *The Hour-Glass Sanatorium*). Although Has was recognized as an immensely talented director, since the late 1980s he wasn't able to finance movies that would match his visions, and he chose to retire. His last movie, *The Tribulations of Balthazar Kober* (1989; based on a novel by Frederick Tristan), was another effective venture into the realm of the fantastic, and in most cases it was very well received by the critics.

Those who adore Jan Potocki's labyrinthine novel *The Manuscript Found in Saragossa* may find its adaptation by Wojciech J. Has disappointingly tight, but the movie aptly recreates the book's atmosphere and does its best to squeeze the multitude of plots into the three-hour frame. Watching *The Saragossa Manuscript* is, quite literally, like stepping into the uncharted territories of the odd, the horrible and the fantastic.

Dr. Terror's House of Horrors

DIRECTOR: Freddie Francis
CAST: Peter Cushing, Christopher Lee, Donald Sutherland, Neil McCallum,
Alan Freeman, Roy Castle, Ann Bell, Ursula Howells, Michael Gough,
Kenny Lynch, Jennifer Jayne, Bernard Lee
UK, 1965

In the late 1950s Hammer Films discovered a successful formula for horror movies and, not surprisingly, several other companies soon tried to use the formula for their own purposes. One of Hammer's main competitors was Amicus, founded in Great Britain by two Americans, Milton Subotsky and Max J. Rosenberg. Even before the Amicus name was used, Subotsky offered the viewers a sample of the horrors to come in the Christopher Lee–starring *Horror Hotel* (1960; aka *The City of the Dead*), for which he wrote the main story (as well as produced it, together with Rosenberg). Although shot in black-and-white, *Horror Hotel* was as effective as the horrors from Hammer, and after a stretch of average comedies — like Richard Lester's directorial debut *It's Trad, Dad!* (1962) and *Just For Fun* (1963) with cinematography by Nicolas Roeg — Subotsky and Rosenberg decided to follow a similar path in future. The first official Amicus horror movie, now in lush color reminiscent of the Hammer productions and starring the iconic duo of Peter Cushing and Christopher Lee, was *Dr. Terror's House of Horrors*.

Actually, this handsome portmanteau horror wasn't just a rendition of the Hammer style. Its very format — five separate episodes and a wraparound story — was bringing to mind the classic horror from Ealing Studio, *Dead of Night* (1945). Therefore, it's no coincidence that when Cushing's character, Dr. Schreck (or Dr. Terror), enters an already crowded train compartment, he asks his fellow passengers whether there is "room for one more," which is a memorable line from *Dead of Night*. There is, indeed,

In *Dr. Terror's House of Horrors* (1965), art critic Franklyn Marsh (Christopher Lee) is stalked by the severed hand of an artist he used to mock.

room for one more, and Schreck joins a group of five travelers: sneering art critic Franklyn Marsh (Lee), jokey jazz musician Biff Bailey (Roy Castle), silent Bob Carroll (Donald Sutherland), and two reserved, serious-minded fellows: Jim Dawson (Neil McCallum) and Bill Rogers (Alan Freeman). When Dr. Schreck takes a nap, a bag falls from his lap and Tarot cards are scattered on the floor. This makes everyone except for the art critic interested in learning something about their future, and the mysterious doctor promptly agrees to read the cards for them. The five stories that follow are possible turns of events for each of the men. In *Werewolf,* Jim Dawson renovates an old house and is shocked to find a hungry werewolf living in it; *Creeping Vine* sees the plant of the title terrorize Bill Rogers' family; *Voodoo* is a warning against stealing music: Biff Bailey does that when on a trip in the Caribbean and is then stalked by a spooky stranger; in *Disembodied Hand* Franklyn Marsh drives a hated artist (Michael Gough) to suicide, but the artist's severed hand exacts revenge on him; finally, *Vampire* shows Bob Carroll coming to terms with the fact that he's married to the titular creature.

As is often the case with omnibus horror movies, not all episodes are equally good (the first three have no climax to speak of, actually) and the way in which the wraparound story ties them all together turns out to be a cheat (unlike in *Dead of Night,* where the finale added a punch to the preceding episodes). But somehow *Dr. Terror's House of Horrors* still manages to work remarkably well as a whole. Perhaps it's because of all the great performances on display: Cushing is both funny and intriguing with the fake bushy eyebrows and speaking with exaggerated German accent, while the scenes between Lee and Gough are a delight. Perhaps the main reason is Freddie Francis's direction and his eye for captivating shots (like the one where Dr. Schreck is silently scanning the faces of the five passengers). Or, more controversially, it may be Subotsky's script that made the movie a success: it no doubt operates on some of the most worn-out horror themes and doesn't try to invest them with much originality, but aren't genre enthusiasts drawn to what is familiar? And are there any horror fans who wouldn't be interested in seeing a movie that combines all their favorite elements? Subotsky knew exactly what he was doing, as he was a die-hard genre fan himself, and by putting together all the many pieces of popular movies — the Hammer horrors, *Dead of Night*, *Dracula* (1931), *The Wolf Man* (1941), *The Beast with Five Fingers* (1946) and *The Day of the Triffids* (1962), to mention the most obvious ones — the scriptwriter-producer clearly wanted to create a horror magnum opus. He didn't achieve that, but instead managed to reinvent the formula of an anthology and successfully introduced Amicus to the horror-hungry British viewers.

The next offering from Amicus was an underrated horror based on a story by Robert Bloch, *The Skull* (1965; again directed by Francis and with an impressive cast: Cushing, Lee, Gough, Patrick Wymark and Patrick Magee). But some more anthologies soon followed, too; Francis directed *Torture Garden* (1967; with Cushing, Jack Palance and Burgess Meredith) and *Tales from the Crypt* (1972; with Cushing, Magee and Joan Collins), while Roy Ward Baker took care of *Asylum* (1972; with Cushing, Magee, Britt Ekland and Herbert Lom) and *The Vault of Horror* (1973; with Denholm Elliott and Michael Craig). All of these are highly entertaining, with *Tales from the Crypt* and *Asylum* (the latter based on four stories by Bloch) joining *Dead of Night* and *Dr. Terror's House of Horrors* as the best omnibus horrors ever made. Other directors who helped build the studio's horror anthology reputation were Peter Duffel (who made the thrilling 1971 *The House That Dripped Blood* with Cushing, Lee, Elliott and Ingrid Pitt) and Kevin Connor (the fine 1973's *From Beyond the Grave* with Cushing, Ogilvy, Donald Pleasence and Lesley-Ann Down). Out of the standard movies produced by Amicus, the most interesting ones are Baker's gothic ghost story *And Now the Screaming Starts!* (1973; with Cushing, Lom, Magee, Stephanie Beacham and Ian Ogilvy) and Paul Annett's crazy werewolf film *The Beast Must Die!* (1974; with Cushing, Calvin Lockhart, Charles Gray, Michael Gambon and Tom Chadbon). In the mid–1970s, Hammer-type horror movies were losing popularity and Amicus turned to prehistoric fantasy-adventure with Connor's *The Land That Time Forgot* (1975; starring Doug McClure), which was the company's greatest financial success and spawned two sequels, *At the Earth's Core* (1976) and *The People That Time Forgot* (1977). The latter, however, was officially produced by American International Pictures, as Amicus was already dissolved by then.

Francis, who before joining Amicus worked for Hammer (for example, he directed 1964's *The Evil of Frankenstein*) and was a praised cinematographer (an Oscar for 1960's *Sons and Lovers*), made — to quote him — "too many horror movies" after *Dr. Terror's House of Horrors*. Some of them were very good, like his best Amicus output, Tigon's

The Creeping Flesh (1973; again with Lee and Cushing) and the retelling of the Burke and Hare scandal, *The Doctor and The Devils* (1985; starring Timothy Dalton, Jonathan Pryce, Twiggy, Stephen Rea, Patrick Stewart and Julian Sands). Some, on the other hand, were utterly horrible, like the infamous *Trog* (1970; starring Gough and Joan Crawford). Thanks to director David Lynch, Francis returned to working as a cinematographer with *The Elephant Man* (1980), and went on to shoot such pictures as Karel Reisz's *The French Lieutenant's Woman* (1981), Lynch's *Dune* (1984), Edward Zwick's *Glory* (1989; which brought him the second Oscar) and Martin Scorsese's *Cape Fear* (1991).

This horror anthology is a vintage production from Amicus, the company that tried to compete with Hammer during the 1960s and 1970s. It stars Peter Cushing and Christopher Lee, and takes the viewer on an exciting tour around the genre's most popular themes: vampires, werewolves, voodoo rituals, aggressive plants and a disembodied hand. It's all here, aptly directed by Freddie Francis and with some juicy performances to boot.

The Reptile

DIRECTOR: John Gilling
CAST: Ray Barrett, Jennifer Daniel, Noel Willman, Jacqueline Pearce,
Michael Ripper, Marne Maitland, John Laurie
UK, 1966

Several years after the success of Terence Fisher's *The Curse of Frankenstein*, people started wondering whether it was possible for the good men at Hammer to come up with a horror movie that wouldn't be lifting monsters from other films. And eventually, after revamping Frankenstein, Dracula and the Mummy, Britain's most famous horror company did give us their very own creatures in Fisher's *The Gorgon* (1964) and John Gilling's *The Reptile* (1966). Both movies are today regarded as powerful and underrated but it's the reptilian beast from Gilling's entry that is usually remembered as the more shocking of the two. (Which comes as no surprise; overall, *The Gorgon* may be an interesting movie, but its she-beast with snakes for hair looks plain ridiculous.)

The opening of *The Reptile* tells us that what we have here is one of the best horror offerings from Hammer. It's a calm evening in a small village in Cornwall, when the soothing silence is interrupted by a strange tune — not exactly loud or particularly unpleasant but decidedly eerie. A man (David Baron) leaves his house to check where the sounds are coming from and this leads him to a mansion nearby. Curious, the man enters the building and before he can hear a word of warning from its owner, Dr. Franklyn (Noel Willman), he is attacked and bitten by a furious creature we can hardly see. The man's face turns black, he starts foaming at the mouth, and he falls dead just after running out of the house. People in the village and the victim's family are informed that the man died of "the black death" but with the arrival of his brother, Harry Spalding (Ray Barrett), this official version will soon be challenged. When another man dies with his face turned black and snake bites near his neck, Harry, accompanied by the only friendly villager, Tom Bailey (Michael Ripper), decides to exhume the body of his

The Spaldings (Jennifer Daniel, Ray Barrett) and Tom Bailey (Michael Ripper) prepare to meet the title monster in John Gilling's *Reptile* (1966).

brother, and see if it, too, bears similar bite marks. Harry's wife, Valerie (Jennifer Daniel), meets Dr. Franklyn's daughter, Anna (Jacqueline Pearce), who seems to be eager to make friends with her, and consequently Harry and Valerie are invited to the doctor's mansion. There they will discover the source of the exotic melody that always precedes the deaths — and they will realize they have to start worrying about their own lives. The title of the movie is explained when we learn about Dr. Franklyn's brush with a snake cult during a trip to Borneo, and we meet yet another menacing character — the doctor's supposed manservant Malay (Marne Maitland), who turns out to be controlling his "master" for some reason.

The Reptile cleverly mixes the realistic (the characters of Harry and Valerie, the setting) with the bizarre (the creature, the typically "horror" cellar), and it moves at a steady pace from one good scene to another, scattering nice scares along the way (the first face-to-face encounter with the monster is an especially memorable shock moment). And although Gilling masterfully creates funereal atmosphere, he never forgets to lighten it up from time to time with a surprising comedy scene (like the one where the reserved Spaldings are having dinner with a crazy villager) or with the introduction of an apparently helpful protagonist (Tom Bailey and Anna). Consequently, *The Reptile* is a movie of contrasts and metamorphoses, as in the end many characters emerge as completely different beings than those we initially thought them to be.

In fact, for a movie from a company usually associated with "guilty pleasure" horror films, *The Reptile* plays with some of the genre's intricate themes with surprising effectiveness. The bodily metamorphoses we witness are shocking and exotic (one character changes into a half-human half-reptile; the bodies of the victims turn black), the uncertain identities of some protagonists keep us guessing about the power play between them, and the issues of Otherness — i.e., being perceived by the majority of people as different and threatening — are plentiful and presented in a very interesting way. Dr. Franklyn and his daughter are Others because the trip abroad changed them forever, but Harry and Valerie are Others, too — they are newcomers in a village and the local people are clearly afraid of them and don't want them around. Then there's the Asian manservant: an enigmatic and seemingly menacing figure isolated from everyone else.

And, typically for horror movies that consciously and skillfully deal with Otherness, there are some homoerotic subtexts to be found in *The Reptile* as well. The relationship between Valerie and Anna is not unlike the one between Dr. Frankenstein and his monster — or Frankenstein and Dr. Pretorius — in *Bride of Frankenstein* (1935): the two women feel drawn to one another, yet they are also uncertain whether they should continue their friendship. Also, for both of them, the tightening of the friendship would entail liberation from the dominant male — in Valerie's case — the husband, and in Anna's case — the father. Therefore, *The Reptile* can also be viewed as a movie that reflects upon the ideology of feminism.

Gilling shot *The Reptile* back to back with *The Plague of the Zombies* (1966), often using the same sets and even hiring two of the same actors, Jacqueline Pearce and Michael Ripper. *The Plague of the Zombies* seems to be a bit more conventional Hammer horror and it certainly doesn't have a creature as spectacular as the one in *The Reptile* but it, too, is effectively creepy and puts the Cornwall setting to good use. Yet more importantly, though, it also addresses the issue of Otherness and does it in an inspired way; the threat still has its source in a trip to a remote place (this time to the Caribbean) but some of the relationships presented in Gilling's previous movie are virtually reversed. Most strikingly, the status of the ethnic Others is completely changed here: the black people who work for the movie's villain actually *are* harmless slaves, not just act like ones.

A Hammer horror without either Lee or Cushing but with a wonderfully uncanny reptilian creature instead. Fresh, suspenseful and brooding, this is one of their finest efforts.

The Fearless Vampire Killers, or:
Pardon Me, But Your Teeth Are in My Neck

aka *Dance of the Vampires; Vampire Ball*
DIRECTOR: Roman Polanski
CAST: Jack MacGowran, Roman Polanski, Sharon Tate, Jessie Robins,
Alfie Bass, Ferdy Mayne, Iain Quarrier, Terry Downes
USA-UK, 1967

That night, penetrating deep into the heart of Transylvania, Professor Abronsius was unaware that he was on the point of reaching the goal of his mysterious investigations. In the course of which he had journeyed throughout Central Europe for years accompanied by his one and only faithful disciple, Alfred. A scholar and scientist whose genius was unappreciated, Abronsius had given up all to devote himself body and soul to what was to him a sacred mission. He had even lost his chair at Königsberg University, where for a long time his colleagues used to refer to him as "The Nut."

With these lines, spoken by a gravelly-voiced narrator, begins Roman Polanski's parody of Hammer horror films, *The Fearless Vampire Killers*. We see the characters of Professor Abronsius (Jack MacGowran) and Alfred (Polanski himself) arriving in a small village and finding there some clues that the vampires they've been so eagerly seeking may be somewhere near. At a local inn, Alfred also spots beautiful, red-haired Sarah (Sharon Tate) and immediately falls for her, so when the girl is kidnapped and taken to a nearby castle, the two wannabe vampire killers hurry to rescue her. Count von Krolock (Ferdy Mayne) hospitably welcomes them to the castle, but he won't be as happy to let them out. His son, Herbert (Iain Quarrier) apparently has a crush on boyish Alfred.

The kitsch, sexy and often gratuitously violent horrors from Hammer, so popular in the 1960s, definitely demanded a good parody. Yet, no one expected it to come from Polanski, a praised young director who had made three grim black-and-white features by that time (*Knife in the Water*, 1962; *Repulsion*, 1965; *Cul-de-sac*, 1966). In his autobiography *Roman* the director recollects that whenever he would watch a horror movie at the theater, he saw that the audience wasn't treating it seriously. That was when, together with Gérard Brach, Polanski decided that it might be a good idea to make a horror that would be intentionally funny. Another idea that struck him while skiing to relax after the troublesome shoot of *Cul-de-sac*, was that a place surrounded by snow-capped woods and majestic mountains would make a perfect setting for this type of movie. Producer Martin Ransohoff of Filmways, a company that had a distribution deal with MGM, was in

Gorgeous Sarah (Sharon Tate) is a vampire magnet in Roman Polanski's *The Fearless Vampire Killers* (1967).

awe after having seen *Cul-de-sac* and he quickly decided to buy the rights to screen it in the U.S. *and* to finance the director's next film. He also convinced Polanski to hire a relatively unknown actress, Sharon Tate, for one of the main roles, an idea which turned out to be life-changing for the director, as the two soon became a couple.

Watching *The Fearless Vampire Killers* today is perhaps even more rewarding than it must have been when the movie premiered. After all, we now know that throughout the four decades that have passed, there was no tribute to Hammer horrors as charming and beautifully shot as this. Back in the 1960s some critics complained that the movie is slow and not funny enough: Roger Ebert, who didn't appreciate Polanski's sense of humor at all, famously reported that not a single person laughed during the screening he attended ("One or two people cried, and a lady behind me dropped a bag of M&Ms which rolled under the seats, and a guy on the center aisle sneezed at 43 minutes past the hour. But that was about all the action," he wrote in his review). Truth be told, the movie is *amusing* rather than *hilarious*, but some scenes have a perfect comic timing (see the excellent interaction between the actors when the gay vampire is trying to seduce Alfred). Polanski's role as shy and cowardly Alfred shines with comedic brilliance, as in the scene where Sarah asks Alfred whether he'd allow her to have "a quick one"; or when he gets to the crypt of the vampires, but is too scared to use the hammer and the stake properly. Also, typical horror themes and props are often debased here to a funny effect; we see, for example, a Jewish vampire refusing to be scared off with a crucifix. The movie is not scary—and most probably it never aimed to be so—but the horror atmosphere is maintained via the overwhelming snowy setting and Krzysztof Komeda's suspenseful score, one of the best in the genre.

Despite all the enthusiasm and talent invested in the movie, it was anything but an instant success. The contract allowed producer Ransohoff to edit the film in any way he desired, and it soon turned out that this was exactly what he was about to do. Polanski's 107-minute cut was shortened to 91 minutes, and an unnecessary cartoon summary of the plot was added to the opening credits. This version annoyed the director so much that he wanted to withdraw his name from the movie (the contract wouldn't allow this, though), and it didn't please the audience, either, bringing poor box office results. Polanski's original cut, when released later in Europe (as *Dance of the Vampires*), had a much better reception, but perhaps these weren't just the restored scenes that were responsible for the discrepancy—this movie, aiming to make fun of British rather than American horrors, was simply much better suited for the cinematic taste of Europeans. Throughout the years its cult reputation was constantly growing, though, and today it has a huge number of enthusiasts, as well as detractors, on both continents. In 1997 a curious stage version of the story, again bearing the title *Dance of the Vampires*, premiered in Vienna. The musical was directed by Polanski himself, with music by Jim Steinman and libretto by Michael Kunze. Its tone was a bit different than that of the movie, and the inclusion of Steinman's old hit "Total Eclipse of the Heart" as the main theme was no doubt controversial, but all in all the musical was a success, and in the following years it was performed on some of the most prestigious stages around the world, including Broadway.

As a result of the conflict with Ransohoff, Polanski was apprehensive of making another movie for a big company. However, when Robert Evans, vice-president of Paramount, offered him an adaptation of Ira Levin's *Rosemary's Baby*, the director didn't hesitate. This movie, released in 1968, was the real breakthrough for Polanski and is still regarded as one of the creepiest and at the same time most artistic horror films in history. The director was about to experience an even greater horror in real life: in August 1969, pregnant Sharon Tate was murdered by the members of Charles Manson's "family." Polanski kept on making movies after the tragedy, but neither his ultra-violent version of Shakespeare's *Macbeth* (made in 1971), nor the weird, sexy and utterly ridiculous *What?* (1972) were received with enthusiasm. He wouldn't give in, and his next movie, the noir thriller *Chinatown* (1974), was another masterpiece. Since then he has been continually making high-quality movies; his dramas are always beautifully shot and moving (*Tess*, 1979; *The Pianist*, 2002; *Oliver Twist*, 2005), the thrillers typically suspenseful (*Frantic*, 1988; *Death and the Maiden*, 1994), and the more controversial pieces are truly shocking and disturbing (*The Tenant*, 1976; *Bitter Moon*, 1992). Even the critically denounced *Pirates* (1986) and *The Ninth Gate* (1999) are very enjoyable for those who adore Polanski's style. The former marks his welcome return to comedy, and the latter is another horror movie with elements of parody, just a hue darker than *The Fearless Vampire Killers*.

Not everyone will laugh during *The Fearless Vampire Killers*, and hardly anyone will be frozen with fear, yet there never was a better parody of Hammer horrors. Typically for Polanski's movies, the movie has great photography, brilliant actors (with a marvelous turn from the director himself), and a chilling, evocative soundtrack by Krzysztof Komeda.

The Sorcerers

DIRECTOR: Michael Reeves
CAST: Ian Ogilvy, Boris Karloff, Catherine Lacey, Elizabeth Ercy,
Victor Henry, Susan George, Sally Sheridan
UK, 1967

After making a camp, makeup-heavy horror movie called *The She-Beast* (also known as *Revenge of the Blood Beast*), 23-year-old director Michael Reeves clearly wanted to create something more original and contemporary. He hired horror legend Boris Karloff for one of the main roles, but this was perhaps yet another way of playing with our expectations; instead of making Karloff's character sinister and monstrous, Reeves chose to make him helpless and kind-hearted, while the movie's real monster turned out to be the character played by the seemingly fragile and innocuous Catherine Lacey.

The Sorcerers starts with Professor Monserrat (Karloff) and his wife Estelle (Lacey) getting ecstatic about the prospect of trying out his new invention, a machine that will enable them to control other people and feel whatever their mental prisoners feel. The first person they subject to the experiment is an egoistic young man named Mike Roscoe (Ian Ogilvy). The professor lures him into his apartment, talks him into putting on a pair of futuristic-looking headphones, then tortures him with some awful sounds and blinds him with some wildly colorful lights. When Mike leaves the Monserrats' apartment he remembers nothing of the visit, and goes back to his normal life. The hypnotists are, however, eager to see how much pleasure they can get from controlling the man. After they experience Mike's night swimming in a local pool, the Monserrats start to disagree about how they should use the invention. The professor would like to "help other old people," while wicked Estelle would rather check what the subject of their experiment feels when he's stealing things, pummeling his friends and killing people. His clubbing companions Nicole (Elizabeth Ercy) and Alan (Victor Henry) feel that something is off but will they succeed in preventing all the killings Estelle plan for Mike? Or will they end up becoming two more victims of the remote control killer?

The movie gives the impression of being a rather uneven piece of work, where the adrenaline-fueled scenes are mixed with ones that are either predictable or overlong. The acting of Karloff and Lacey is impeccable and makes for a nice contrast: Karloff plays his role with great subtlety, while Lacey makes her character grotesque and mad. It's a pity, then, that after good introductory scenes, the portions of the movie focused on Mr. and Mrs. Monserrat become somewhat repetitive, and these are mostly the episodes with Ogilvy, Ercy and Henry that make *The Sorcerers* an unforgettable experience. Ogilvy (Reeves' childhood friend and favorite actor) has no problem dealing with the huge amount of screen time he gets here, and even though his character must have been quite unlikable in the script — even before the Monserrats trap him, he is cold and conceited — the actor invests him with a healthy dose of charisma and charm. Ercy and Henry are in Ogilvy's shadow throughout most of the movie, but when they finally step into the limelight they both do well; a scene worth mentioning is the one in which the characters played by Ercy and Henry question Ogilvy's Mark to find out whether he is a killer or not. The tension between them rises with Mark's every nervous blink and with every unclear answer, and it all inevitably leads to an energetic, wonderfully photographed fistfight.

In a review in the respected British magazine *Empire*, we read that *The Sorcerers* is to be enjoyed as a "simple horror film," and we are advised to not "try and make it more than that." But Reeves' movie refuses to be a simple horror. Even if we do our best to not interpret it in an overly sophisticated way, *The Sorcerers* is a wonderful portrayal of the 1960s (with the everpresent swing, the eye-catching mini-skirts and cute singer Sally Sheridan in one of the roles), and also a tale of getting old and disjoined from this hip, colorful world (the Monserrats, through their dream device, desperately want to reconnect with the world). And if we do look a little bit deeper, we can even start perceiving the movie as a metaphor for the movie-watching experience itself. After all, it too boils down to "becoming" somebody else for a while. *The Sorcerers* is equally convincing on both levels, but it's true that it works well as a "simple," very austere horror as well.

Paul Maslansky (producer of Reeves's previous feature film) says in the documentary "Blood Beast — The Films of Michael Reeves" that the director "might have become the English Spielberg" because he "knew the vocabulary of film so well." *The Sorcerers* shows that on one hand it seems to be true, as he surely knew how to push the emotional buttons (an awkward and very realistic car chase scene from the final part of the movie is a good example); on the other hand, however, *The Sorcerers* is definitely not a crowd-pleaser of the Spielbergian kind (there are truly viewer-unfriendly moments here, like the one where Mike is listening to ear-piercing sounds — and the audience has to listen to them, too). Who knows, though, what would have happened if Reeves was ever allowed to make a big-budget movie. Perhaps *The Sorcerers* could have been what Spielberg's *Duel* now is to *Jurassic Park*?

A year after finishing *The Sorcerers*, Reeves had another movie ready, and it was one to be forevermore cited as the director's masterpiece — *Matthew Hopkins: The Witchfinder General*. This time Vincent Price was offered one of the main roles, but that didn't stop the ambitious filmmaker from advising the star on how to act; famously, when Price said to Reeves, "I've made 84 movies, young man. How many did you make?" the director replied, "Two good ones." And there's no denying that the pieces of advice Reeves offered Price really worked — the character of merciless Matthew Hopkins belongs to the very best in Price's career. Reeves was then getting ready to helm *The Oblong Box* but he died during pre-production from an overdose of sleeping pills. *The Oblong Box* (1969) was eventually directed by Gordon Hessler, with Vincent Price and Christopher Lee in the main roles.

While it may be too raw, patchy and weird for some viewers, *The Sorcerers* undoubtedly oozes the atmosphere of 1960s London, sports some fine acting and includes several very effective scenes. A foreshadowing of the talent that would be fully revealed in director Michael Reeves's next effort — *Matthew Hopkins: The Witchfinder General*.

Viy

DIRECTORS: Georgi Kropachyov, Konstantin Yershov
CAST: Leonid Kuravlyov, Natalya Varley, Nikolai Kutuzov, Aleksei Glazyrin,
Pyotr Vesklyarov, Vadim Zakharchenko, Vladimir Salnikov
Soviet Union, 1967

Although horror never became an immensely popular genre in Russia and the Soviet Union, its filmmakers have been flirting with supernatural themes since the early years of cinema. Such directors as Yakov Protazanov (*Dance of the Vampire*, 1914; *The Queen of Spades*, 1916; *Satan Triumphant*, 1917) and Wladyslaw Starewicz (*The Terrible Vengeance*, 1913; *The Portrait*, 1915) were said to have made some very unsettling films, often drawing their inspiration from the works of Nikolai Gogol, Alexander Pushkin, or Fyodor Dostoevsky. Unfortunately, most of their earliest works are now partially or entirely lost, and we can only glimpse their brilliance in the surviving, often badly scratched excerpts (though the condition of what remained of *Satan Triumphant* and *The Portrait* is relatively good). Starewicz soon moved to France and became a world-famous master of the stop-motion technique, but the Soviet Union already had his successor: Aleksandr Ptushko, a director, writer, art director, cinematographer, producer and — most importantly — an effects specialist, also very much interested in stop-motion filmmaking.

Ptushko's first works were usually fantasy adventures with some remarkable effects-laden set pieces, and occasional ghoulish moments. He was responsible for the retelling of Jonathan Swift's *Gulliver's Travels* with the use of puppets (*The New Gulliver*, 1935), directed the Soviet Union's stunning first full-color feature (*The Stone Flower*, 1946), followed it with several similarly beautiful fantasy films (*The Magic Voyage of Sinbad*, 1954; *The Tale of Tsar Saltan*, 1966), and made a movie based on Finnish folklore epic Kalevala (*The Day the Earth Froze*, 1959). "His stories came from fairy tales," Nancy Ramsey of *The New York Times* wrote of the director, "but unlike filmmakers who used folk tales to subtly criticize the Soviet system, Ptushko's films were straightforward: good was good, and evil was evil." That is certainly true if we consider most of Ptushko's early films, but near the end of his career, he took a chance and made something more controversial: *Viy*, an imaginative horror movie deeply rooted in Ukrainian folklore and based on Nikolai Gogol's well-known short story. Officially, *Viy* was directed by Georgi Kropachyov and Konstantin Yershov, with Ptushko being responsible for art direction, special effects and parts of the script, but today the movie is largely recognized as a realization of Ptushko's vision.

Gogol was not an overly optimistic writer and his story "The Viy" definitely wasn't of the "good is good, evil is evil" kind, but Ptushko (together with his fellow writers and directors) decided against introducing too many changes into the plot. Gogol's depiction of Russian society as, to put it mildly, unenlightened, made it into the movie version, and though it's not quite as depressing as the writer's famous novel *Dead Souls*, some viewers may still regard it as provocative and unjust. But it seems that hardly anyone does. Perhaps the fiendish finale tends to turn everyone's attention away from all other things in the movie.

There are no likable characters in this story. The main man is Khoma Brut (Leonid Kuravlyov), a young seminarian who just started his vacation and, accompanied by two friends (Vadim Zakharchenko, Vladimir Salnikov), is looking for a place to stay the night. As a dark and foggy evening approaches, the three men start fearing that they will have to sleep outside, but eventually they find a house and convince its owner, an old lady (Nikolai Kutuzov), to put them up. Khoma goes to sleep on a haypile in a barn, away from his companions, but before he dozes off, the old lady enters the barn and approaches him, as if she wants to seduce him. Scared and disgusted, Khoma tries to run away, but the woman turns out to be a witch and uses her powers to stop the man, then gets on his back, reaches for a broom and the two of them fly away for a little joyride. When they come back to the ground, Khoma beats the witch unconscious with a stick, and before he runs away back to his Monastery, he sees that the old lady transformed into a beautiful young girl. In the Monastery, however, the rector (Pyotr Vesklyarov) informs the man that a famous Sotnik (Aleksei Glazyrin) has contacted him and asked for Khoma to say prayers for Sotnik's dead daughter Pannochka (Natalya Varley). The seminarian is not willing to do that, but he is given no choice. For three consecutive nights he has to go to church and, with Pannochka's body lying in a coffin next to him, pray for her salvation. Obviously, this turns out to be the witch's revenge for the beating she received, and the nights in the church become Khoma's darkest nightmare, with Pannochka trying to claw his eyes out, a wide variety of otherworldly creatures crawling out of the walls, and Viy — the king of the monsters with huge, heavy eyelids and sight that kills — paying him a visit.

Khoma is by turns amiable, funny and annoying, but after the encounter with the witch it's difficult to feel for him. After all, not only had he severely thrashed an old woman just because she invited him to ride the broom, but afterwards he also left the probably dying, innocent-looking girl on the ground without trying to help her or at least feeling remorse. Actually, the poor old witch is a bit more likable than Khoma, and her vengeful actions seem justified. The rest of the characters are either disloyal (Khoma's friends), despotic (the rector, Sotnik), or mindless and constantly inebriated (the Cossacks who keep an eye on Khoma in Sotnik's village). This causes some scenes in the middle part of the movie to drag. (It's much more pleasant to listen to dialogues exchanged by characters we like.) But it doesn't affect the suspense of the final scenes; Khoma may be a dimwit, but somehow we don't want to see him devoured by the church-dwelling monsters. Ptushko, Kropachyov and Yershov achieved this effect of sudden empathy for the main character by an inventive use of the camera: it circles wildly around Khoma to show his sudden panic, and it "attacks" him, as if presenting the point of view of the witch. Not all special effects employed in *Viy* are great (the rear projection often looks very poor), but the concluding creature-heavy showdown makes up for all the dull moments and is easily one of the finest, most original moments in the history of the genre.

Following *Viy*, Ptushko only made one more movie, the ambitious and suitably dark fantasy tale *Ruslan and Ludmila* (1972), based on a poem by Alexander Pushkin, directed and scripted by Ptushko himself. In 2006 another adaptation of "The Viy," and called *The Power of Fear*, had Oleg Fesenko at the helm, with a Russian cast struggling to speak English. The movie employed some good special effects in several scenes, and it's curious to see Gogol's story being given a modern spin, but overall it is tedious and lacking suspense. For 2009, which marks the bicentenary of Gogol's birth, another version of the tale is planned, this time directed by famous genre actor Robert Englund.

Viy was the much desired "dark piece" in the filmography of Russian stop-motion virtuoso Aleksandr Ptushko, and the movie's climactic summoning of various monsters and demons belongs to the genre's most memorable moments. The pacing may be patchy and not all special effects stood the test of time, but there is a one-of-a-kind flair about *Viy* that just has to be witnessed.

Hour of the Wolf (Vargtimmen)

DIRECTOR: Ingmar Bergman
CAST: Max von Sydow, Liv Ullmann, Erland Josephson, Gertrud Fridh,
Naima Wifstrand, Georg Rydeberg
Sweden, 1968

Hour of the Wolf is hardly ever regarded as Ingmar Bergman's best film (an honor that usually goes to 1956's *The Seventh Seal*, 1957's *Wild Strawberries*, or 1986's *Fanny and Alexander*), but many horror directors point it out as their favorite genre movie, and one that inspired them to pursue certain themes and adapt a similar dreamlike tone in their own movies. It's a pity that Bergman never made another horror movie—

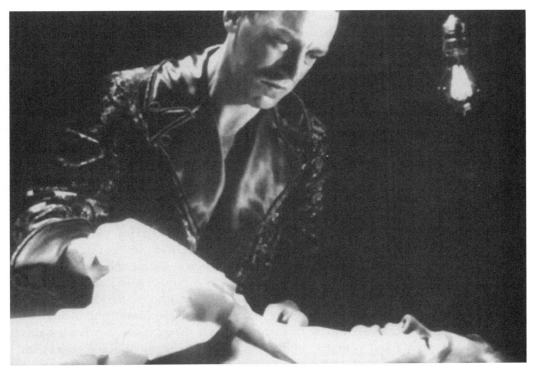

Max von Sydow (standing) and Ingrid Thulin in Ingmar Bergman's *Hour of the Wolf* (1968).

though some slight horror elements did appear in several of his films — as *Hour of the Wolf* infuses the viewer with a different kind of fear than any other genre movie. Even if Bergman's visual style and his trademark obsession with existential dread can be traced back to the works of Victor Sjöstrom (especially *The Phantom Carriage*), and some of his tricks are these days effectively used by Michael Haneke (*Benny's Video* and *Funny Games* shock the viewers with similar nightmarish mood that is by turns realistic and deliberately contrived), *Hour of the Wolf* remains an inimitable achievement.

Bergman's previous film, *Persona* (1966), was a close look at the disintegration of personality as well as the disintegration of cinema, and it started a series of somber pieces on the same theme. *Persona* opened with the image of a film projector at work, as if to remind the viewers that they're about to watch fictitious characters in made-up situations. *Hour of the Wolf* employs a similar gimmick: the opening credits are accompanied by the sounds of a film crew making preparations to shoot a scene, and when the credits end, Liv Ullmann approaches the camera and introduces the movie — either as if she was simply explaining something to the director, or as if she wanted to turn directly to the audience. She is not out of character, though; she speaks as Alma, wife of a painter who recently disappeared on the island of Baltrum after a string of menacing occurrences. The woman still lives on the island, and still cannot believe that her husband is gone. "Johan was uneasy," she says. "He always grew uneasy when his work didn't go well, and it hadn't gone well for some time now. And he became sleepless. He was frightened, as if he was afraid of the dark." But Johan (Max von Sydow) was not so much afraid of the dark as he was of the "hour of the wolf"—the time around 3:00 A.M., when most people die and most children are born. Since arriving at the desolate island, Alma and Johan made a tradition of sitting through this dreadful hour, with Johan talking about his fears, and showing Alma the paintings and sketches he had done during the day. It's on one of these nights that the man first mentions the "cannibals" who bother him when he's painting away from home; he's not quite sure whether the creatures are real or imaginary, but whichever is true, his art suffers, as from the time when they started appearing he cannot properly concentrate on the canvas. Alma tries to understand Johan, but this is clearly difficult for her. She is not an artist, and all she wants is to be close to him, spend more time together, and—since she's pregnant—make sure that Johan will be a caring father; she wants to be more like her husband so as to be able to empathize with him, and she also wants her husband to be more like her, more interested in their relationship. Unfortunately, only the first part of her wish comes true. When one day Alma leaves her house, she sees an old woman, one of the demons Johan has been lately encountering and putting in his sketches.

Generally speaking, *Hour of the Wolf* is indeed—like *Persona*—about human personality falling apart; here it is a problem for both Johan, whose inner demons do the damage, and Alma, who loves her husband too much, and starts sharing his obsessions. It is also about the deconstruction of filmmaking (via the everpresent reminders that "it's only a movie"), but on both levels Bergman manages to get to different places than the ones he explored in *Persona* and several later movies. For one, the movie can be seen as a sort of warning, apparently. "If you live with somebody who's not at peace, you may lose your peace, too," Ullmann said in an interview, referring to the ill-fated relationship between Alma and Johan, as well as to her own relationship with Bergman at the time. The actress was pregnant with Bergman's baby during the shoot of *Hour of the Wolf*, and she later admitted that it would have been much better for her to leave the director and raise the child on her own. She stayed, though, and after some time her lover's demons started biting at her soul, too—just like Bergman had predicted it in the movie.

The thing is, Bergman didn't aim at making *Hour of the Wolf* a documentary on his own problems and obsessions, he just wanted to use them to construct an effective horror movie. Hence all the references to classic horrors (a Bela Lugosi look-alike, Gothic settings, German Expressionism–influenced photography), and the whole scheme to keep reminding us that we're watching a movie. In the book *Conversation avec Bergman*, Olivier Assayas asks whether it is possible to present a real-life drama on screen in such a way that the audience feels exactly what the person who was going through it had felt; Bergman, one of the greatest directors of all time, replies that this is something cinema is incapable of: "You can do a fairy tale or a horror movie out of it," he says, "but to express it in a straightforward way—that's impossible." And that's what *Hour of the Wolf* is, too: a haunting horror movie, this artificial vessel, at the heart of which lies a much more painful human tragedy, impossible to be translated into the language of cinema.

In the Bergman movie made right after *Hour of the Wolf*—the wartime drama

Shame (1968) — he kept away from horror imagery, but he didn't abandon the theme of a relationship falling apart, with the troubled couple again played by von Sydow and Ullmann. The two actors returned for another bleak Bergman outing, *The Passion of Anna* (1969), an especially difficult piece for both, as it was filmed just when they were breaking up; not surprisingly, the character played by von Sydow is a man who has to come to terms with being left by his wife. *Cries and Whispers* (1972), *Face to Face* (1976), and *The Serpent's Egg* (1977) were also dark, emotional works that should appeal to those who came to love the atmosphere of *Hour of the Wolf*, and the director's masterpiece *Fanny and Alexander* is an atypical ghost story.*

Nightmares tormenting an artist didn't let go of the director until the very end of his life, it's just that they have been changing shapes throughout the years. Interviewed in *Time* in August 2007, shortly after Bergman's death, Woody Allen said that he used to talk to him by phone and got to know some of his recent fears. "He confided about his irrational dreams," relates Allen, "for instance, that he would show up on the set and not know where to put the camera and be completely panic-stricken. He'd have to wake up and tell himself that he is an experienced, respected director and he certainly does know where to put the camera. But that anxiety was with him long after he had created 15, 20 masterpieces." And where was Bergman having these dreams? In the setting of *Hour of the Wolf*— the windy ghost island of Faro, where he spent the last years of his life.

With its desolate setting, odd characters and peculiar narration, *Hour of the Wolf* provides the best existential scares cinema has ever had to offer. The performances of Max von Sydow and Liv Ullmann are unnervingly convincing, and the movie is all the more frightening, as we know that at the time Bergman had been tormented by nightmares that must have been similar to the ones he captured here.

The Cremator (Spalovač Mrtvol)

DIRECTOR: Juraj Herz
CAST: Rudolf Hrusínský, Vlasta Chramostová, Ilja Prachar, Milos Vognic,
Jana Stehnová, Zora Bozinová, Jirí Menzel
Czechoslovakia, 1968

There weren't many other countries in post–World War II Europe where making movies was more difficult than in the communist Czechoslovakia; there, the censors would rather completely rewrite and re-edit a film than risk releasing any remotely controversial work. It was only due to a lucky coincidence that director Juraj Herz managed to sneak his brilliant anti-totalitarian horror *The Cremator* past the censors. It was only Herz's second feature-length movie (after 1967's hospital-set detective story *Znamení Raka*, from which all the eroticism was typically excised), but his directorial talent

---

*A number of films from Bergman's earlier period also show his fascination with horror motifs: there's the confrontation with Death in *The Seventh Seal*, the evil hypnotist in *The Magician* (1958), and the shocking tale of revenge in *The Virgin Spring* (1959; remade by Wes Craven in 1972 as the brutal *The Last House on the Left*).

had already been shining bright in it. The script was based on the Ladislav Fuks novel *Spalovač mrtvol* (*The Corpse Incinerator*), but Herz took his time to shape the story according to his own vision, and in the end, with the help of Fuks, came up with a plot that was unlike anything ever made by the Czechoslovakian film industry. To make it all the more confusing to his countrymen, for the role of the devilish main character Herz chose Rudolf Hrušínský, an actor who in the previous decade became a national comedy icon by playing tubby soldier Josef Svejk in 1957's *Dobrý Voják Svejk* and 1958's *Poslusne Hlásím*.

In *The Cremator*, Hrušínský appears as Roman Kopfrkingl, an individual obsessed with the idea of becoming a man of success. He often says that he wants to be wealthy because he cares about his "blessed family," but in reality he cares about no one except himself: he wants to be rich so that people admire him; he wants to be admired so that he can influence people; and as soon as he becomes influential enough, he is tempted to abuse the power he was entrusted with, and betray his family, friends and colleagues to climb another rung of the social ladder. However fanatical Roman clearly is from the very beginning, he at least appears to be a man of principles and good taste: he abhors addictions, cares about his health, takes great pleasure in art and Buddhist philosophy, and is nothing short of perfect in his profession of running a crematorium. But when a Party member offers him a "better life," Roman rejects everything that used to be dear to him and agrees to sign a Faustian pact with the Party; he even has an idea on how his crematorium could be used now that he's been assigned an almost God-like position.

The movie takes place in 1930s Prague and the Party members are obviously Germans coming in to occupy Czechoslovakia. However, Herz intentionally avoided naming the Party members as Nazis, so that the whole story could be seen as a metaphor for the contemporary situation of the country, with the Party standing for the communists who had replaced Germans by then, and Roman being a caricature of all Czechoslovakians who were brainwashed by the new occupants. "Given the fact that Soviet forces occupied Czechoslovakia just after *The Cremator* was released, the line 'we live in Europe in the 20th century, in a civilized world,' which is stressed several times throughout the film, seems both ironic and sadly absurd," writes Adam Schofield in "A Black Pearl of the Deep: Juraj Herz's *The Cremator*"; but he also adds that although its focus is on the history of East Central Europe, "those unfamiliar with the region's political past can surely enjoy it as a work of black comedy or psychological horror" since it is "an ingeniously orchestrated film, full of complexities, and capable of giving the horror genre a better name." Which is true, as from the opening scene at the zoo — which introduces the viewers to Roman and is filled with distortions, weird camera angles and symbols — Herz proves that he feels comfortable with any sort of visual tricks, while Hrušínský flawlessly plays the fanatic-turned-opportunist-turned-murderer. Compare Roman's speeches at the beginning and near the end of the movie to fully appreciate Hrušínský's skill at showing the metamorphosis of his character: during the former he speaks almost like a caring priest and during the latter he's a full-blooded Hitler.

Peter Hames in *The Cinema of Central Europe* contrasts the relatively good — even if also riddled with censorship — state of filmmaking business in Poland and Hungary during the late 1960s with this in Czechoslovakia; he states that except for a brief period of liberalization during Prague Spring (from January 5 to August 21, 1968) filmmakers had their hands tied by the censors. "After 1969," he writes, "over a hundred films were banned and culture (including film) was subjected to an extensive suppression that was to last twenty years. Many directors emigrated and others found their careers at an end." This is another thing that makes *The Cremator* an exceptional movie: it was finished within this short period of liberalization, and could be released without cuts, despite its controversial content. Therefore, *The Cremator* remains Herz's only film made in his home country that the director is satisfied with. He admitted in a recent interview with Ivana Košuličová: "During shooting, it became clear that this was a unique chance which wouldn't come again.... I had absolute liberty in my work. I could film whatever I wanted to." Herz could also travel throughout Europe to see how the movie was received in different places: "[T]he reactions of the audience were completely different in every country," he says in the interview. "In Prague, people were depressed; in Slovakia, they laughed; in the Netherlands, it was a comedy from the beginning to the end; in Italy, the spectators went from the cinema right to the bar because cremation is just impossible, awful and unacceptable in their country." But even this most fortunate of all Herz's early movies didn't revel in success for too long: it managed to become one of 1969's box office hits, but was soon banned as the influence of the Soviet Union on the country's culture was getting stronger.

Herz probably realized that it would be extremely difficult to keep on making good movies in Czechoslovakia under the Soviet occupation, but he would rather try than immediately emigrate. Consequently, the next several of his films were very disappointing for the director himself, though not always for the viewers, who weren't aware of how much was cut out of them or how drastically the scripts had to be modified to appease the censors. *Kulhavý Dábel* (1969) was supposed to be an erotic musical, but all the raunchy scenes were deleted. *Petrolejové Lampy* (1970) was a drama set at the turn of the 20th century which helped avoid accusations of it being a direct comment on contemporary events, but some controversial scenes still had to be cut. *Morgiana* (1972), one of the director's best works, was a dark and beautiful Gothic tale of two sisters/doppelgangers, but according to Herz the movie was missing a whole second half, which he envisioned as shedding new light on preceding events. And even the severely cut *Morgiana* was labeled a "masochistic movie" and banned. After the incident, Herz wasn't allowed to make movies for more than a year. Eventually, he was handed a story by communist Jaromíra Kolárová and was asked to adapt it, but the result (*Holky z Porcelánu*, 1974) again wasn't satisfactory for the administration, as instead of praising the proletariat, Herz "presented the workers as whores." In the late 1970s he was given a choice: either make strictly controlled political movies or fairy tales; he chose the latter. His best known work from that period is *Panna a Netvor* (1978), an attractive, if not very innovative, version of "Beauty and the Beast." In the 1980s Herz tried to return to the horror genre with a story about a vampire car, *Upír z Feratu* (1981), but the censors first trimmed all the most controversial parts of the script, and when the movie was finished they proceeded to make further cuts, so that the final product hardly resembled the director's original idea. But even in such difficult conditions Herz managed to make one more masterpiece: a depiction of a concentration camp nightmare, *Zastihla Mě Noc* (1986), which was based on another story by Kolárová, but also allowed the director to draw from his own childhood experience (at the age of 10 he went to a camp in Ravensbrück). "I think that the film *Zastihla Mě Noc* is my greatest horror," says Herz. "It is a real horror. There is no blood, but it is unwatchable for people with weak nerves." After finishing the fairy tale *Galose Stastia* (1986; based on a story by Hans Christian Andersen), Herz finally made the decision to move to Germany. There he mainly worked for television and kept on adapting fairy tales (like 1991's *Zabí Král* and 1994's *Císarovy Nové Saty*). His last great movie to date, the Kafka-esque *Pasáž* (1997), was made after coming back to Czech Republic, which had been by then transformed into a post–Velvet Revolution democracy.

The Cremator is a rare horror made in the communist Czechoslovakia and the only movie made during this period by director Juraj Herz that wasn't mutilated by the censors. Cue a whole lot of political metaphors, and a critique of conformity and totalitarianism given a Gothic treatment.

Murder à la Mod

DIRECTOR: Brian De Palma
CAST: William Finley, Margo Norton, Andra Akers, Jared Martin,
Jennifer Salt, Laura Rubin
USA, 1968

As the decade of the 1960s was nearing its end, the most "uncomfortably successful" directorial career was born: *Murder à la Mod*, shown proudly at New York's Gate Theater in 1968, was the first sign of the dazzling cinematic genius of Brian De Palma. Truth be told, not everyone was *dazzled* by the director's first feature-long release — a rather peculiar, "acquired taste" piece of work. Let's not forget, however, that De Palma was only 27 years old back then: a restless and ambitious young man first trying out the tricks of the trade. (Before *Murder* he made *The Wedding Party* starring Robert De Niro, but it was not released until 1969.) Yet even at this young age De Palma proved that he was able to create something that could be easily called the essence of cinema.

The core idea for *Murder à la Mod* was not new: we observe a certain situation from different points of view, and each time the point of view shifts, we have to re-evaluate the whole story. Akira Kurosawa did this in *Rashomon* (1951) many years before and several other directors utilized the gimmick since, but De Palma, typically, replaces content with style and aims to prove that the same plot can spawn three completely different movies: a drama, thriller and comedy. And the most intriguing thing is that the situation the three genres are woven around doesn't belong to any of them, as it's a horror set piece showing a girl having her eyes taken out with an ice-pick. To make things even more spicy, in the background of the ambiguous set piece De Palma puts the moviemaking business and one of the themes he's most obsessed about: that of a film director forcing young girls to disrobe in front of his camera.

De Palma was never afraid of teasing the audience with blatant artificiality of the worlds he created, yet his movies always have been incredibly involving — especially the ones where the plot itself was not the most important piece of the puzzle. Please note that De Palma's "fanbase favorites" are not his most critically acclaimed or most popular films — like, respectively, *The Untouchables* (1987) or *Mission: Impossible* (1996) — but rather the experimental, unpredictable, mood-oriented works *Phantom of the Paradise* (1974), *Blow Out* (1981), *Raising Cain* (1992) and *Femme Fatale* (2002); *Murder à la Mod* no doubt belongs to the latter group — and holds a special place in it. Josh Ashbrook recounts in his book *Brian De Palma* that even the director himself, who usually didn't care much about being accused of favoring style over substance, thought that *Murder* was a bit too much: "confusing and too shallow ... the deliberate artifice of the idea actually worked against it." *Murder à la Mod* may then be, if you will, too De Palma–esque for De Palma himself, but is at the same time a treat for his most faithful fans, as even with no split screen it is everything they love about the director's works: it has multiple points of view, hypnotizing rhythm, beautiful girls, scenes of voyeurism and grotesque violence, a bagful of twists, the feel of an homage to classic filmmakers, great energy, a hilarious title song and, last but definitely not least, it has the great William Finley in one of his craziest roles.

Seen through the eyes of a horror fan rather than through the eyes of a Brian De Palma fan, *Murder* is a much tougher thing to love. Suspenseful and gruesome at times, the movie generally escapes clear genre definitions. Just when you think it's on its way to turning into a bloodbath, De Palma shifts gears and treats you to a Laurel and Hardy–inspired comedy; and just when you think it's safe to laugh, things suddenly turn bloody again. But perhaps that's why De Palma is so often perceived as "the most European of the great American directors." He's not interested in telling us easy-to-digest, linear stories, but wants to fill them with as many unexpected punches as possible — the movie's coherence be damned. The comedy/horror duality was later visible in several other De Palma's movies, all of them loved by his fans, but usually panned by the critics. These are, most notably, *Sisters* (1973), the aforementioned *Phantom of the Paradise* and *Body Double* (1984).

Back in 1968, *Murder à la Mod* was presented on a double bill with Paul Bartel's *The Secret Cinema* (1965), a 30-minute movie that, according to some critics, was the better one of the duo (Vincent Canby of *The New York Times* called it "a cool, hilarious study of madness that is absolutely believable"). Like *Murder*, *The Secret Cinema* is a celebration of the title medium in its purest form, a movie-within-a-movie that manages to be playful and involving at the same time. ("In the context of most of today's moviemaking," wrote Canby of both *Murder à la Mod* and *The Secret Cinema*, "it's fun to see directors who are willing to acknowledge the movie form, and who do not try to convince us that what we see on the screen is necessarily 'real.' When they don't try — curiously — we often do believe, which is what movies are all about.") Bartel's story about a woman who suspects that her life is being filmed, from today's point of view often perceived as a predecessor of Peter Weir's *The Truman Show* (1998), in fact bears more than a passing resemblance to De Palma's early films — just think of all the Peeping Toms trying to make movies out of other people's lives in *Murder à la Mod*,

Greetings (1968) and *Hi, Mom!* (1969). De Palma was later trying to reach a healthy compromise between his natural tendency for quirkiness and the need to make financially successful movies (which compromise, as the likes of 2000's *Mission to Mars* prove, didn't always bring best results), while Bartel — three years older than De Palma — chose to barricade himself within the confines of cult cinema, following *The Secret Cinema* with the comedy about murders, voyeurism and family secrets *Private Parts* (1972), the infamous Sylvester Stallone-David Carradine vehicle *Death Race 2000* (1975) and the cannibalistic farce *Eating Raoul* (1982); in 1986 Bartel reworked *The Secret Cinema* as an episode of the TV series *Amazing Stories*. The perfectly matched Gate Theater double bill spawned two very different careers, then, but if you look back on these early efforts from De Palma and Bartel, you will still see them as two examples of fresh and fascinating cinema made by young guys clearly in love with filmmaking.

Murder à la Mod shows us De Palma at a learning stage (see how he employs Hitchcock's technique to create an early suspense scene; or how he constructs his trademark violent set pieces), but based on this piece of evidence you can easily tell he was a brilliant pupil. For the perfect 1960s cult cinema experience, watch *Murder* back-to-back with Paul Bartel's *The Secret Cinema*.

The Bird with the Crystal Plumage (*L'Uccello dalle Piume di Cristallo*)

DIRECTOR: Dario Argento
CAST: Tony Musante, Suzy Kendall, Renato Romano, Enrico Maria Salerno, Eva Renzi, Umberto Raho
Italy-Germany, 1970

The term *giallo* was originally associated with cheap Italian-made crime books with yellow covers (hence the name *giallo*, meaning "yellow"). It was, however, the movie format that made the term internationally recognizable. Luchino Visconti's film noir *Ossessione* (1942) is sometimes called an early attempt to bring *giallo* to the screen, but the first proper *gialli* were made by Mario Bava: the suspenseful duo of *The Girl Who Knew Too Much* (1963) and *Blood and Black Lace* (1964) set the rules that were to be closely followed by other filmmakers specializing in the subgenre. With very few exceptions, a *giallo* movie depicts bloody crimes of a serial killer whose identity is not revealed until the finale; the killer usually wears black gloves; the murders stem from a childhood trauma; the victims are beautiful girls; there are many suspects and many red herrings; and the ending has to include a surprising twist. Just when Bava got slightly bored with the whole concept and started focusing on grisly deaths rather than on the plot (as can be observed in 1970's *The Twitch of the Death Nerve*, aka *Bay of Blood*— the movie that inspired the slasher subgenre), Dario Argento made his debut as a director with *The Bird with the Crystal Plumage*, a *giallo* that was on one hand quite traditional, and on the other felt very fresh. It stunned audiences with elaborate set pieces, as well as with the mesmerizing rhythm that was unlike anything experienced in cinema so far.

The plot itself, however, is based on a typical — if very involving — *giallo* story-line taken from the novel *Screaming Mimi* by Fredrick Brown. American writer Sam Dalmas (Tony Musante), who came to Italy to relax and get easy money by writing a book on birds, witnesses a murder attempt at an art gallery. Although he is not able to do much, his arrival at the door of the gallery scares away a black-clad figure before the blow is dealt, and the injured victim (Eva Renzi) survives. Sam later confesses to the police that there's something strange about the scene he witnessed, but he can't quite put his finger on it — and saying this turns out to be his greatest mistake (apparently, the person who fled the crime scene is a dangerous serial killer.) Hoping that several more days in Italy may refresh the writer's memory, the police confiscate his passport and encourage him to do some thinking. That he does, and soon he even comes up with an important clue concerning the identity of the killer, but at the same time he and his lovely girlfriend (Suzy Kendall) become the next names on the psycho's hit list.

Argento has been accused of misogyny and using gratuitous violence far more often than other directors of *giallo* movies. Surprisingly, he doesn't seem to be bothered by this too much, and his own statements concerning onscreen violence usually add to the controversy instead of relieving it. There's a wonderfully awkward moment in the documentary *Dario Argento's World of Horror* (1985; directed by Michele Soavi) when Argento admits that to him, murder is "very beautiful," and that after having directed so many *gialli*, he would "make a pretty good murderer"; he later adds that "between the victim and the murderer there is something sensual, something erotic." This fascination with the eroticism of murder is apparent in most Argento's movies and is the main reason for the accusations of misogyny. This is jumping to conclusions, though, as Argento's female characters are usually very likable, much more complex and interesting than the male leads. When the killer stalks them, we do feel for them and don't want them to die (unlike in many truly misogynistic slasher movies, for example 1982's *Slumber Party Massacre*). This is, of course, why Argento handles the suspense scenes so well. In a memorable moment from *The Bird*, we see a woman imprisoned in her apartment and literally paralyzed with fear, while the killer is at the door, closer and closer to getting inside. We want the victim to do *something* to try to save herself when she just screams and waits for the killer to get her, which means that no matter how beautiful murder can be in an Argento movie, we instinctively still don't want it to happen.

But it has to happen, obviously, and not just once; after all, it's *giallo* we're talking about here. Argento's novelty method for the subgenre was to make the victims sympathetic, as well as to have murderers intriguing enough for us to make attempts to understand their motivation. In the director's best movies — *The Bird* among them — he pulls off the rare trick of forcing the audience to root for both the killer and the victims. In the aforementioned documentary, Argento says that near the end of the movie he, in a way, cheers for the murderer — as, in his opinion, do the viewers. "Not that they would like him to kill again," explains the director, "but they want him to get away, or at least don't want him to get punished. They seem to decide that his reasons are justified."

After *The Bird with the Crystal Plumage*, Argento made two more movies with fancy animal-themed titles, *The Cat O'Nine Tails* and *Four Flies on Grey Velvet* (both 1971); in 1975 he created his *giallo* magnum opus *Deep Red.** In later years, Argento chose to make his *gialli* bloodier and more shocking — like *Tenebre* (1982), *Terror at the Opera* (1987), *Trauma* (1993) and *Sleepless* (2001) — but recently came back with another suspenseful Hitchcockian entry similar to his early works, *Do You Like Hitchcock?* (2005). So as not to be labeled as a *giallo*-only director, Argento also made several fantasy-horrors, and he turned out just as great with them as he was with *gialli*; *Suspiria* (1977), *Inferno* (1980), and *Phenomena* (1985) certainly belong on any list of his best works. The recent *The Third Mother* (2007) has moments of greatness, but is ultimately spoiled by excessive use of digital effects and some ridiculously gory sequences.

Not as complex or otherworldly as the director's later works, *The Bird with the Crystal Plumage* nevertheless remains a powerful and hypnotizing movie. It is also Argento's most humorous work to date (though most of the funny moments are, understandably, very odd — scenes with the cat-eating artist being highlights), and his only collaboration with great Italian cinematographer Vittorio Storaro (*Last Tango in Paris*, *Apocalypse Now*, *The Sheltering Sky*). The box office success of the movie seems to have inspired many other directors to follow in Argento's footsteps, and within the two years from the premiere of *The Bird* such *giallo* classics were made as Lucio Fulci's *Lizard in a Woman's Skin* (1971), Paolo Cavara's *Black Belly of the Tarantula* (1971), Sergio Martino's *Blade of the Ripper* (1971), Aldo Lado's *Short Night of the Glass Dolls* (1971), and Massimo Dallamano's *What Have They Done to Solange?* (1972).

Argento's directorial debut is a model example of his unique style, and a great introduction to the half-realistic, half-imaginary world that is further explored in his later movies. Still one of the finest *giallo* films ever made.

Lizard in a Woman's Skin
(Una Lucertola con la Pelle di Donna)

aka *Schizoid*
DIRECTOR: Lucio Fulci
CAST: Florinda Bolkan, Jean Sorel, Stanley Baker, Leo Genn, Silvia Monti,
Mike Kennedy, Penny Brown, Anita Strindberg
Italy-Spain-France, 1971

Lucio Fulci is a director who wasn't afraid to try his hand in most genres that were popular between the late 1950s and the early 1990s, and he proved at least adequate with most of them. He was no stranger to comedy (his 1959 debut *The Thieves* and several films that followed), musical (1959's *The Jukebox Kids*, 1960's *Howlers at the Dock*), drama (1963's *The Swindlers*), adventure (1964's *Two Public Enemies*), or western (1966's *Massacre Time*). At the end of the 1970s he successfully broke into the hor-

---

*Argento claimed in interviews that *Deep Red* is much different from the *giallo* that make up the animal trilogy, but plot-wise it is strikingly similar to his debut: here again, a likable and helpless foreigner witnesses a crime, and has to recollect one tiny detail to reveal the identity of the killer.

ror genre with *Zombie Flesh Eaters* (1979)—an unofficial follow-up to George A. Romero's *Dawn of the Dead* (1978)—but even before that he made several violent thrillers often based on horror imagery, starting with *One on Top of the Other* (1969), an interesting story that echoed the works of Alfred Hitchcock and Mario Bava. However, it wasn't until two years later and *Lizard in a Woman's Skin* that Fulci could really show the full scope of his talent as a master of the shocking and the bizarre. And even though it is often pointed out that *Lizard* was made to exploit the popularity of *giallo* movies and it copied the style of Dario Argento's recent hit *The Bird with the Crystal Plumage* (1970), Fulci's film is too stunning to be simply regarded as a quick cash-in— in the same way as *Zombie Flesh Eaters* is too frighteningly beautiful and unique to be ever called a clone of *Dawn of the Dead.*

Fulci used to say that he and Argento were making very similar movies, and the only difference was in the budgets. This sounds true if we only compare the *gialli* the two directors have made (after all, Argento never made a musical or a straightforward comedy), as Fulci's efforts do seem to be more savage, rough-at-the-edges takes on similar themes. Even the title *Lizard in a Woman's Skin* sounds like it wants to be a supplement to Argento's "animal trilogy" (*The Bird with the Crystal Plumage* plus the 1971 duo of *The Cat O' Nine Tails* and *Four Flies on Grey Velvet*), but the sheer strangeness of the title promises a trip yet weirder than whatever Argento had prepared for the viewers by that time—and that's exactly what we get.

Gorgeous Brazilian actress Florinda Bolkan plays Carol Hammond, a woman troubled by perverse dreams in which she is drawn to sexy blonde Julia Durer (Anita Strindberg). Carol, married to a handsome man (Jean Sorel), is so unsettled by the lesbian dreams that she talks about them to a psychoanalyst (Georges Rigaud), who calmly explains that she shouldn't get worried—it's just her subconscious at work. But is it? The dreams soon turn into a violence-filled nightmares in which Carol repeatedly stabs Julia in the chest with a letter opener; after the woman confesses this to the psychiatrist, it turns out that Julia really is dead—killed with a letter opener, wearing the same clothes she wore in the dream, and Carol's fingerprints are all over the crime scene. Now it's up to the inquiring Inspector Corvin (Stanley Baker) to solve the mystery death. Did Carol's unfaithful husband frame her? Or perhaps the murderers were a hippie couple (Mike Kennedy and Peggy Brown) who used to attend the victim's wild parties?

Fulci's movies are an acquired taste, and *Lizard in a Woman's Skin* is no exception. Like most of the director's works, *Lizard* is zoom-happy, has pacing problems and does not always adhere to logic. Also, at a first glance, it may seem that some violence was somewhat gratuitously squeezed into the script, especially in the scene that sees Carol exploring rooms of a private clinic and stumbling across several "living dead dogs," sad creatures apparently being experimented upon, squeaking pathetically, with their beating hearts exposed and numerous tubes protruding from their mutilated bodies. This effects show-off (by Carlo Rambaldi, author of some of the cinema's most memorable visual effects, who in this case had to prove in court that he did no harm to live animals) comes from out of nowhere and leads nowhere, but it is *not* gratuitous; it adds a lot to the movie's mood and lets us see the world from the point of view of the main character — as dangerous and full of inexplicable cruelty. But Fulci doesn't stop at including occasional shocks and gore to build the right atmosphere: he also uses wild editing, slo-mo, overexposure and split-screen, and blurs the boundaries between the dream and reality, while Ennio Morricone's foreboding score aptly supports the nightmarish imagery.

Another interesting aspect of the movie is its depiction of sexuality. The characters who are too concerned about their social status find sexual fantasies and relationships embarrassing — like Carol, who is at the same time fascinated and repelled by Julia's uninhibited attitude towards sex because she realizes that had she herself been involved in any sort of a scandal, she would have ruined her father's career; and vice versa. The characters who don't care all that much about their position in society, tend to enjoy sexuality in all its forms, and without any pangs of conscience — like Julia, the hippies and Carol's adulterous husband. The movie being set in hippie heaven — London during the "swinging sixties" — Carol feels overwhelmed with the forbidden sexuality, which presumably generates the lesbian dreams she's so ashamed of, and makes her a primary suspect in the case of Julia's murder. As the twist ending shows, the murder itself is also strongly connected with the issue of repressed desire and the fear of losing social status — and it's at this point that Fulci tells us whose side he's on.

Lizard in a Woman's Skin remains one of Fulci's best — and most coherent — mixtures of horror and thriller, even though it precedes the era when he became a truly recognizable and controversial filmmaker. His next effort *Don't Torture a Duckling* (1972) was another powerful *giallo* (again with Bolkan in the main role), and it was to become the director's personal all-time favorite; this time Fulci didn't just shock the viewers with the graphic violence but also with the harsh criticism of the Catholic Church (which got him in trouble and prevented the theatrical premiere of the movie in the U.S.). Several years later, Fulci returned to the *giallo* subgenre with the brilliant *Murder to the Tune of the Seven Black Notes* (1977; aka *The Psychic*), and then changed the face of cinematic horror with the likes of *Zombie Flesh Eaters*, *City of the Living Dead* (1980) and *The Beyond* (1981). His output in the late 1980s wasn't very impressive (1989's TV movie *The Sweet House of Horrors* being the nadir of his career), but in 1990 he made one last great movie, *A Cat in the Brain*, in which he played Dr. Lucio Fulci, a director haunted by horrors from his own films. (Fulci later claimed that Wes Craven borrowed the concept for 1994's *New Nightmare*, a postmodern horror that was, ironically, often called "highly original" and "reinventing the genre.")

Not as popular as Lucio Fulci's later horror feasts, *Lizard in a Woman's Skin* is an intriguing and suspenseful giallo, and a sign of bloodier things to come — especially in the uncut version that features an infamous scene with Carlo Rambaldi's shocking special effects. Setting the movie in London at the turn of the 1960s adds a psychedelic aura to the proceedings, and raises some interesting questions about sexuality.

Blood on Satan's Claw

aka *Satan's Skin*
DIRECTOR: Piers Haggard
CAST: Patrick Wymark, Linda Hayden, Anthony Ainley, Barry Andrews,
Wendy Padbury, Michele Dotrice, Simon Williams
UK, 1970

When you think of great British horror movies that have been overlooked by large audiences, it's usually Michael Reeves's *Witchfinder General* (1968; produced by Tigon, a new, promising film company at the time) and Robin Hardy's *The Wicker Man* (1973) that come to mind. However, within the five-year period in between these films (that are now established must-see genre classics, with *The Wicker Man* already adopted for modern cinema-goers by Neil LaBute via a 2006 remake), a yet better example of a fine, little-seen UK horror is to be found: Tigon's *Blood on Satan's Claw*.

"I didn't really know much about horror films," admitted director Piers Haggard while talking about being first approached by the Tigon executives to film *Blood on Satan's Claw*. Then he went on to confess something even more shocking: "I'd seen the Hammer films, but I wasn't a huge fan of those, I wouldn't go out of my way to see one. I was a rather serious young man, and didn't like the overdone quality of those. I was more interested in a more poetic sort of cinema." This attitude might have spelled disaster, especially to everyone who adored the "overdone quality" of the horrors from Hammer. In the end, however, Haggard's movie became one of the greatest genre pieces made in the 1970s, and even though it really was much different from the Hammer films, it didn't turn out to be "a poetic movie in a horror disguise" but rather a genuine, graphic and unsettling horror movie with a poetic touch to it.

The often cited similarities between *Blood on Satan's Claw* and *Witchfinder General* are visible even if we only compare the settings and the main plotlines of the two movies. *Witchfinder General* took place in 17th century England and depicted the hell brought to a small village by one wicked person (Vincent Price's title character); *Blood on Satan's Claw* takes place in the 17th century and it, too, depicts the hell being brought to a small village by a single person, just as wicked as the general. But to make things more complicated, this person is young, cute and innocent-looking blonde Angel Blake (Linda Hayden), who turns into a devil-worshipper after finding the claw of the title while playing in the fields. To summon the dark lord, Angel needs to muster a sizable group of followers, impress the creature with a proper number of rapes and sacrifices, and collect patches of the devil's skin that will, in the end, form a giant, hairy puzzle in the form of the Master himself. The greatest nuisance for the villagers is that the devil's skin starts growing on their own bodies, and whatever part becomes hairier than normally accepted, they have to cut off and give back to its rightful owner. Some people are happy to give away pieces of themselves for as worthy a cause as composing the devil, and some are not, because for some reason they resisted the temptation of Angel. The latter group consists of a judge (Patrick Wymark), the Rev. Fallowfield (Anthony Ainley), plowman Ralph (Barry Andrews) and Peter Edmonton (Simon Williams), who already survived a personal nightmare as first his fiancée's and then his own hand turned into devilish claws. These men will have to face Angel's murderous cult and find a way to interrupt their violent ritual.

Blood on Satan's Claw is an engaging spectacle that uses all the right tricks to invite us to its equally gorgeous and frightening world, and later to anger us, surprise us, shock us and move us. The movie's crowning brilliance, however, relies on Linda Hayden, so angelic and yet so perverse in the role of Angel Blake that you will feel unable to hate her and too guilty to adore her. When she was asked to star in Haggard's movie, Hayden was just teasing the whole world with the label of a "British Lolita" that she was marked with after her debut performance in Alastair Reid's *Baby Love* (1968). A single scene from *Blood on Satan's Claw*— the one in which Angel disrobes in front of the pure-hearted Rev. Fallowfield and attempts to seduce him — affirmed the fact that the label was correct, but the most important thing Hayden proves here is that she can truly *own* a movie; her screen time is not all that impressive if you care to measure it, but after the movie ends, she seems to have been the main character. That there are other great parts here (Patrick Wymark's smooth, seemingly improvised role as the judge brings to mind Anthony Hopkins's best performances of two decades later) only makes Hayden's accomplishment more impressive. And although *Blood* remained the undisputable peak of her career, she starred in some other genre movies that are worth seeing: *Taste the Blood of Dracula* (1969, with Christopher Lee, made just before *Blood*), *Madhouse* (1974, with Vincent Price and Peter Cushing) and *The Boys from Brazil* (1978, an adaptation of Ira Levin's novel, with Gregory Peck).

Tailored to become a hit with the contemporary audiences, *Blood* had to include some references to the contemporary era, as people generally like to see themselves mirrored in a movie, even if it's a period piece. The unbearable eroticism of Angel, making her a perfect example of a rebellious, independent 1970s kid, living life to the full, was connection number one. Connection number two was Mary Bell, an 11-year-old girl from Newcastle-upon-Tyne, who strangled two other children, and didn't seem to feel any remorse afterwards. The Mary Bell headlines shocked scriptwriter Robert Wynne-Simmons so much that he decided to mold the character of Angel, also a ruthless child-killer, on Mary. (Several years later, John Carpenter would form the character of Michael Myers after looking into the eyes of a kid who was, in his own words, "pure evil.")

Haggard has received much praise for the movie since its 1971 premiere. (*Blood* was never a huge box office hit but it gained much more popularity in the late 1970s and early 1980s when it was regularly shown on late night TV.) His later efforts weren't quite as thrilling or memorable as his first feature: *The Quatermass Conclusion* (1979, also confusingly titled *Quatermass*) was usually deemed an unnecessary exploitation of the famous moniker, *The Fiendish Plot of Dr. Fu Manchu* (1980, starring Peter Sellers) was nothing more than a light, entertaining piece of cinema, and *Venom* (1982), an interesting and well-acted thriller, could perhaps be much better if it weren't for the constant fights between its two hot-blooded leads, Klaus Kinski and Oliver Reed. Similarly, since 1970 the Tigon company never produced a horror movie as good as *Blood*. Together with the aforementioned *Witchfinder General*, Haggard's debut feature still remains the studio's finest genre input.

Blood on Satan's Claw is weird, suspenseful, sexy and it's a dozen other things, not least of them — as director Piers Haggard would have it — it's a poetic horror movie. If that wasn't enough, it also stars "British Lolita" Linda Hayden, who puts in the performance of her life. Had the Tigon company made more movies like this, it could actually have become equal to Hammer.

Vampyros Lesbos

DIRECTOR: Jesus Franco
CAST: Soledad Miranda, Ewa Strömberg, Dennis Price, Heidrun Kussin,
Victor Feldman, Jose Martinez Blanco, Jesus Franco, Paul Müller
Spain-Germany, 1970

By 1970, Spanish director Jesus Franco had already made over 30 movies, most of them cheap and fun genre hybrids with catchy titles like *The Awful Dr. Orloff* (1961), *Attack of the Robots* (1966) and *Sadist Erotica* (1969). His most classic title didn't come into being until he decided to give a homoerotic spin to Bram Stoker's *Dracula*. Truth be told, Franco's *vampyros* are far more interested in being *lesbos* than in drinking human blood, but the movie is so mesmerizing and so outright sexy that you really shouldn't mind that.

Shortly before *Vampyros Lesbos*, Franco had made a more straightforward and rather disappointing adaptation of Stoker's novel, *Count Dracula* (1970), so this time he chose to play with the familiar plot instead of becoming its slave. Turning the characters of Dracula, Jonathan Harker and Renfield into homosexual females was not enough to satisfy the director, though, and in effect *Vampyros Lesbos* became one of the least predictable variations on the theme.

Dracula's name is actually mentioned in Franco's movie, and it grates when we hear it. The name slips out in a scene where Countess Nadine Carody (Soledad Miranda) is revealing the juiciest bits from her past to a woman she hardly knows, Linda Westinghouse (Ewa Strömberg). Dracula, it turns out, was once Nadine's lover and left her something more than just his inheritance. The "Dracula" pronounced by lovely, suntanned Miranda in the bright of day sounds artificial and out of place, as the movie doesn't even try to evoke the atmosphere of the novel. Nadine is a vampire, but for the most part she refuses to behave like one: she does drink blood and avoids reading the Bible, but she doesn't care about hiding away from the sun or metamorphosing into a bat. When Linda first visits Nadine's house on a picturesque island off Istanbul, she is not invited to a dark and cold room, but to join the countess for a swim in the sea. The two women soon feel they belong to one another: Linda had been dreaming of Nadine long before she met her, and Nadine is convinced that there is no better person than Linda to mix blood with. The similarities to "Dracula" are mostly to be found in the depiction of the characters: apart from the Vampire and the Visitor we also meet a Doctor (Dennis Price) and a Vampire's Mad Servant (Heidrun Kussin) along the way. The rest of the plot explores territories that were not covered by Stoker (for example, Franco's doctor is hardly as tough and honest as Stoker's Van Helsing, and his version of Jonathan Harker not nearly as powerless as his counterpart in the novel).

"A kitsch artifact from an era devoid of style or taste. Memorable for all the wrong reasons" is what Essi Berelian of the usually dependable *Total Film* magazine wrote about *Vampyros Lesbos*. Never mind the value of Franco's movie — it's always a tricky thing to praise or defend his works — but the criticism of the particular era in which it was made sounds very much off. The era of the early 1970s was one of the most colorful in the history of the genre: it was the peak of the sexual revolution and the filmmakers were unashamedly using the obsession with eroticism to sell their works. David J. Skal wrote in *The Monster Show: A Cultural History of Horror*, "By the end of the sixties, the big American sex party was in full swing.... As in the twenties, sexual abstinence was distinctly unfashionable." And whatever you think of Franco's way of making movies, he surely had a knack for showing us that sexual abstinence indeed is unfashionable. In a very poignant scene near the beginning of *Vampyros Lesbos*, Linda, deeply confused by the dreams about another woman, consults a doctor, and a piece of advice he gives her is: "Find yourself a better lover." The whole vampire/lesbian adventure that follows may, therefore, be a projection of Linda's mind — an effect of not being able to achieve sexual satisfaction in her heterosexual relationship. Curiously, when Linda then meets her dream partner, Nadine, she feels that whatever she may gain in this new relationship, it is still not worth giving up her personal freedom. The ending of *Vampyros Lesbos* is effectively ambiguous, and leaves us with a convincing and complex picture of a woman torn between her sexual needs and the fear of becoming dependent on the person who finally manages to satisfy her.

After making *Vampyros Lesbos*, Jesus Franco kept on churning out similar mixtures of horror and erotica that, unfortunately, had the tendency to be less and less impressive as the years passed. Worth mentioning are: *She Killed in Ecstasy* (1971), *Bare Breasted Countess* (1973), *A Virgin Among the Living Dead* (1973, also known under a title invented to lure Lucio Fulci's fans: *Zombi 4*), *Barbed Wire Dolls* (1975), *Demoniac* (1979), *Barbarian Goddess* (1980, aka *Mondo Cannibale*), and more recently *Killer Barbys* (1996). Apart from the fact that he did make a handful of truly good movies, Franco is a fascinating director because he's been using a record number of aliases in the credits, from relatively simple ones like Jeff Manner and J. Frank Manera, through more sophisticated — say, Frarik Hollman and David J. Khune — to utterly mysterious, in the vein of Candy Coster or Rosa Maria Almirall; and there's about five dozen more, mind you. There aren't many people on Earth who can claim they saw all his works (it seems that Franco makes movies quicker than most people can digest them).

With around 200 movies under his belt, Jesus Franco must have got some of them right, and *Vampyros Lesbos* is without doubt one of these. Franco's metaphors might seem forced and the characters are not always fully fleshed out, but just watch the sparks flying when Soledad Miranda gets anywhere near Ewa Strömberg and you'll immediately forget about most of the movie's weaknesses. To get genre credibility, *Vampyros Lesbos* gets its teeth deep in Bram Stoker's *Dracula*, and actually injects some new life in it. All this to the rhythm of a wonderfully psychedelic soundtrack that is almost as difficult to shake off as the movie's sexiest scenes.

Raw Meat

aka *Death Line*
Director: Gary Sherman
Cast: Sharon Gurney, David Ladd, Donald Pleasence, Hugh Armstrong,
Christopher Lee, Norman Rossington, James Cossins
UK, 1972

Here's a horror movie that cannot be compared to anything that preceded it. It was made in England, with a mostly British cast (David Ladd being the only exception), but due to the European atmosphere and acting style having been mixed with the sensitivity of American director Gary Sherman, the final outcome was neither a copy of the horrors from Hammer, nor a simple rehash of gruesomely realistic movies in the vein of *Night of the Living Dead* (1968). In *Raw Meat*, unnerving violence stands next to offbeat humor, sentimentality, and biting socio-political commentary — all of them quite effective but at the same time refusing to form one coherent piece. Normally, this wouldn't be a good thing, but Sherman's movie somehow works despite being a string of sequences rather than a polished whole; here you have Donald Pleasence doing his comedy routine with the teabags, there you see Hugh Armstrong biting a rat's head off, and you are also treated to David Ladd talking about how it pays off to be insensitive in the modern world. Sherman doesn't give us a movie that is evenly paced, includes obligatory twists or has a neat ending, but perhaps this is why after watching it you feel you've experienced something that reflects real life better than most other horror movies.

Ugliness and sorrow suddenly enter the lives of two carefree students, Alex (David Ladd) and Patricia (Sharon Gurney), when they find an unconscious — or perhaps dead — man in the Russell Square tube station. They leave the body and go for help but upon their return the man is gone. A strange thing this, since he couldn't have left by train (it was late and the train Alex and Patricia took was the last one) and couldn't have sneaked past them and exited the station, either. The conundrum is presented to Inspector Calhoun (Donald Pleasence), and he only takes interest in it because the missing man turns out to be a prominent official named James Manfred (James Cossins). Apparently, not long ago, some other people also went missing in the same area, but they were not important enough for Calhoun to start a proper investigation. Now, with help from Detective Sergeant Rogers (Norman Rossington), the inspector sets out to solve the mystery — even though a man from MI5, Stratton-Villiers (Christopher Lee), suddenly pops out of nowhere and tries to convince him it's none of his business. After some brainstorming, Calhoun realizes that the body snatcher of Russell Square may be a descendant of the male and female workers who were trapped in the tube back in the 1890s and were left there for dead. The thing is, some of them might have survived by turning to cannibalism and they might have bred as well; right now they have perhaps run out of food and started searching for it amongst the passengers arriving at the station late at night.

"But how could the hardy band of ghouls have fed themselves for five generations without the police catching on, until now, that the Russell Square tube stop had a problem? And why, if the survivors can move freely from their old tunnel to the new one, didn't they simply escape? And if the original survivors couldn't escape, why ... didn't they consume each other before the nine month reproduction cycle?" Roger Ebert clearly asks too many questions in his witty and otherwise favorable review of *Raw Meat*. Had the movie's script covered all the possible plot holes Ebert mentions, it wouldn't be so much fun, just like forcing Pleasence's character to be more useful plot-wise would no doubt make him much less enjoyable. (As it is, Pleasence's Calhoun is a lazy, sarcastic bastard who talks a lot, but is not of much use to anyone around — and that's the way we want him to be.)

Pleasence's energetic, truly unforgettable performance is one of the movie's greatest assets — and one of the best in his career, on a par with the wild performance in Roman Polanski's *Cul-de-sac* (1966), and much different from his most popular horror part (Dr. Loomis in John Carpenter's *Halloween*). Another striking thing about *Raw Meat* is the impressive cinematography by Alex Thomson that reaches its peak during a long tracking shot showing us the dirty, rotten and infinitely sad lair of the cannibals; and since we're there, the convincingly nasty makeup of the male cannibal and his victims (by Harry and Peter Frampton) is quite exceptional, too. Interestingly, as off-putting and brutal as the movie's killer is, he is also rather sympathetic: constantly repeating "Mind the doors" — the only human phrase he has learned — and putting his victim's watch on his dead wife's breast, so that he can keep on believing her heart is still ticking. This makes "The Man" (as Hugh Armstrong is credited in the movie) more similar to the tragic monsters from the early days of sound cinema (for example Frankenstein and the Wolf Man) than to the mindless creatures and heartless killers from most horror movies of the 1970s.

In some aspects, however, *Raw Meat* is proudly rooted in the 1970s: all the interaction between Calhoun and Alex aims at pointing out the then-hot issue of a generation gap. Yet more emphasized is the problem of class exploitation (the tube workers left to die; the missing people unworthy of a police investigation), and the emotional coldness within the modern society is illustrated by the actions of both the young (it's obvious that Alex and Patricia don't care much about each other) as well as the elder (egoistic Calhoun), and is juxtaposed with the touching tenderness of "The Man." When a couple years later Tobe Hooper made his most important movie and the most influential cannibalistic horror ever — *The Texas Chain Saw Massacre* (1974) — he made sure it also portrayed the society of the times (this time from the American point of view), but he wasn't so much interested in eliciting sympathy for the villains, which makes his work completely different from Sherman's.

Sherman's follow-up to *Raw Meat* was another original and highly entertaining horror movie, *Dead & Buried* (1981), but since then he's been either covering other genres (quite successfully so in case of 1982's *Vice Squad* and 1987's *Wanted: Dead or Alive*, both gritty thrillers), working for TV (1990's *After the Shock* among several other titles) or ruining his horror CV with some unimpressive titles (1988's *Poltergeist III* was a shock to most fans of the director).

Good cannibal horror movies are extremely hard to find, so *Raw Meat* — no doubt one of the best examples of the man-eat-man cinema — scores big even before you realize it actually preceded the big daddy of onscreen cannibalism, *The Texas Chain Saw Massacre*. It should also be seen by all those who like to argue that the role of Dr. Loomis in *Halloween* was Donald Pleasence's only memorable genre input.

Flesh for Frankenstein

aka *Andy Warhol's Frankenstein*
DIRECTOR: Paul Morrissey
CAST: Udo Kier, Jose Dallesandro, Monique Van Vooren, Arno Juerging,
Srdjan Zelenovic, Dallia Di Lazzaro
USA-Italy-France, 1973

Trying to find a review of *Flesh for Frankenstein* without the word "gall bladder" in it, is a near impossible task. That's because it's a key word in one of the movie's most offensive scenes, one that best captures the atmosphere of the whole affair. And since it's so helpful in depicting this demented take on Mary Shelley's story, let's get it over with and have the excerpt here as well. We are in Dr. Frankenstein's cold and empty "laboratory" (that looks more like an operating room), and we see him lying on a beautiful woman who is, however, quite clearly dead. Strained and with fanatical sparkles in his eyes, Frankenstein rapes the lifeless body through a wound in the ribcage and pronounces the following words of wisdom to his crazed helper Otto: "To know life, you have to fuck death in the gall bladder." Spoken in the thickest German accent possible, this simple line tells you everything you need to know before deciding to watch the movie: *Flesh for Frankenstein* is about sex, death and innards — and it's not to be taken seriously.

Apart from "knowing life," Baron Frankenstein (Udo Kier) also wants to improve life, and with the help of Otto (Arno Juerging) he tries to build a perfect couple. To do this, he has to kill the peasants for body parts that could be useful for either the male or the female monster. The baron hopes that when he sews all these most attractive body parts together, he will get a pair of creatures so sexy, that as soon as he brings them to life they will be interested in nothing else but the intercourse, and will therefore procreate with no end. When we meet Frankenstein, he's very close to achieving his goal: the she-monster (Dallia Di Lazzaro) is almost ready for the resurrection, while the he-monster is just waiting for a handsome head to be found. But when Frankenstein finally spots a manly villager (Srdjan Zelenovic), cuts his head off and attaches it to the body of his monster, it turns out that since the victim didn't originally have much interest in the opposite sex, after being brought from the dead he refuses to bed his perfect bride. At the same time, the baron's sister and wife, Katrin (Monique Van Vooren), gets herself a young lover (Jose Dallesandro), who happens to be a close friend of the baron's latest head-donor. No wonder that when Katrin's new boyfriend sees his companion's head on a freakish body, he starts planning bloody revenge on Frankenstein — all this in amazing 3D, to heighten the viewers' pleasure.

The main question after watching *Flesh for Frankenstein* is whether director Paul Morrissey intended to do anything other than an exercise in excess. He probably did — though it's not easy to see the satire he was aiming at through all the blood, body parts and perverse sexual rituals that fill the screen for most of the running time. *Flesh for Frankenstein* may be, however, seen as a derogatory comment on the hippie movement; back when the movie was made, the movement was just several years old (it was started in 1966) but as much as it was adored by some, it was also looked down on by others, and Morrissey must have belonged to the latter group. His Mr. and Mrs. Frankenstein family seems to be a cruel parody of die-hard hippies some years after their 1966 initiation: bored with sex, nervously looking for new ways to satisfy themselves, and at the same time hypocritically teaching their children that sex is filthy. Morrissey, bold and independent filmmaker that he was, wasn't criticizing the concept of freedom that the hippies were proclaiming, but he was pointing an accusing finger at certain features of the movement, those that struck him as a bit too fanatical. While "being free" undoubtedly sounds great to everyone, making "free love" doesn't necessarily have to — and in *Flesh for Frankenstein* Morrissey shows us the vision of free love gone bad, or perhaps even "gone fascist." (Kier's heavy accent was not just used for a laugh, apparently. Also, let's not forget that this particular Frankenstein was not creating his own humans just to satisfy his ambitions as a scientist: he was hoping to create a better new race by sewing together the perfect body parts of his victims.)

Whether Morrisey's effort is or isn't a horror film is debatable. On the one hand, it uses one of the genre's most recognizable characters and there's enough gore in it to put to shame most of the 1970s horror titles; yet on the other hand, it doesn't even try to be scary. As a result, it's more like a macabre performance piece than a straightforward horror movie with elaborate suspense and real scares. Still, since the movie is such an unexpected twist on a horror icon, it should be viewed by all the fans who want to decide for themselves whether it fits within the boundaries of the genre.

The director's companion piece to *Flesh* is *Andy Warhol's Dracula* (1973), a somehow less controversial yet equally weird "adaptation" of Bram Stoker's vampire classic. *Dracula* also doesn't have many of Warhol's fingerprints on it, because the famous artist didn't have much to do with it; apparently, it was one of the cases where he was merely lending his name to help promote works that were as bold and innovative as his own. And in this regard the two movies do not disappoint: even if they are not typical pieces of horror cinema, they are both fresh, funny and outrageous.

Tired of Dr. Frankenstein being constantly portrayed as a tidy, cultured scientist? This Andy Warhol–produced version of the story may turn out to be just right for you. Not only does the doctor finally get his hands awfully dirty, he also speaks with Udo Kier's wonderfully exaggerated German accent.

Scream Blacula Scream

DIRECTOR: Bob Kelljan
CAST: William Marshall, Pam Grier, Richard Lawson, Don Mitchell,
Michael Conrad, Barbara Rhoades
USA, 1973

Until the 1970s there weren't many influential horror movies with black actors in significant parts. Jacques Tourneur's *I Walked with a Zombie* (1943; with Darby Jones

Blacula (William Marshall) is reaching new heights in the blaxploitation classic *Scream Blacula Scream* (1973).

as a very mysterious undead) comes to mind, as does George Romero's *Night of the Living Dead* (1968; with Duane Jones cast against the trends as the main character), but not much else. This changed with the rise of blaxploitation cinema in 1971, when *Sweet Sweetback's Badasssss Song* and *Shaft* prompted film historians to an endless dispute over which of these two movies is the first *real* example of blaxploitation. The audiences applauded the new subgenre, and soon more projects with mostly-black casts followed, horror films among them. Of the latter group, two variations on the Dracula mythos, William Crain's *Blacula* (1972) and Bob Kelljan's sequel *Scream Blacula Scream*, were the definite highlights.

In *Blacula* we see Prince Mamuwalde (William Marshall) being bitten by Dracula (Charles Macaulay), then spending nearly 200 years imprisoned in a coffin, and finally getting out to suck the blood of the funky 1970s crowd, and seduce Tina (Vonetta McGee), the reincarnation of his beautiful wife. After the initial fistfight between Mamuwalde and Dracula, *Blacula* doesn't hold any more surprises, but Marshall makes a marvelous vampire, McGee is endearing in the conventional role of a love interest-victim, and the mixture of pop and soul by The Hues Corporation that permeates the movie, gives it an addictive feel and enlivens the proceedings. The sequel, however, was not about to simply replicate the atmosphere of the original: a new director was chosen (Bob Kelljan, who by then had made the very entertaining horror duo of 1970's *Count Yorga, Vampire* and 1971's *The Return of Count Yorga*), new themes were added to the typical vampire story, and the songs of The Hues Corporation were nowhere to be heard. *Scream Blacula Scream* resurrects Prince Mamuwalde (Marshall again) via voodoo practices performed by vengeful Willis (Richard Lawson), who naively thinks that the powerful blood-drinking creature will make *him* more powerful, too. But as soon as Mamuwalde, who now urges people to call him Blacula, returns to the 1970s, he forces his way to Willis's neck and makes him his slave. This means double trouble for the annoying voodoo priest: not only is it now more difficult for him to overpower his main adversary, Lisa (Pam Grier), but being a bona fide vampire he can't see his cool clothes in the mirror, either. To make matters worse, Blacula is conspicuously affectionate towards the foxy Lisa, and plans to use her voodoo skills to be put out of the misery of the undead.

This, perhaps, is the most distinctive difference between *Scream Blacula Scream* and the first movie. Here, Prince Mamuwalde is not just a depressed romantic character looking for his lost love; now he is even more tragic, a monster whose main aim is to try to take away Dracula's curse. The absence of *Blacula*'s mesmerizing soundtrack is a letdown, but the lead actors are strong again (Marshall owning his character by now, and Grier trying to play a heroine and a victim at the same time), the scares are more effective than the first time around (especially in the vampire attack scenes), and the plot is much more complex, leading to a better conclusion. Still, some critics refused to appreciate such a formula for a black vampire. After the premiere of *Scream Blacula Scream*, Roger Ebert wrote in his review, "Marshall has the kind of pseudo–Shakespearean dialog and delivery that Vincent Price and others have been polishing at Hammer. And Miss Grier, a real beauty, has a spirit and enthusiasm that's refreshing"; however, he didn't think that the movie worked as a whole, and his conclusion was that if one wants to make a good blaxploitation horror, "just hiring black actors, and giving them false fangs won't do."

Not all critical responses were so harsh, though. In *The Horror Film*, Peter Hutchings analyzes points of view of David J. Skal, an expert on all representations of Dracula (who doesn't consider the *Blacula* movies very clever) and Harry M. Benshoff, an expert on blaxploitation (who thinks they are quite significant). Hutchings doesn't seem to be very enthusiastic about Skal's opinion, and clearly favors the theory according to which Prince Mamuwalde "has the potential to become a metaphor both for black enslavement and, as a powerful black male, for black resistance to that enslavement." It may not be as obvious in *Blacula* (in which Mamuwalde discusses with Dracula the idea of putting an end to slavery, but the following events entirely ignore the issue), but is much more clearly put in *Scream Blacula Scream* where the prince becomes a serious-minded character. (Upon meeting two pimps, he blames them for "imitating their masters," and then swiftly finishes them off.)

Throughout the 1970s, blaxploitation horror movies were flourishing, though not many of them were good and none as interesting as the two parts of *Blacula*. Only William Girdler's *Abby* (1974; an update of 1973's *The Exorcist* for the blaxploitation-hungry audiences) and Paul Maslansky's *Sugar Hill* (1974; starring Richard Lawson from *Scream Blacula Scream*) delivered adequate amounts of fun and chills, and some were genuinely bad (for example, William E. Levey's *Blackenstein*, made in 1973, and 1976's *Dr. Black, Mr. Hyde* directed by *Blacula* helmer William Crain, and starring Bernie Casey). Near the end of the 1970s, blaxploitation movies were causing more and more controversy, as it was argued that they only perpetuated certain harmful stereotypes, so the Coalition Against Blaxploitation was formed, and by the end of 1970s the subgenre has perished. Horror movies focused on black characters still do pop up occasionally, for example Bernard Rose's *Candyman* (1992), Wes Craven's *Vampire in Brooklyn* (1995) and Stephen Norrington's *Blade* (1998); but they are totally different from the blaxploitation horrors in both appearance and tone.

This follow-up to the entertaining, if rather unsophisticated, blaxploitation horror *Blacula* is weirder and less predictable than the original. Plus, the lovely Pam Grier is in fine form as Blacula's love interest, and the film even carries a sociological message.

Horror Express

aka *Panic on the Trans-Siberian*
DIRECTOR: Eugenio Martin
CAST: Christopher Lee, Peter Cushing, Alberto de Mendoza, Silvia Tortosa,
Helga Liné, Alice Reinheart, Julio Peña, Juan Olaguivel, Telly Savalas
USA-Spain, 1973

Whenever the names Christopher Lee or Peter Cushing appear in a movie's credits, the interest of a horror fan rises. Obviously, not all films starring the two actors are genre classics, and some of them are truly awful (Lee's *Howling II: Your Sister Is a Werewolf* and *Police Academy 7: Mission to Moscow* are perfect examples of these). Starring both, *Horror Express* is a very enjoyable, over-the-top effort that never tries to pretend to be a masterpiece. Or to pretend to be a logical movie with a coherent script, for that matter. The good thing is that we get to see both Lee and Cushing, plus the always welcome Telly Savalas, here in a wildly overacting mode.

In 1906 Manchuria, Sir Alexander Saxton (Lee) has just discovered the two million-year-old body of a strange animal. He hopes it is the missing link in the theory of evolution, so he puts it in a crate and takes it on board the Trans-Siberian Express, anxious to study it as soon as possible. He is joined by a fellow Brit, Dr. Wells (Cushing), and his assistant Miss Jones (Alice Reinheart). Even before the train starts moving, Sir Saxton's monster takes the life of an unlucky thief who had a bit too much interest in the unguarded crate sitting on the platform. Seeing that the death was caused in some mysterious way (the thief's eyeballs turned to white and started bleeding), odd-looking monk Father Pujardov (Albert de Mendoza) proclaims the content of the crate "unholy" which, rather unsurprisingly, inspires some people to try and take a peek inside. When the journey begins, more characters die, always ending up with their eyes white and bleeding. In no time the creature breaks free from the chained crate and its magical powers are revealed: apparently, when the monster looks in its victim's eyes the person's brain is "erased" in a matter of seconds. Moreover, the creature can also leave its own body and enter the body of the victim, which will at one stage make us wonder which of the passengers is the monster. Sir Saxton, Dr. Wells, Miss Jones and a group of secondary characters — two attractive ladies among them (Silvia Tortosa and Helga Liné) — will have to do their best to survive the journey with the beast, but it's when hyperactive Captain Kazan (Savalas) boards the train that the real horror begins.

Hiring respectable actors doesn't necessarily mean that their characters have to get lines that make sense. When Cushing's Dr. Wells performs an autopsy on one of the victims and sees that the brain is unusually smooth (it looks like the top of a rubber ball, to be precise), he promptly and without much surprise diagnoses that it "has been drained" and "the memory has been removed like chalk erased from a blackboard." This is as scientific as *Horror Express* gets. Later in the movie we also hear the explanation of the creature's origin and it is just as wonderfully goofy. The script is packed with camp dialogue, the more hilarious for the fact that it is pronounced by the two serious-looking horror icons. The most famous exchange is between a police inspector and Dr. Wells. "What if one of you is the monster?" asks the policeman, looking with concern at Lee and Cushing; Cushing, clearly shocked, replies, "Monster? We're British, you know!"

The movie's other great asset is that it is impossible to lock it within one of the horror subgenres. First it aims at being a full-blooded monster movie, then it unexpectedly changes into an old-fashioned sci-fi–scented mystery, only to finally morph into something that resembles a zombie movie (there's a chilling scene with a group of white-eyed passengers chasing the frightened survivors). The plot moves briskly from one ridiculous set piece to another (here the creature fries someone's brain, there Dr. Wells performs a quick lobotomy, and soon after this the first "possession" takes place...), so in the end, no matter what our particular taste in horror is, we can't complain that the movie lacks good pacing or crazy twists and turns.

What it doesn't lack, either, is showy acting, often balancing on pretentiousness but not once failing to stay on the safe side of it. Cushing gets all the best lines and mustachioed Lee looks funny enough in most of his scenes (especially at the beginning, when we aren't yet used to his outlandish facial hair), but wait till you see Telly Savalas forcing his way onscreen, wearing a bright red Cossack uniform and holding the cigarette in his trademark devilish way (think *On Her Majesty's Secret Service*'s Bloefeld). Savalas tended to overact at the time — his turn in Mario Bava's *Lisa and the Devil* (1973) is yet more evidence to prove it — but the role of the violent and sarcastic Captain Kazan should perhaps make it to World's Top 5 Over-the-Top Acting, should such list be ever made. His part is not much more than a cameo but one that gets rooted in your memory and that gives the plot the final adrenaline shot. Just watch Savalas' sly smile during his interaction with the character played by Silvia Tortosa: "I'll have you sent to Siberia!" the woman warns him, to which Savalas responds, "Madam, we are in Siberia"; there goes the half-macho/half-psycho smile and the actor's eyes send off sparks of self-satisfaction.

As non-competitive and unambitious as it seemed to be, *Horror Express* marked a period of prosperity for the legendary duo of Lee and Cushing: it preceded Lee's famous *The Wicker Man* (1973) and another enjoyable Lee-Cushing pairing, *The Satanic Rites of Dracula* (1974). To this day *Horror Express* also remains the best horror movie set on a train, Roger Spottiswoode's *Terror Train* (1980, starring Jamie Lee Curtis) being the only other important contender.

A wild mixture of a monster movie, a classic train-confined whodunnit and a zombie horror, all the more appealing for the charismatic presence of Lee, Cushing and Savalas.

Seizure

aka *Queen of Evil*
DIRECTOR: Oliver Stone
CAST: Jonathan Frid, Martine Beswick, Joseph Sirola, Hervé Villechaize,
Anne Meacham, Henry Baker, Christina Pickles
USA-Canada, 1974

Ambrose Bierce's eerie short story "An Occurrence at Owl Creek Bridge" inspired many horror films, some of them very popular among the fans of the genre: for example, the hallucinatory 1962 classic *Carnival of Souls*, Robert Enrico's award-winning short film *La Rivière du Libou* (aired in the U.S. in 1964 as part of *The Twilight Zone* series), and Adrian Lyne's nightmarish tale of the demons of war, the 1995 *Jacob's Ladder*). The story's most distinguishing and influential feature was the twist ending that forced the viewers to question much of what was shown before. Oliver Stone, back in the early 1970s a wannabe filmmaker and a relatively inexperienced scriptwriter, thought that weaving his own plot around Bierce's final surprise would render a movie to launch his career as a director. The outcome was *Seizure*: on the one hand, a proof that at that time Stone was not yet ready to join the mainstream; and on the other, the best opportunity ever for us to peek into the wildest parts of the director's imagination (almost literally so, as according to some sources the movie is based on one of Stone's dreams).

In the film, Edmund Blackstone (Jonathan Frid), a writer working on "a horror story for children," admits to using his nightmares as a source of inspiration for the grim tale. During a party hosted by Edmund and his wife (Christina Pickles), a strange and terrifying event takes place: three bloodthirsty figures, thus far dwellers of Edmund's imagination, break free and enter the real world. From this moment on, the innocent party changes into a cruel game with the lives of the guests at stake, as the trio of dreamed-but-real characters — the Queen of Evil (Martine Beswick), the Spider (Hervé Villechaize) and Jackal the Giant (Henry Baker) — force the boring humans to take part in a series of deathly contests. Edmund's only hope is to find a way to regain control over the phantasmal creatures, but as the action progresses we are led to think that he no longer has the strength to do that.

Often labeled incomprehensible, *Seizure* is, ironically, a movie about desperate attempts at grasping the meaning of life; or to put it more precisely: about an *artist's* attempts at grasping the meaning of life. Edmund is terrified by the possibility of dying

Henry Judd Baker as the deadly Jackal in Oliver Stone's debut *Seizure* (1974).

before he manages to create another worthwhile piece. At some point, as his friends and the members of his family are being executed by the grotesque party crashers, Edmund selfishly screams that "an artist is not allowed to die"; he can easily come to terms with the idea of everyone else losing their lives (even his wife and his young son) but it's just inconceivable for him that he could end up a victim, too. There is, after all, a horror story that needs to be finished! Stone's portrayal of an artist in *Seizure* is backbiting then, not only because the main character turns out to be ready to sacrifice his family in order to survive, but also because as petty a thing as a horror story seems to be his only excuse to do that. (He does try to justify his selfishness by speaking of "many other families he can have," most probably meaning families to be created in his future books, but the viewer knows that the sad horror story is the only thing Edmund can think of at the moment — and, truth be told, even this he cannot handle properly.) Eventually it's the artist who is the sole loser here. He may have despised everyone around him for wasting their time on trivialities but it's his constant focusing on "artfulness" that is disclosed to be the greatest triviality of all. To show us this, Stone uses the highly impressive, Bierce-influenced *coup de grâce*, and leaves the viewer in awe.

However, *Seizure* is not a typical, flashy Stone movie that keeps the viewers in awe throughout. It is occasionally rambling and repetitive, its philosophizing tends to be over-the-top, and the characters are often annoying (but purposely so: it's how the main protagonist perceives them, and the audience sees everything through his eyes).

The real pleasure of viewing *Seizure* is not so much in the *viewing* itself, as it is in trying to notice all the signals and metaphors along the way, and piecing them together after the epiphanous finale.

After *Seizure*, Stone made only one more all-out horror movie (the straightforward but enjoyable 1981 effort *The Hand*, starring Michael Caine), but his debut bears more resemblance to two movies from his wild period in the 1990s: *Natural Born Killers* (1994) and *U-Turn* (1997). Still, no matter how entertaining and energetic these latter two are, they won't leave scratching your head as madly as after having seen *Seizure*, nor will they tell you quite as much about Stone's opinions on the fellow artists or, indeed, about your own subconscious. Don't we all think of ourselves as "artists" from time to time?

Oliver Stone's first feature-length movie is crazier than anything he did afterwards (though *Natural Born Killers* and *U-Turn* are worthy contenders). And even if the director himself doesn't speak very fondly of *Seizure* these days, it still makes for powerful viewing, one that will put you on better terms with your subconscious.

Frightmare

DIRECTOR: Pete Walker
CAST: Deborah Fairfax, Kim Butcher, Sheila Keith, Rupert Davies,
Paul Greenwood, Fiona Curzon, Jon Yule
UK, 1974

Harvey Fenton, the editor of *Ten Years of Terror: British Films of the 1970s*, introduces director Pete Walker in the following way:

> By directing what he termed "terror films" set in the instantly recognizable surroundings of contemporary middle class Seventies society, Walker was bucking the British horror cinema trend of the time. The "English Gothic" horror films, as exemplified by the works of Hammer, Tyburn et al., were essentially period-piece costume dramas spiced up by dollops of gore, mad science, supernatural chills and buxom wenches in peril. Walker's films however dwell on the mundane possibility that beneath the surface of life in the Home Counties there might be an untamed beast lurking.

The director's 1974 effort *Frightmare* is a perfect representation of this approach: here the "untamed beast" being an old lady who lives in a cozy little house with a loving husband, but after some time reveals an insatiable appetite for human flesh. These two characters, Dorothy and Edmund Yates (Sheila Keith and Rupert Davies), have spent 15 years in a mental asylum after Dorothy's earlier attempt at eating some poor guy (Edmund was treated as an accomplice), but now they're back to society, apparently "cured." The Yateses are parents of two young girls: older and more responsible Jackie (Deborah Fairfax) and reckless Debbie (Kim Butcher). When Jackie sees that her mother is on the verge of returning to the old cannibalistic habit, she tries to satisfy her (the mother's) craving by bringing her pieces of raw meat she can munch on. This soon ceases to work, though, as Momma decides that she needs the thrill of the kill just as much as she does the taste of meat. Edmund, just like 15 years ago, is unable to prevent his wife from doing whatever she wishes to do. Jackie becomes more and more depressed about the whole situation, and Debbie seems to be enjoying the violence as much as her mother does. Jackie's boyfriend (Paul Greenwood) tries to help the two sisters by resorting to psychology, but this turns out to be of little use. It becomes obvious that Momma *will* eventually kill again — and to make the experience more exciting, she's going to treat her victims to a power drill.

Frightmare was Walker's second collaboration with scriptwriter David McGillivray, who afterwards worked with him on *House of Mortal Sin* (1975, aka *The Confessional*) and *Schizo* (1976), and actress Sheila Keith, who soon became famous for playing vicious ladies. (Keith appeared in several more movies by Walker, right up to the director's last feature, *House of the Long Shadows* [1983], in which she was accompanied by Vincent Price, Peter Cushing and Christopher Lee.) McGillivray was partly responsible for the change of direction of Walker's filmmaking (that was previously focused on eroticism rather than on horror), as with *House of Whipcord* (1974) the duo found a formula for making controversial movies that sell not *despite* being controversial but *because* of it. As soon as Walker found out that all the bad reviews his films were getting could, ironically, sound enticing to potential viewers, he decided to use them for promotional purposes. In consequence, people were lured to see *Frightmare* because it was said to be a "horrendous chiller," "a despicable film" and "a moral obscenity."

While it is easy to see why some critics were so appalled by this cannibalistic tale, *Frightmare* is hardly just a "moral obscenity." Steve Chibnall writes in *British Horror Cinema* that Walker's output is, in a way, similar to that of Roger Corman as he, too, "is able to combine a feeling for past cinema ... with a keen sense of current controversy." According to Chibnall, Walker's finest 1970s movies "capture an essence of the period" and "encode key cultural issues and attitudes together with the residues of his own biography into the mythic structures of the Gothic" (though at the same time the writer admits that Walker "is no Godard or Buñuel," as he has "no aspirations to deconstruct bourgeois ideology or the codes of cinema"). *Frightmare* is indeed deeply rooted in the previous decade of British horror: like Alfred Hitchcock's *Psycho* (1960), it expresses doubts in the effectiveness of psychiatry; like Michael Reeves's *The Sorcerers* (1967), it depicts the old generation "feeding" on the youth; and like John Gilling's *The Reptile* (1966), it deals with the concept of the "monstrous feminine." Then again, *Frightmare* also tackles such themes as the punishment for hedonism (similarly to what Ken Russell did in 1971's *The Devils*) and the "monstrous family" (as in 1972's *The Fiend*, directed by Robert Hartford-Davis), in consequence becoming an eclectic collection of the most distinctive fears and obsessions of its time (that is, of the pre–Thatcherite Britain). But if anything could be called Walker's trademark (apart from, as many critics would claim, the depiction of excessive violence), it's the fact that his movies aren't favoring either the old or the young generation, but are rather pointing out what is "scary" about both of them: "Walker almost gleefully depicts his age as one of moral dissolution in which hypocrisy is challenged by a hedonism which is only slightly less ethically repellent," concludes Chibnall.

Premiering the same year as *The Texas Chain Saw Massacre*, and several years before *The Toolbox Murders* (1978) and *The Driller Killer* (1979), Walker's *Frightmare* was an early attempt at using hand tools to scare the audiences and force them to perceive the era they were living in and their community from a different perspective.

Black Christmas

Director: Bob Clark
Cast: Olivia Hussey, Margot Kidder, Keir Dullea, John Saxon,
Andrea Martin, Art Hindle, Lynne Griffin
Canada, 1974

The enjoyable documentary *Going to Pieces: The Rise and Fall of the Slasher Film* (2006) traces the history of the title subgenre back to Michael Powell's *Peeping Tom* (1960) and Alfred Hitchcock's *Psycho* (1960), points out the huge influence of Mario Bava's *Bay of Blood* (1971), takes a good look at the most successful early slasher movies, most notably John Carpenter's *Halloween* (1978) and Sean S. Cunningham's *Friday the 13th* (1980), and moves on to the titles that revived the slasher cinema in mid–1990s, Wes Craven's *Scream* (1995) leading the way. Typically, the significance of Bob Clark's atmospheric chiller *Black Christmas* is completely overlooked, and it yet again remains the missing link in the evolution of the violent subgenre. Watch Clark's movie, though, and you will realize that there really was something highly inspiring in the 18-year gap between *Psycho* and *Halloween*.

If a proper slasher movie requires a mysterious, hardly seen killer, an atmospheric place where the murders occur, a "final girl" (usually the most attractive female character who survives until the final credits), peculiar ways of eliminating the victims, and an ambiguous ending, then *Black Christmas* fits the definition perfectly. The movie's unidentified villain is a psycho who cannot help making obscene and threatening phone calls to a sorority house where several young girls are spending their time just before Christmas; obviously, at some point the man decides that it's high time to support the calls with actual killing, and he does that in a variety of ways (one character is suffocated with the use of a plastic bag, another stabbed with the spiky part of a glass unicorn, and so on). The best bet on who may become the final girl seems to be either the sweet but strong Jess (Olivia Hussey) or the constantly drunk, annoying, provocative and sexy Barbie (Margot Kidder). When Jess and Barbie's housemates start disappearing one by one, Lieutenant Fuller (John Saxon) tries to find the crazed caller, and in one hilarious sequence reminds us of the near-impossibility of tracking a phone number back in the 1970s. It takes a lot of time before the characters realize that the calls are, in fact, "coming from inside the house."

Perhaps the main reason for the movie being perpetually overlooked by genre historians is that it lacks the suspense, swift pacing and payoff characteristic of a *Halloween* or *Friday the 13th*. It does, however, creep us out nicely with the atmosphere of mystery, fleshes out several interesting characters (the one played by Kidder being a standout), and leaves us puzzled with its bold, vague ending. Interestingly, Clark chose to avoid employing overly bloody effects for the death scenes, even though he worked with the maestro of bloody makeup, Tom Savini, on his previous movie *Dead of Night* (aka *Deathdream*, 1974). In effect, *Black Christmas* is a movie at the same time surprisingly restrained and shockingly perverse (the insane phone calls sound oddly convincing, and the idea of intercutting one of the killings with children singing carols makes for a twisted effect).

Apart from being a pioneering and atmospheric slasher movie, *Black Christmas* is also reverberation from the sociopolitical problems in Canada and the U.S. in the early 1970s. The inefficiency of police work as depicted by Clark may be understood as a travesty of the aftermath of the October Crisis (the Canadian government gave the police the right to arrest anyone suspected of helping the terrorists; many people viewed this as a desperate move that wouldn't do much good but *would* become a threat to civil liberties), and the very concept of "the killer in the house" may be interpreted as a metaphor for the fear of terrorism (a terrifying number of bombings, shootings and kidnappings was noted in Canada, the U.S. and many other countries at the time). Yet more strikingly, the movie's subplot concerning abortion (the character played by Hussey finds out that she is pregnant but doesn't yet want to get married and become a mom) seems to be a hint at the 1973 Roe v. Wade case (a controversial decision of the Supreme Court that allowed women to choose abortion for any reason until a certain point in the pregnancy). Hussey's Jess is a woman who's just making the hardest decision of her life, all the more difficult for the fact that her boyfriend begs her to have the child and marry him. Her likable and empathic portrayal seems to be Clark's personal pro-choice vote. It's not an easy task to find another slasher movie that deals with similar emotions and with such difficult questions.

Black Christmas was not Clark's first horror effort: just before it he made the aforementioned collaboration with Savini, *Dead of Night*, and also — *Children Shouldn't Play with Dead Things* (1972). The educated horror enthusiasts still regard Clark as the genre's cult icon, even though after *Black Christmas* he switched his interests to comedy and gave us *Porky's* (1982), *Porky's II: The Next Day* (1983), *Loose Cannons* (1990), and the rather infamous trio of *Baby Geniuses* (1999), *SuperBabies: Baby Geniuses II* (2004) and *Karate Dog* (2004). The director's death in a 2007 car accident shattered all hope for his return to darker themes, though he did perform the producer duties on two tongue-in-cheek horror movies, *Popcorn* (1991) and the modern remake of *Black Christmas* (2006), the latter a very grotesque take on Clark's original vision.

This semi-forgotten movie helped carve the slasher genre years before Carpenter's *Halloween*. By no means an immaculate work, *Black Christmas* nevertheless oozes creepy atmosphere, introduces a faceless killer far less subtle than *Psycho*'s Norman Bates and defines the "final girl" phenomenon.

The Rocky Horror Picture Show

DIRECTOR: Jim Sharman
CAST: Tim Curry, Susan Sarandon, Barry Bostwick, Richard O'Brien,
Patricia Quinn, Nell Campbell, Peter Hinwood, Charles Gray,
Jonathan Adams, Meat Loaf
UK-US, 1975

As previous sections of this book show, there are many reasons for a movie to be regarded as a cult favorite. *Freaks* (1932) shocked the viewers with its unflinching look

Dr. Frank-N-Furter (Tim Curry, center) looks sexy and mean in *The Rocky Horror Picture Show* (1975), flanked by Riff Raff (Richard O'Brien, left) and Magenta (Patricia Quinn).

at sideshow attractions and was promptly banned; *Plan 9 from Outer Space* (1959) turned out to be an addictive mixture of some of the genre's favorite motifs and utter silliness, but needed to be re-discovered decades after the premiere; *Blood Feast* (1963) splattered the audience with amounts of gore not seen onscreen before, and had to be cut by the censors; *The Saragossa Manuscript* (1968) wasn't painfully realistic, silly or gory, but its plot was said to be very challenging and — until recently — not many people were able to see it. *The Rocky Horror Picture Show*, on the other hand, gained its cult status because the audience at some point decided that it was a perfect movie to talk to.

According to J. Hoberman and Jonathan Rosenbaum, the authors of *Midnight Movies*, talking to the *Rocky Horror* characters started with Louis Farese Jr., a teacher from Greenwich Village, who during a 1976 screening couldn't help commenting on certain parts of the story. (Apparently, Farese's first remark was "Buy an umbrella, you cheap bitch!" said when Janet is seen using a newspaper as protection against the rain.) This habit then spread like an infection and soon started taking on more complex forms: members of the audience weren't only adding lines to the movie's dialogues, but were dressing up like the main characters, joining them for the song and dance routines, and using props in order to actually *feel* the movie (squirt guns are traditionally shot in the air when it's raining in the movie, and rice is thrown during the wedding scene). Originally *Rocky Horror* was a stage musical: *The Rocky Horror Show* premiered in 1973, with performances by Tim Curry, Richard O'Brien, Patricia Quinn and Nell Campbell (as Little Nell). Perhaps this fact, too, encouraged future movie-goers to try to "interact" with the onscreen characters. It's as if they wanted to pretend the new version of the story is just as alive as the stage musical. They eventually succeeded, literally bringing the movie back to the stage — only this time these were the members of the audience themselves who were doing the *live* acting.

There are slight differences between the stage version of the show and the movie (e.g., the former didn't feature the wedding scene or the cannibalistic dinner feast), but generally the two follow a very similar plot. The attractive yet somehow boring couple, Brad Majors and Janet Weiss (Barry Bostwick and Susan Sarandon in the movie version), decide that it's high time they got engaged. As soon as they do, however, they have to face all sort of problems: their car breaks down in the middle of nowhere and despite the heavy rain and nightmarish thunders they have to go out and look for help. Since an uninviting gothic castle is the only building in sight, Brad and Janet knock on its doors to ask if they may use a telephone. However, instead of calling for help, they will join Dr. Frank-N-Furter (Curry) and his freaky helpers — the deathly pale hunchback Riff Raff (O'Brien) and two frisky girls, Magenta (Quinn) and Columbia (Campbell) — in celebrating the creation of Rocky Horror (Peter Hinwood), a blonde, muscular male whom Frank-N-Furter, a bisexual transvestite and proud of it, plans to use for "relieving his tension." In the course of events, Brad and Janet will both be seduced by the transsexual doctor, and things will get violent with the arrival of the manly, leather-clad Eddie (Meat Loaf) — one person Frank-N-Furter badly wants to see die. The plot is regularly interrupted by the narration from "The Criminologist" (Charles Gray), and each important incident eventually explodes into a pop-rock song, best of which are "Science Fiction/Double Feature" (a tribute to classic horror and sci-fi movies performed during the opening credits by the iconic huge red lips floating in the blackness), "Time Warp" (a song that unnerves Brad and Janet when they enter the castle), "Sweet Transvestite" (an unforgettable introduction of Dr. Frank-N-Furter), and "Hot Patootie" (Eddie's high-powered piece).

The participation of the audience was directly responsible for the movie's success (when it first premiered in 1975, as a "normal" movie, it didn't draw crowds to the theatres). There were several other factors that greatly helped *Rocky* be embraced by audiences: Curry's stunning performance (he had a distinctive singing voice, and was curiously sexy as a man in drag — to both male and female viewers), O'Brien's catchy songs (although they were very simple and not all of them worked equally well), and a clever capturing of the social and political context of its era. Jeffrey Weinstock writes in his book on *The Rocky Horror Picture Show* (part of the crafty Cultographies series) that the movie "includes or was influenced by ... the American Vietnam war, the development of the birth control pill in 1960, the Stonewall Inn riots in 1969, the development and spread of television, British immigration patterns and education reform in the late 1960s, fashion designer Mary Quant's mini-skirts and hot pants, Britain's imposition of direct rule over Northern Ireland in 1972 and entrance into the Common Market in 1973"; according to Weinstock, the "social unrest" was crucial in the process of shaping the movie:

> Women, persons of color and homosexuals advocated vocally — and sometimes violently — for a more egalitarian reformation of American, British and Western society more generally, and *The Rocky Horror Picture Show*'s sexual politics cannot be divorced from the highly visible Women's and Gay Liberation movements of the time and the accompanying "sexual revolution" that altered Western ideas about sexual practices and morality.

It comes as no surprise that after the brilliant role of Dr. Frank-N-Furter, Curry was typecast. Doing his best to change this, he never reprised the character and therefore no direct sequel to *The Rocky Horror Picture Show* has ever been made. Instead Curry could be seen in many great stage musicals like "Amadeus," "The Pirates of Penzance," "The Threepenny Opera," "My Favorite Year" and, most recently, "Spamalot" (a stage version of 1975's laugh riot *Monty Python and the Holy Grail*). As a movie actor, he never got a role that would equal that of Frank-N-Furter, though he was perhaps one step from it: if Jack Nicholson had said "no" to playing the Joker in Tim Burton's *Batman* (1989), the director would have asked Curry to do it. Still, some of the actor's post–*Rocky Horror* roles are memorable, for example his audacious turn as the Lord of Darkness in Ridley Scott's *Legend* (1985), the killer clown in Tommy Lee Wallace's *It* (1990; TV mini-series based on Stephen King's epic novel), and even Gomez Addams in the otherwise unfunny *Addams Family Reunion* (1998), in which he was given the hard task of replacing Raul Julia who owned the character in the two previous *Addams* movies.

Unlike Curry, director Sharman and writer-actor O'Brien were both eager to try to recreate *Rocky*'s magic, and their best shot was *Shock Treatment* (1981), a musical in which Brad (Cliff De Young) and Janet (Jessica Harper) test their marriage on a TV show. Many cast members returned (O'Brien, Quinn, Campbell and Gray, among others) the songs were again catchy and it was great to hear Harper singing again after her mesmerizing turn in Brian De Palma's *Rocky Horror* doppelganger *Phantom of the Paradise* (1974), but the overall mood of *Shock Treatment* was much different than that of *Rocky Horror*, and the movie disappointed most fans of the first movie. As an all-singing critique of media invasion in people's lives, Sharman and O'Brien's new effort worked very well, though, and it would be perhaps much better received if it wasn't attached to the *Rocky Horror* phenomenon at all.

The Rocky Horror Picture Show may be flawed as a movie, but it is absolutely perfect as a phenomenon inviting audiences to dance, sing, act and shout mild obscenities at the screen. And whoever hasn't seen Tim Curry in *that* role, has missed out on one of the greatest, most energetic performances ever.

The Beast (La Bête)

DIRECTOR: Walerian Borowczyk
CAST: Lisbeth Hummel, Sirpa Lane, Elisabeth Kaza, Pierre Benedetti,
Marcel Dalio, Guy Tréjan, Pascale Rivault, Roland Armontel
France, 1975

If horror movies are, as some critics and fans of the genre would claim, all about mixing sex and violence in the most effective ways, then having an erotica auteur introduce a hungry, otherworldly beast to his usual gathering of beautiful females might seem like a genius idea. And it indeed worked well in the case of Walerian Borowczyk, a Polish director living and working in France, and his 1975 movie *The Beast*. Already famed for the equally outrageous and impressive *Immoral Tales* (1974) and *The Story of Sin* (1975), Borowczyk dipped his next project in horror not so much to scare the viewers, as to tell them a highly convincing tale of the force of the primal instincts.

There are two layers to *The Beast*. The first one, originally intended to become a part of the erotic anthology *Immoral Tales*, takes place in 1700s France and involves the innocent yet very seductive Romilda de l'Esperance (Sirpa Lane) being chased in the woods by a werewolf-like creature that sports a grotesque erection. The monster clearly wants to rape the frightened woman but she is not an easy catch, and the beast has to find sexual satisfaction in performing quick oral sex on the fleeing victim, in getting a footjob from her hanging on a branch of a tree, and in masturbating with her blonde wig. Having this weird and highly fetishistic episode on his hands, Borowczyk eventually decided to exclude it from *Immoral Tales* and give it an even more controversial spin by adding a present-day wraparound story. Within this second layer of the plot, the main character is Lucy Broadhurst (Lisbeth Hummel), a young English girl just as innocent and attractive as the monster magnet Romilda. Lucy is brought to a chateau that was home to Romilda two centuries before, and she is supposed to get married to Mathurin de l'Esperance (Pierre Benedetti), a savage-looking man who takes pleasure in observing two fiercely mating horses (an act presented to the viewer in a series of long, untiring close-ups). There is a certain problem with the nuptials, however, as a cardinal is in no hurry to arrive and bless the young couple, and so Lucy retreats to her room to have a nap. There, inspired by her Polaroid photos of Mathurin's mating horses, and by the story of Romilda's date with the beast as told by Duke de Balo (Marcel Dalio), the girl spends most of her free time masturbating and dreaming a possible scenario of what might have happened to Romilda and her hairy lover.

Not surprisingly, Borowczyk's movie caused quite a stir upon its original release in the mid–1970s: Guy Flatley of *The New York Times* called it "a sleazy blend of fairy tale, Freudian foolishness and Eighth Avenue peep show." Many people seeing it at the London Film Festival were outraged, and the censors quickly started thinking of the most brutal ways to cut all the most interesting parts out of the picture. A shame, obviously, as *The Beast* only works when all the elements — the satire, the dark humor, the eroticism and the horror — are balanced just as Borowczyk intended them to be. Plus, there's much more to this movie than just a nicely controversial subject matter and lots of nudity.

For the genre enthusiasts, *The Beast*'s greatest asset will be the previously mentioned masterful mixture of sex and violence. Which is, in fact, a trick mastered by very few filmmakers. Even *Playboy*'s Hugh Hefner admits in the documentary *100 Years of Horror* (where he is somewhat awkwardly squeezed between such horror legends as Christopher Lee and John Carpenter) that he doesn't usually appreciate sexiness being put next to violence; most probably, however, he would still enjoy *The Beast*, as the violence here is never mind-numbing or disgusting, while the eroticism is surprisingly effective and works on many levels — from the subtle depiction of Lucy's sexual energy, as she impatiently takes in the world that's new to her upon her arrival, through the funny/sexy relationship between another female character (played by Pascale Rivault) and her servant (Hassane Fall), and culminating in the sequences where the characters dream of fierce, "beastly" sex (either by admiring the mating horses or by imagining Romilda being chased by a monster). It almost feels like Borowczyk aimed to mock the horror genre here: his beast, no matter how big and hairy, is never truly scary, and we never get to see the bloodbath typical for the 1970s genre movies. Which is, perhaps, yet another reason for the movie being so special. After all, it isn't often that cult horror circles embrace a piece of work that treats the subject matter in such an irreverent way. Especially since it was made within the decade that spawned some of the most brutal and painfully realistic movies in the history of cinema. Borowczyk's light take on the subject must have seemed risky, but eventually turned out to be a success. The creature attack sequence is memorable and fittingly odd, but it doesn't spoil the erotic feel of the movie nor does it overshadow the more important wraparound story.

Saying that Borowczyk just wants to shock or arouse the viewer would not be quite fair, though. The main story is full of meaningful details: the mating horses a metaphor for forced marriage, the constantly interrupted sex between a white woman and a black male a critique of class division, and an old priest kissing an angelic boy a strong criticism of the hypocrisy of the Church. These days *The Beast* is often accused of being racist (some reviewers see the black lover as a parallel to the movie's "sexual animal" — either a horse or the Beast itself, both of which are indeed black here), which is far off the director's intentions, which were to describe the powerful animal instinct common to people of both sexes and all races. Certainly, though, Borowczyk was not a politically correct director — he wasn't afraid of touching upon controversial subjects and he didn't much care whether some of the scenes were ambiguous or not. This is exactly why *The Beast* feels so honest and so bold after all these years.

Surely not one of the scariest horror movies ever made, but it may well be one of the sexiest and most provocative works of the genre. Plus, it shows us the somehow hackneyed figure of a hairy, wolfish beast in a completely new light.

Shivers

aka *They Came from Within; The Parasite Murders*
DIRECTOR: David Cronenberg
CAST: Paul Hampton, Lynn Lowry, Susan Petrie, Barbara Steele, Allan Kolman,
Joe Silver, Ronald Mlodzik, Fred Doederlein, Kathy Graham
Canada, 1975

Shivers is often referred to as David Cronenberg's first work, a movie that helped him unchain the phobias and fantasies that would then reappear in most of his future projects. The truth is, *Shivers* was Cronenberg's first remarkable success, but hardly the first ever public exhibition of his nightmares. At the beginning there were two short movies he directed as a student — *Transfer* (1966) and *From the Drain* (1967) — and they were already a promise of the nastiness to come. (*Transfer* touched upon the subject of psychiatry that would later return in 1981's *Scanners*; and *From the Drain* featured a scene in which a man is attacked by a monstrous plant that reaches for him from the bathtub drain. Several years later, this would metamorphose into a parasite attack scene in *Shivers*.) Then there were two films that clocked in at over 60 minutes each, and they were a yet deeper examination of the themes that would haunt most of Cronenberg's full-length films. *Stereo* (1969) is a study of telepathy and a description of cruel experiments aimed at enhancing the skill: the subjects have parts of their brains and vocal chords removed, so that they have no choice but to communicate with thoughts.

The epidemic spreads: Lynn Lowry (left) and Paul Hampton in David Cronenberg's *Shivers* (1975).

Crimes of the Future (1969) further explores the theme of dangerous experiments, one that would keep returning in the director's future output, and again features a heartless institution that becomes a threat to mankind — another one of Cronenberg's favorite motifs. *Crimes of the Future* tells the story of a mysterious disease that threatens to destroy mankind. These two films established both the wide range of controversial issues on which the director would feed from then on (experiments, institutions, diseases, mad scientists, the human body, supernatural powers, sexual perversions), but also the particularly cold, emotionless style of his filmmaking. *Shivers* — a movie that was initially called *Orgy of the Blood Parasites* and then renamed several times to fit different markets — draws from all of Cronenberg's earlier works and is his first fully fleshed-out effort: unsettling, disgusting and intelligent.

The intelligence of *Shivers* was apparently an easy feature to overlook upon the movie's original release, as many distinguished critics stuck to just being unsettled and disgusted with it (the most quotable of them was *Saturday Night*'s Robert Fulford who called *Shivers* "a disgrace" and "sadistic pornography"). One could perhaps argue that Cronenberg was asking for such reaction, as he deliberately stuffed the movie with violence, nudity and perversions. Still, mistaking him for a B-movie hack must have been a deep source of shame for some of these merciless reviewers; even if *Shivers* remained *Orgy of the Blood Parasites*, it would still demand *some* respect from the world's most serious critics.

The movie's main character is Starliner Towers, a snobbish modern high-rise on an island in Montreal. As we observe a young couple being shown around the building to admire all the state-of-the-art amenities, we can also peek in one of the rooms and see a tenant (Fred Doederlein) butchering a young, topless girl (Kathy Graham). After slitting open her chest, he pours acid in the opening, and then commits suicide. Shortly afterwards, the viewer learns — as does Roger St. Luc (Paul Hampton), the doctor at the complex — that the killer was in fact a scientist performing experiments on parasites, and one of his little creatures recently escaped; the man was hoping that by killing the girl he would kill the parasite as well. No such luck; now all the people living in Starliner Towers are in danger of being attacked by the penis-like monster — and, as a consequence, becoming sexually obsessed zombies. This plot device validates the upcoming string of perverse scenes, and the only question that remains to be answered is who — if anyone — will survive the attacks. Nicholas Tudor (Allan Kolman) and his wife Janine (Susan Petrie) seem to be doomed from the start, as does the sensuous Betts (Barbara Steele), but doctor Roger and his ice-cold assistant (Lynn Lowry) look like survivors — and possibly saviors, too.

According to the most popular interpretation of the plot, *Shivers* can be seen as a metaphor for a venereal disease — some critics say syphilis, others say AIDS (the latter option being quite impossible, as AIDS wasn't to be recognized until the early 1980s). Another less obvious interpretation sees the movie as a critique of the 1970s Canadian society, trying to lead "antiseptic" lives and therefore nearing self-destruction. However, Cronenberg himself wouldn't fully approve either of these views, as in his opinion one should identify with the parasite, not with the human characters, and therefore perceive the plot as a tale of the conquest rather than as a tale of defeat. Professor of film studies Adam Lowenstein writes in his book *Shocking Representation* that the introductory scenes of the movie show Starliner Towers as "eerily underpopulated" and "uniformly cold and disappointing"; "[I]t is only with the onset of the parasite epidemic that the hallways come alive and residents are able to express a delirious passion for each other." Elsewhere in the book, Lowenstein states: "In Cronenberg's cinema, disease is not just the enemy of identity, it is also the source of identity. Parasites, plagues, and mutations in Cronenberg's films surely bring pain and death, but they simultaneously endow his 'diseased' characters with a savage life, an undeniable power." Therefore, *Shivers* could also be perceived as a diseased but hopeful depiction of Canada in the 1970s, with Trudeau's invocation of the War Measures Act to detain separatists and terrorists.

Cronenberg's next movie, *Rabid* (1977), was very similar to *Shivers* in the cold tone, the subject matter (an injured girl undergoes an experimental surgery and in effect becomes a source of dangerous epidemic), the setting (Montreal again), and the possible subtexts (as the epidemic spreads, the streets burst with chaos and violence, which could be seen as a metaphor for the separatist groups standing against Trudeau). With the exceptions of 1979's *Fast Company* and 1993's *M. Butterfly*, Cronenberg's obsession with disease, surgery and the human body featured prominently in all his films until 1999's *eXistenZ*. But even if his latest works — *Spider* (2002), *A History of Violence* (2005) and *Eastern Promises* (2007) — all have a mainstream feel to them and are not as intense as the movies he used to make, they are nevertheless linked by one common denominator: an emotionless male character who has to find his place in society — or die. Paul Hampton in *Shivers*, Frank Moore in *Rabid*, Art Hindle in *The Brood* (1979), Stephen Lack in *Scanners* (1981), James Woods in *Videodrome* (1982), Christopher Walken in *Dead Zone* (1983), Jeff Goldblum in *The Fly* (1986), Jeremy Irons in *Dead Ringers* (1988) and *M. Butterfly*, Peter Weller in *Naked Lunch* (1991), James Spader in *Crash* (1996), Jude Law in *eXistenZ*, Ralph Fiennes in *Spider* and Viggo Mortensen in the last two films — they are all the same troubled person who finds it difficult to communicate with the rest of the world; a person much like Cronenberg himself, perhaps: a brilliant filmmaker, whose intentions have been misinterpreted since the first time one of his movies reached a broad audience.

Cronenberg's first big success and first huge controversy, *Shivers* still disgusts and impresses in equal measure. It's very raw in comparison with the director's polished-to-perfection recent works, but it has the edge most of them lacks. It's also a very "Canadian" picture, convincingly displaying some of the country's worst fears and obsessions.

The House with Laughing Windows
(La Casa dalle Finestre Che Ridono)

DIRECTOR: Pupi Avati
CAST: Lino Capolicchio, Francesca Marciano, Gianni Cavina,
Pietro Brambilla, Giulio Pizzirani, Eugene Walter
Italy, 1976

Many great Italian *gialli* had already been made when director Pupi Avati decided that he, too, should contribute to the violent subgenre. Not discouraged by the fact that his movie would have to compete with masterpieces such as Mario Bava's *Blood and Black Lace* (1964) and Dario Argento's *The Bird with the Crystal Plumage* (1970), Avati created what is by many considered a perfect *giallo*. Typically for the subgenre, the movie's title was made of two nouns and the identity of its killer was kept secret until the unnerving finale but overall the film was also far less violent than most other Italian horrors and thrillers, and it moved at a very lazy pace. The fact that *The House with Laughing Windows* is now remembered with fondness despite being so untypical and so challenging for impatient viewers is the best proof of its quality.

Avati uses the slow pacing to create a dreamlike atmosphere that lulls and imprisons the viewers, making them all the more vulnerable when the shocks start coming. We get a wonderful sense of this at the beginning, when the main character, Stefano (Lino Capolicchio), arrives in a small Italian village on a ferryboat; one of the boat's passengers is gorgeous Francesca (Francesca Marciano), and Stefano has a hard time taking his eyes off her during the unhurried passage. Forcing himself to look elsewhere, he focuses on a small, overdressed man waiting for him on the shore. That's Mr. Solmi (Bob Tonelli), who hired Stefano to help restore the painting of St. Sebastian in the village's small church. This seemingly unimportant scene actually dictates the mood for the rest of the movie: our attention, just like Stefano's on the boat, will be often turning from the beautiful to the odd and uncanny, and the impression of moving too slowly and always getting everywhere too late will become the main character's curse. Since Avati takes his time to unleash the horror, we get acquainted with the movie's important supporting characters: handsome but clearly disturbed altar boy Lidio (Pietro Brambilla), friendly priest (Eugene Walter) and nervous but likable drunk Coppola (Gianni Cavina). We also get to see more of Francesca when she has an inevitable affair with Stefano, though it must be said that Avati shies away from gratuitous nudity as much as he does from gratuitous violence. We learn, too, about the legend of the painting that Stefano is restoring; it appears that its creator, Buono Legnani (Tonino Corazzari), was as mad as he was talented, and he used to kill the models to perfectly bring out the needed pain and suffering in his works. The long introduction is all dialogue, Amedeo Tommasi's enchanting score and Pasquale Rachini's ethereal photography, but when the main character is eventually brought to a mysterious "house with laughing windows," we know that there are thrills on the way, too.

As beautiful as it is, Avati's movie wouldn't be quite as remarkable if it weren't for the suspense and the surprisingly grotesque ending. There's a scene in which Stefano finds an old recorder and promptly pushes PLAY to listen to what turns out to be the mad artist's voice. The voice itself is convincingly creepy and haunted, and the atmosphere of the house where the recording was found adds to the strangeness of the event: The door closes on its own, the windows squeak, the wind starts howling suddenly.... And soon there's another scene with the player, this time working quite differently, with a nice little twist in the end. It is yet another sign of Avati's need for playing with the expectations of the viewers — and his undeniable talent for it.

Set in post-war Italy, *The House with Laughing Windows* is not just a unique and masterly done *giallo* but also a metaphor for the guilt and bitterness over the country's alliance with Hitler during World War II. There are, after all, similarly uncomfortable secrets buried in the memory of the movie's villagers, and no one has the courage to do anything about them, no one even dares speaking of them (unless inebriated, that is). People seem to be focused on their daily duties, they do their best to try leaving the past behind, but it seems that their hidden sins are slowly destroying them from the inside, and the possibility of the past horrors returning to the village becomes more and more likely.

In later years, the director of *The House with Laughing Windows* was famed for criticizing and diminishing his own horror movies, yet he also had the habit of returning to the genre every decade. In the 1980s he produced Lamberto Bava's early movie *Macabre* (1980) and directed the unforgettable zombie movie *Zeder* (1983; also known as *Revenge of the Dead*); in the 1990s he wrote the script for Maurizio Zaccaro's *Dove Comincia la Notte* (1991), produced and helped to write Fabrizio Laurenti's *Bitter Chamber* (1994; alternative title *The Room Next Door*) and directed another great horror, *The Mysterious Enchanter* (1996). Interestingly, *The House with Laughing Windows*, *Dove Comincia la Notte* and *Bitter Chamber* are sometimes referred to as an unofficial trilogy of slow-burning horrors, and *Bitter Chamber* is occasionally labeled as a sequel or remake of *The House with Laughing Windows* even though it most certainly isn't either of these.

A gorgeous and suspenseful example of what *giallo* movies should be like. Yes, it does move at a slow pace, but with all the beauty around — the dreamlike Italian landscapes and the alluring Francesca Marciano — you most probably won't mind that.

Eraserhead

DIRECTOR: David Lynch
CAST: Jack Nance, Charlotte Stewart, Jeanne Bates, Allen Joseph,
Judith Roberts, Laurel Near, Jack Fisk, Jean Lange
USA, 1977

David Lynch's early short films reveal surprisingly much about what he would have in store for his viewers. *Six Figures Getting Sick* (*Six Times*) (1966) showed human shapes with bulging stomachs and heads that eventually caught fire; in *The Alphabet* (1968) another tormented figure is giving birth to the letters of the alphabet; an old lady grows from a seed planted by a boy in *The Grandmother* (1970); and *The Amputee* (1974) sees a male nurse trying to stop profuse bleeding from the title character's stump. All these motifs — getting sick, the horror of birth, planting seeds and bleeding that can't be stopped — reappear to an even more overwhelming effect in the director's debut feature *Eraserhead*.

Henry Spencer (Jack Nance), a man with a shock of hair and consternation plastered onto his face, lives in a dehumanized, industrial area, with seemingly no other people around and the constant machinery noise a soundtrack to his life (and to the movie). When he visits the house of his girlfriend Mary (Charlotte Stewart), he finds it impossible to communicate with Mary's family, as they all behave as if they were saddened automatons using the presence of Henry for nothing else but channeling their frustration. The girl's father (Allen Joseph) talks of his many health problems and the burden of being a plumber; the mother (Jeanne Bates) asks Henry whether he had sex with Mary and then tries to seduce him herself; Mary seems depressed and has constant crying fits; the grandma (Jean Lange), on the other hand, is an unmoving zombie who can do nothing but smoke cigarettes. Before the family can feast on tiny "man-made" chickens ("Little damn things. Smaller than my fist. But they're new," the father says of the dish), Henry is about to discover that Mary recently gave birth to a baby — only, of course, the doctors are "still not sure it *is* a baby"...

Naturally, Henry now has to marry his girlfriend and do his best to bring up the alien-looking offspring. At the same time, he looks forward to having an affair with his sexy neighbor (Judith Roberts), fantasizes about a puffy-cheeked girl (Laurel Near) living in a radiator, has visions of a spooky God-like figure operating a set of gears, and sees his own head falling off and being used as a material for pencil erasers.

Due to the lack of funds, it took Lynch about six years to finish *Eraserhead* (which was perhaps most troublesome to Jack Nance who had to keep his wacky hairdo unchanged all that time), but the result was astonishing — a truly original and deeply unnerving movie that is at the same time alluring and repugnant. "One thing I thank my mother for is that she refused to give me coloring books, because it's like a restricting thing," said the director in one of the interviews, and that's the best possible explanation for the uniqueness of *Eraserhead*: it doesn't follow the rules of traditional cinema,

Henry (Jack Nance) has lost his (eraser)head in David Lynch's stunning debut.

and it is not limited by adhering to the canons of "good taste." Lynch claims that he hasn't yet read an accurate interpretation of the movie's plot, but he can't hide the fact that most of it was inspired by what was happening to him at the time: he moved to Philadelphia, a city that he saw as "fantastically beautiful," but also "filled with violence, hate and filth"; he married and divorced Peggy Lentz, with whom he had an unplanned child born with deformed feet; he wanted to devote himself to art, but the responsibility towards the family and serious money problems made it impossible, and he had to work part-time as a plumber. *Eraserhead* is also a very Kafka-esque film, with Henry being an incarnation of K./Gregor Samsa, a man in the teeth of the system, who is here at one point put on trial and undergoes a nightmarish metamorphosis. And Lynch does admit to being the writer's enthusiast: when asked what books he can't get out his mind, he replied, "I only pick books that give me a good mood. Kafka, for example." Seen from such a perspective, *Eraserhead*— bleak and shocking as it is — should perhaps be regarded as a feel-good movie, too.

John Alexander, the author of *The Films of David Lynch*, is likely to agree with this. He writes in his book that in the end the movie's main character has "traversed his psychosis for on the other side of madness lies redemption. He has regained his identity." Jeff Johnson, who wrote the controversial but interesting *Pervert in the Pulpit: Morality in the Works of David Lynch*, also recognizes the optimistic side of *Eraserhead*: "Lynch promotes a return to the values inherent in a mythological, post–World War II America, embracing wholeheartedly Reagan's reification of the fifties that he ... considers America's greatest generational decade." Johnson therefore sees Lynch as "a puritanical, hyper-patriotic, idealistic conservative on a reformer's mission, bent, actively through his films, on correcting what he sees as the scourges of American youth culture: drugs, alcohol and hedonism," and reads *Eraserhead* as "a save-sex-for-marriage propaganda parable."

The movie wasn't everyone's darling (*Variety* called it "sickening" as well as lacking in "substance or subtlety") and it's not difficult to understand why; then again, it also impressed several Hollywood decision-makers and opened the gates to the world of serious filmmaking for Lynch. Mel Brooks and George Lucas both offered him the chance to helm their latest productions, and Lynch agreed to work on Brooks's *The Elephant Man* (1980), deciding that he wouldn't be able to make a *Star Wars* movie his own (it is indeed difficult to imagine 1983's *Return of the Jedi* directed by Lynch). With the help of talented cinematographer Freddie Francis and some great actors — Anthony Hopkins, John Hurt, Anne Bancroft and John Gielgud — *The Elephant Man* became the director's second masterpiece, again inviting the viewers to look differently on ugliness. This success was followed by a colossal flop in the form of the big-budgeted *Dune* (1984), but with the dark and perverse *Blue Velvet* (1986) Lynch won his enthusiasts back and gained many new ones. *Wild at Heart* (1990) was another success and another controversy: it won the Golden Palm at the Cannes Film Festival despite being "offensively violent" (Roger Ebert objected to the verdict, calling the movie "repulsive and manipulative"). Between 1990 and 1991 the director was busy working on two seasons of the TV phenomenon *Twin Peaks*, and when it came to an end, he prolonged its existence via a feature-length prequel, *Twin Peaks: Fire Walk with Me* (1992). Unfortunately, the movie wasn't anywhere near as thrilling as the TV series; what's more, Lynch's next TV projects — the quirky comedy *On the Air* (1992) and the dark mystery *Hotel Room* (1993) — misfired, too, and were both canceled after several episodes. Four years later the director returned with style, though, with the schizophrenic, puzzling and very creepy *Lost Highway* (1997). In *The Straight Story* (1999), on the other hand, he proved he's just as good with more down-to-earth dramas, while *Mulholland Dr.* (2001) marked a U-turn to the darkest and weirdest cinematic territories, and was another chilling, mind-blowing piece. Sadly, after having shot the pretentious and overlong *Inland Empire* (2006) on digital video, Lynch swore to never come back to traditional filming. This may mean that the viewers who fell in love with the gorgeous, meticulously composed images from *Eraserhead* will lose interest in the director's future projects altogether, as there's hardly any beauty about the way in which he handles the camera in *Inland Empire*.

Eraserhead is a beautiful exercise in ugliness. It is shocking and disgusting, but once it draws you in, you can't look away from the screen; it is seemingly incomprehensible, yet you *feel* that you understood it better than you will be ever able to express it. David Lynch took his time preparing this unsettling chiaroscuro vision, but it was definitely worth it. Grabs you by the unconscious so hard, you'll never forget the experience. Ever.

Martin

DIRECTOR: George A. Romero
CAST: John Amplas, Lincoln Maazel, Christine Forrest, Elyane Nadeau,
Tom Savini, George A. Romero, Sara Venable, Francine Middleton
USA, 1977

After having stirred up the world of horror with the concept of flesh-eating zombies in *Night of the Living Dead* (1968), director George A. Romero was having serious trouble re-establishing his name. Several movies that followed *Night* were interesting but also uneven and not nearly as groundbreaking as his debut feature. They were not all horror movies, either — there was a drama (*There's Always Vanilla*, 1971), as well as sport documentaries on Romero's pre–1980s CV, while the genre efforts *Hungry Wives* (1972; aka *Season of the Witch*) and *The Crazies* (1973) were rather light on gore and suspense, thus disappointing the viewers and critics who were waiting for another merciless chiller. The director's return to what he does best was 1977's *Martin*, a modern take on the vampire mythos: bleak, bloody, and throwing away all the supernatural elements.

The teenage boy of the title (played by sad-eyed John Amplas) is pale, shy and seemingly innocuous; the catch is, however, that he believes himself to be an 84-year-old vampire, and when he starts craving blood, he turns into a methodical and ruthless psycho who stalks attractive women, puts them to sleep with a shot of anesthetic, undresses them, and then opens their veins with a razor. We learn of his wicked ways in the opening scene, when during a journey on a train he kills one of the passengers

(Francine Middleton), and then makes the murder look like a suicide. But even after finding out that Martin's looks are misleading, it's impossible not to feel for him. He doesn't seem to understand the world he lives in, he's hopeless with women unless they're unconscious, and his religious uncle (Lincoln Maazel) confirms him in the belief that he indeed is "nosferatu," and that if need be, he will be offed with the use of a traditional wooden stake. The boy tries to explain to the uncle that he is *not* a vampire that can resort to magic and supernatural powers, like the ones in the books and movies, but his plea for understanding is totally ignored. Fortunately, one day Martin meets seductive and lonely Mrs. Santini (Elyane Nadeau), who may help him overcome the fear of sexuality and thus lift the vampiric "curse."

"Vietnam, the Civil Rights movement, feminism, the Kent State shootings, the oil embargo ... all of these images, played out to the incessant screams, filtered into the American horror movie," wrote critic Jamie Graham of the genre output in the 1970s, at the same time tracing its style back to *Night of the Living Dead*; "Romero's dead-eyed, shuffling zombies took ragged bites out of the American Dream," concluded Graham. Then, in the course of the decade, the cadaver of the American Dream was further mutilated and eventually torn to pieces by the likes of *The Last House on the Left* (1972), *The Texas Chain Saw Massacre* (1974), *Eaten Alive* (1977), *The Hills Have Eyes* (1977), *Halloween* (1978), and Romero's second zombie movie *Dawn of the Dead* (1978). *Martin*, powerful as it may be, was hardly ever mentioned in the same breath with the above titles, even though it does exactly the same job — sinks its teeth deep in the American Dream and spits out bloody chunks of it. The movie was shot on location in Braddock, Pennsylvania: once a thriving industrial town, starting to lose its importance with the collapse of the steel industry during the 1970s. Romero immediately fell in love with its ugliness; he would later say that in Braddock, "the sense of the American Dream crumbled was incredible," and this was very effectively translated to the screen. (There are several scenes in which Martin simply wanders around the town taking in the views of its slow decay.)

Most telling in the movie is the contrast between the scenes of Martin's brutal assaults on his victims, and the interwoven black-and-white parts, in which the victims become volunteers, smiling and inviting the boy to drink their blood. It's as if Martin wished to romanticize his crimes, or perhaps the other way around — as if what he does in reality wasn't exactly what he had planned, and even when he ultimately gets what he wanted (the sex and blood), the satisfaction isn't complete. The same disappointment concerns the American Dream as depicted in so many movies made in the 1970s, and not just horror films, but also mainstream dramas like Martin Scorsese's *Taxi Driver* (1976): the promised successful life doesn't come easily, and the ensuing frustration may change a man into a beast. Seeing Martin as a repressed boy who tries but fails to conform to society, makes much more sense — and is much more interesting — than believing that he actually is an 84-year-old vampire. Still, Romero cleverly avoids making any clear statements about whether the main character is or is not a supernatural creature, which makes the whole story so intriguing — and leaves the viewers scratching their heads long after the suitably austere finale.

After *Martin*, Romero made a movie that put him back on the map of the horror cinema, the already mentioned Dario Argento–produced *Dawn of the Dead*. Since then, with the single exception of the motorcycle action-adventure *Knightriders* (1981), the director has been sticking to the horror genre, though the results weren't always mind-blowing. His collaboration with Stephen King, *Creepshow* (1982), and the continuation of the zombie saga, *Day of the Dead* (1985), are today regarded as genre classics, but back when they premiered, they got mixed reviews. The ridiculous *Monkey Shines* (1988) is often labeled Romero's worst effort, and none of the movies that followed was unanimously praised by the critics or regarded as truly groundbreaking — not even the new, long-awaited zombie movies *Land of the Dead* (2005) and *Diary of the Dead* (2007).

Martin is not just an inventive look at vampirism, and one of George A. Romero's best films, but it also contributes to the depiction of the American Dream crumbling, so typical for the horror movies of the 1970s. Much more subtle than Tobe Hooper's *The Texas Chain Saw Massacre* and Romero's own *Dawn of the Dead*, *Martin* nevertheless remains one of the decade's most powerful movies.

I Spit on Your Grave

aka *Day of the Woman*
DIRECTOR: Meir Zarchi
CAST: Camille Keaton, Eron Tabor, Richard Pace, Gunter Kleemann,
Anthony Nichols, Alexis Magnotti
USA, 1978

I Spit on Your Grave is one of those films that is still remembered only because it once caused a lot of controversy (it made it to the infamous list of the Video Nasties — movies banned from release in Great Britain). Of course, there is no doubt that Meir Zarchi's movie does have many qualities of a worthy cult classic: it is bold, wild, unsettling and at times even suspenseful. Overall, however, it is a bad movie with several good set pieces. And the worst thing is, it's a bad movie that thinks it's clever and tries to deal with themes that are way too big for it — rape, male chauvinism, gender equality and justice.

Wes Craven's rape-and-revenge film *The Last House on the Left* (1972) must have been an inspiration for Zarchi but if we compare the two movies, we can clearly see there's an enormous gap between them. *The Last House on the Left*, though just as raw and bold as *I Spit on Your Grave*, is much more clever and sophisticated (after all, Craven based his script on the plot of Ingmar Bergman's *The Virgin Spring*), infinitely better acted and directed, and it always uses violence to make a point rather than to simply shock the viewers or satisfy their guilty curiosity. That both movies were equally criticized for being gratuitously violent and sexually explicit only proves how superficial the Video Nasties list was. *The Last House* and *I Spit* may deal with similar themes but it is the latter that clearly lacks an interesting script, a good message and talent. So what exactly went wrong here?

Camille Keaton plays Jennifer, an attractive yet very unlikely writer from New York, who decides to spend some time in the countryside in order to finish her latest book. She finds less peacefulness in a house near a lake than in the city, as almost immediately after putting her pen to paper she is abducted, beaten and raped by a group of local males. She survives all this, escapes into the woods, and just when she thinks she's safe she faces the gang of rapists again. Another long, excruciating rape scene follows, and then the men let the victim go. Humiliated, bleeding and hardly alive, Jennifer eventually gets to the safe haven of her house. But is it really safe? Of course it's not. The men are there again, beat the poor woman some more, have another round at raping her, and in the end intend to kill her. Fortunately for Jennifer, the group singles out retarded Matthew (Richard Pace) to perform the execution, and he fails. After the woman recovers, she plans a bloody revenge on the four brutes — and she will not hesitate to castrate or behead them if need be.

The movie's plot may be oversimplified but it does address some important issues. For example, from a feminist perspective it can be perceived as metaphor for the difficulties a female artist faces in order to become appreciated in the world ruled by men (let's not forget that Jennifer, however unconvincingly portrayed by Keaton, is a writer, and just before the final rape scene the men read out loud pages from her book and mock her writing), or at least as a rare display of a scenario in which a woman fights back against the oppressors. (In fact, the feminist circles were divided on the significance of the movie. One group favored the above mentioned interpretations, and the second group quickly wrote it off as being misogynist.) The problem with *I Spit* is not so much in the script, though, as it is in the movie's overall quality. Whatever message Zarchi wanted to convey, the use of one-dimensional and unconvincing characters made the communication with the audience impossible. Roger Ebert, a critic who was responsible for the withdrawal of *I Spit* from theatres soon after the U.S. premiere, called it "a vile bag of garbage" as well as "a film without a shred of artistic distinction," and cited inappropriate behavior of the members of the audience to prove that the movie shouldn't be regarded as pro-feminist. (According to his report, some male viewers greeted the rape scenes with shouts of "That was a good one!" and "That'll show her!") And even though Ebert's efforts to get the movie banned were rather excessive, it is impossible to argue with his main arguments: *I Spit* really is much too silly to try to teach us anything. The movie's "primitiveness" may or may not be intended but in the end it simply doesn't work. Other vengeance films of that period — not just Craven's *The Last House on the Left* but also Sam Peckinpah's controversial *Straw Dogs* (1971) and William Fruet's intense thriller *Death Weekend* (1976) — prove that "primitiveness" can increase the shock quality of a certain work without becoming preposterous. There's no denying that several scenes in Zarchi's film are shocking, especially the ones that involve rape and castration, but since there's no convincing moral message behind them, the sex and the violence in these shock scenes cannot be viewed as anything other than purely gratuitous.

Zarchi allegedly tried to make a sequel to *I Spit on Your Grave* but the idea never came to fruition (to this day Zarchi's only other movie as a director is the obscure 1985 drama *Don't Mess With My Sister*). Instead, in 1993 an "unofficial" sequel was made by Donald Farmer, with Camille Keaton reprising her role as Jennifer (in the credits,

Keaton is listed as Vickie Kehl). Known as *Savage Vengeance* or *I Will Dance on Your Grave*, Farmer's movie for the most part copies the previous plot (Jennifer is again killing off the men who raped her), and it actually shows us that Zarchi didn't deal with the subject in the worst imaginable way. The sequel not only sports much inferior acting and direction — and who could have thought it possible?— but it doesn't even manage to be as controversial as the original was, almost as if the makers had a phobia of censors getting involved, and did their best to keep them at bay. All the flaws of *I Spit on Your Grave* aside, it's to Zarchi's credit that since he set out to tell us an ugly story, he at least had the nerve to illustrate it with fitting onscreen ugliness. It's just a pity that his movie lacked the brains to accompany the courage.

A cult horror gone bad, *I Spit on Your Grave* is much too silly for the serious issues it wants to tackle.

The Driller Killer

DIRECTOR: Abel Ferrara
CAST: Abel Ferrara, Carolyn Marz, Baybi Day, Alan Wynroth, Harry Schultz,
D.A. Metrov, Richard Howorth, Peter Yellen
USA, 1979

Abel Ferrara prefers not to talk about his skin-flick beginnings and his directorial feature debut in which he also acted, *Nine Lives of a Wet Pussy* (1976); when he's discussing his early days as a director, he jumps from his short crime films (1971's *Nicky's Film* and 1972's *The Hold Up*, both scripted by Ferrara's future regular accomplice, Nicholas St. John) straight to *The Driller Killer*. "It was a natural progression, you know what I mean?" Ferrara said about his second feature in an interview with Scott Foundas. "We made things, we made shorts, we started making longer pieces," he continues, "and then we kind of broke through with *The Driller Killer*. We're constantly looking for a way into the business. Back at that period, when something like *The Texas Chain Saw Massacre* [1974] took — whatever it did — $60,000, $75,000 or $150,000 and grossed $30 million, then you could go out to people and say, 'Hey, I could do that.'"

Story-wise, however, *The Driller Killer* is not as close to Tobe Hooper's *The Texas Chain Saw Massacre* as it is to Roger Corman's *A Bucket of Blood* (1959) or Herschell Gordon Lewis's *Color Me Blood Red* (1965) — two tales of an artist gone mad because of the lack of critical appreciation. In Ferrara's movie, the artist is Reno (Ferrara himself disguised as Jimmy Laine), a painter who lives with two girls, Carol (Carolyn Marz) and Pamela (Baybi Day), and is just coming through a very rough period of life, both personally and as an artist. The money's thin, the bills won't stop coming, Reno's latest painting isn't an easy piece to finish, and Carol, who seems to be his true love, is considering going back to her well-off ex (Richard Howorth). When a talentless punk band moves into Reno's building and their loud rehearsals make any sort of artistic work impossible, the painter grabs a battery-powered drill and rushes off to the streets of New York to vent the tension by killing some local derelicts.

You'd think that a movie that became one of the best known "Video Nasties" during the British video witchhunt in the 1980s, and bears *that* violent title, will be a gratuitous gore fest with no place for proper plot in it; when Reno first gets a powerdrill in his hands — several minutes into the movie — in order to help the highly annoying Pamela make a hole in the wall, it seems almost inevitable that he would end up drilling Pam's head instead. But no, Ferrara takes his time before he lets Reno get his drill bloody, and the description of the character slowly losing it is wholly convincing, mainly thanks to great acting from Ferrara and Marz. (The scene of Reno's angry outburst when Carol comments on his painting seems not just improvised but chillingly *real*.) Also, the presentation of the 1970s New York — at the time of the city's nadir, nearing bankruptcy and with crime rates reaching the highest levels ever — looks depressingly sad and realistic enough to think that Ferrara did the bulk of these scenes the documentary style, with no actors (although, for example, Peter Yellen's wacky rant at the bus stop is first-rate acting).

And then there are the infamous powerdrill murders. Piotr Kletowski in his essay on the director ("Abel Ferrara. W poszukiwaniu zbawienia" in *Kino amerykańskie: Twórcy*) compares the study of a murderous artist in *The Driller Killer* with Thomas De Quincey's "appreciation of a murderer" in the 1827 treatise "Murder Considered as One of the Fine Arts." In it, De Quincey jokingly claims that "something more goes to the composition of a fine murder than two blockheads to kill and be killed — a knife — a purse — and a dark lane. Design ... grouping, light and shade, poetry, sentiment, are now deemed indispensable to attempts of this nature." He goes on to "praise" one John Williams, a man accused of murdering seven random Londoners in 1811 with no apparent reason: "Mr. Williams has exalted the ideal of murder to all of us," continues De Quincey, "Like Æschylus or Milton in poetry, like Michael Angelo in painting, he has carried his art to a point of colossal sublimity." Reno, like Williams, doesn't kill people who wronged him (for example, the bothersome punk rockers manage to stay away from the killing drill throughout the whole movie), and he could perhaps be pronounced another "murderer-artist" if it weren't for one tiny detail in De Quincey's theory. Namely, the victim "ought to be in good health" because "it is absolutely barbarous to murder a sick person, who is usually quite unable to bear it." This, of course, disqualifies Reno, as he tends to kill people who are stoned or drunk and who certainly don't belong to the healthiest group in society.

There may be, however, another reason behind the murders Ferrara shows in *The Driller Killer*. Nicole Brenez suggests in her book *Abel Ferrara* (from the Contemporary Film Directors series) that the movie's main theme is not necessarily "an artist gone mad" but rather "capitalism gone wrong." That would be an explanation why so much screen time is devoted not just to Reno, but to the punk rockers and the derelicts as well. The viewer is given a chance to understand and feel for all of them; Brenez writes that in *The Driller Killer*, "capitalism is shown from the point of view of its victims: ... economic castoffs, slowly dying in the street, at anyone's mercy." Is it then possible that Reno is choosing to kill them not just because they are the easiest prey, but actually out of pity? They are, after all, quite similar to him: people devoured by the decaying New York, ones who weren't lucky enough to achieve success or couldn't cope with growing responsibilities. Such an explanation is all the more plausible for the fact that when Reno drills the bodies of the derelicts, it almost always looks like a maniacal sexual act. (In the scene of the first killing, Reno literally mounts his victim, forces the drill into his chest and is clearly aroused when the man writhes in pain under him.)

The Driller Killer later became Part One of Ferrara's unofficial Urban Victim Trilogy (a label used by Nick Johnstone in "Abel Ferrara: The King of New York"), together with the compelling rape-and-revenge film *Ms .45* (1981), and *Fear City* (1984), an uneven thriller about a psycho hunting down Manhattan strippers. Later Ferrara did some work for TV (most notably, he directed episodes of *Miami Vice* in 1985, and *Crime Story* in 1986) and then got to helm his first bigger budgeted features, the successful duo of *China Girl* (1987) and *King of New York* (1990), and also the $20 million flop *Body Snatchers* (1993; shelved for a couple of years and then released as a producer's cut — strangely, Ferrara has always been fond of this movie). In 1992 the director did what many thought impossible by that time: he returned with a movie that caused even more controversy than *The Driller Killer* once did. It was called *Bad Lieutenant*, starred Harvey Keitel at his most obscene and included everything from a rape on a nun, through nasty talks to God, Keitel's frontal nudity and gratuitous masturbation in public, to the cold, shocking documentary-style finale. But if the "badness" of *Bad Lieutenant* seemed a bit overdone, Ferrara's best films — the vampire tale *The Addiction* (1995) and the brutal 1930s crime story *The Funeral* (1996) — managed to keep the perfect balance between the shock effects and the coherence/plausibility of the story.

It might seem a poor idea to remake *The Driller Killer* — it was a sign of its times, after all, and it's hard it imagine the same plot recreated in the 2000s — but at least people behind the idea chose the right director and the right main actor for their cash-grabbing project. Andrew Jones, famous for spending a lot of time with the street derelicts to film his second feature *The Feral Generation* (2007), is at the helm of the new version, and David Hess, best known as the bloodcurdlingly realistic psycho from Wes Craven's *The Last House on the Left* (1972), is set to play the leading role.

The Driller Killer is not the 90-minute-long bloodbath some would perhaps like it to be, but it nevertheless *is* a very nasty movie; only it is nasty in this peculiar "artsy" way that Ferrara has been practicing ever since. The movie packs a punch whether seen as a tribute to several other classic genre pieces or as a twisted social commentary, and Ferrara's rare starring role is a blast.

PART IV:
THE NASTY EIGHTIES

Cannibal Holocaust

DIRECTOR: Ruggero Deodato
CAST: Robert Kerman, Francesca Ciardi, Luca Barbareschi,
Perry Pirkanen, Salvatore Basile
Italy, 1980

"The fault for *Cannibal Holocaust* lies on my son," director Ruggero Deodato confesses in the documentary *Ban the Sadist Videos*. He goes on to explain his intentions for making the movie: "He was only seven then and he would complain about prime time news. They often showed victims of the Red brigades. It was a very gory time. The film was directed at those journalists, the journalists who caused all the fuss. Back then my aim wasn't to do a commercial film, I wanted to make something hard-hitting." And hard-hitting *Cannibal Holocaust* certainly is. Or, to put it more appropriately, it is hugely controversial and painful to watch. Among the many Video Nasties, *Cannibal Holocaust* is arguably the nastiest one: not just because of the very realistic-looking violence towards some characters in the movie but, most infamously, because of the very real violence towards the animals who were unlucky enough to be cast by Mr. Deodato.

Cannibal Holocaust was not the first brutal movie about white adventurers being tortured and eaten by cannibals, and it wasn't the first movie to include real animal cruelty, either, but it was first such movie to employ the technique of a fake documentary (one that two decades later brought a lot of money to the makers of *The Blair Witch Project*). In the movie, the documentary in question is found in the Amazon jungle by anthropologist Harold Munroe (Robert Kerman), who then brings it to New York and wants to show it to the whole world in a series of TV programs. But as he watches the documentary he starts to realize that it's way too much than national television can handle: the crew that made the movie — led by Alan Yates (Gabriel Yorke) — apparently wanted to capture the most savage scenes imaginable, and in order to get them, they themselves started provoking and violating the natives, who finally stood up and killed the white invaders, with the cameras still rolling.

To make the fake documentary as realistic as possible (and from the technical point of view it was very convincing indeed: shot on 16mm, often badly lit and full of scratches), the director asked the actors starring in it to "disappear" for a year. So they did — and put Deodato in serious trouble when he was accused of making a snuff movie and had to prove that all his cast members were alive and well. Eventually the actors were found and the snuff charges were dropped, but there was still one serious problem with *Cannibal Holocaust*: the real cruelty towards the animals. Deodato was trying to defend himself by saying that whatever animals were killed in front of the camera were then eaten by the crew, so it wasn't just killing for entertainment. This might have worked if the movie's animals were simply killed and not slowly dismembered (in case of the turtle) or gutted alive (in case of the musk rat). In the end, Deodato left the court with a four-year suspended sentence, but some *Cannibal Holocaust* co-workers never forgave him for what he did, perhaps the most striking example being Robert Kerman, an actor who also starred in many porn movies, and who to this day claims that *Cannibal Holocaust* is one movie that he honestly hates. (In a Q&A included on the 25th Anniversary Collector's Edition DVD, Kerman speaks of his fruitless protests against the animal cruelty, and admits that he wishes he would have never starred in the movie.)

Apart from the gore-drenched news programs that Deodato mentioned in *Ban the Sadist Videos*, he was also clearly inspired by the shocking documentary series *Mondo Cane* (started in 1962) directed by Gualtiero Jacopetti and Franco Prosperi. Deodato was admittedly disgusted with *Mondo Cane* (which, among other things, depicted cruelty towards animals in various parts of the world), and his own movie was supposed to be criticizing the whole "shockumentary" concept. But it's his movie that ultimately turned out to be more exploitative than the efforts of Jacopetti and Prosperi. Even if the duo filmed all the gore just because they knew it would sell well, they didn't actually order slow tortures for the animals in their movies. Again then, Deodato's need to make a strong statement cannot be wholly justified: sure, *Cannibal Holocaust* does make us think but once the process starts we can't help but also wonder if using such violent means to criticize the display of violence in media is not a bit too hypocritical. Some viewers will argue that the animal cruelty was necessary for the movie to make an impact (Daniel Auty of "The Spinning Image" said: "If part of cinema's role is to challenge and disturb, then this film remains an undeniably important piece of film history"), but this sounds off, if you think about it; isn't it one of the director's main tasks to use various *cinematic tricks* to make the audience think that fictional events are happening for real? What Deodato did here only proves he didn't trust his skills as a filmmaker and had to resort to sadistic butchery. And doesn't it sound ironic when some critics call Deodato a "bold director" particularly because he didn't have the guts to use some more special effects?

Still, *Cannibal Holocaust* stands tall among many other cannibal films of this period, which were usually plotless, gratuitous works that tended to recycle violent scenes from other similarly themed movies, and more often than not also included real animal cruelty; most famous of these were Umberto Lenzi's *Mangiati Vivi!* (1980; aka *Eaten Alive*) and *Cannibal Ferox* (1981), and, incidentally, the main actor in *Cannibal Ferox*, Giovanni Lombardo Radice, felt as jaded about Lenzi's movie as Kerman did about *Cannibal Holocaust*, and he even said that directors who were making films like *Cannibal Ferox* or *Mondo Cane* were just "expressing their longing for fascism" and "titillating the worst and simplest public." (To convince Radice to kill a pig in one scene, Lenzi told him that De Niro would do it, to which the actor replied: "De Niro would kick you in the ass.") Deodato himself also returned to onscreen cannibalism in *Inferno in Diretta* (1985; aka *Cut and Run*), a movie that was quite shocking, yet not as exploitative as *Cannibal Holocaust*. Also, let's not forget that *Cannibal Holocaust* wasn't Deodato's first venture into the jungle: he managed to test a similar formula (though without the use of the fake documentary gimmick) several years before in *Ultimo Mondo Cannibale* (1977; aka *Jungle Holocaust* or *Last Cannibal World*). Like *Cannibal Holocaust*, *Ultimo Mondo Cannibale* is tense and based on an interesting concept, but it is ruined by the inclusion of scenes of animal cruelty.

An understandably controversial movie that could be labeled powerful cinema if it wasn't for one huge flaw: to make his point about the violent-oriented media, director Deodato doesn't stop at using very realistic special effects but feels the need to spill some real animal blood, too — and does it in an alarmingly cruel fashion.

Hell of the Living Dead (Inferno dei Morti Viventi)

aka *Virus; Night of the Zombies; Zombie Creeping Flesh*
DIRECTOR: Bruno Mattei
CAST: Margit Evelyn Newton, Franco Garofalo, Selan Karay, José Gras,
Josep Lluís Fonoll, Bruno Boni, Patrizia Costa, Víctor Israel
Italy-Spain, 1980

One of the most challenging tasks for a genre critic is to praise a Bruno Mattei movie and get away with it. Let's take a look at the following opinion, a convincing piece of writing by reviewer Paul Garcia: "Mattei constructs *Hell of the Living Dead* from the remains of zombie and cannibals past, resulting in a cinematic offal: a film intensely comprehensive in its efforts to cynically plumb and plunder, comical in its bombast and jolting, inappropriate reaction shots, and valiant in its ability to interweave gonzo politics with cultural ignorance. The result is a miserable hodgepodge of genre conventions, so inept in all facets as to transcend its objective badness and become an inadvertent parody." All parts of Garcia's evaluation are true, and yet, somehow, they don't add up to form a true picture of what cinema according to Bruno Mattei really is. Because, the cheapness, stupidity and idea-stealing aside, all of Mattei's works aim to entertain the viewer — and in this respect they very rarely fail.

Hell of the Living Dead is entertaining, too, if you approach it with caution. Expecting a zombie movie to rival Romero's breakthrough masterpieces would be a mistake (though it should be mentioned at this point that *Hell* borrows some of the plotlines and much of the soundtrack from Romero's 1978 hit *Dawn of the Dead*). Expecting re-enaction of the atmosphere from Lucio Fulci's *Zombie Flesh Eaters* (1979) would be equally unwise (you may notice, however, that Mattei does attempt to bring the Fulci spirit back in several scenes). It isn't true that *Hell* works well as a spoof, either: as such, it can only be understood by fans of the horror genre, not by the general comedy audiences (true spoofs rooted in horror — like Mel Brooks' *Young Frankenstein* [1974] — are funny even for the uninitiated in the genre). All things considered, *Hell of the Living Dead* cannot be labeled other than as a pure horror movie: not an especially scary, intelligent or coherent one, but a horror movie nevertheless. It could almost be one of those bland, primitive genre pieces that you forget mere seconds after having watched them, if it weren't for Mattei's desperate attempts at providing us with as much fun as humanly possible. He throws zombies, cannibals, rabid animals and over-the-top gore at us, and before we can thank him properly, he adds unexpected nudity, weird action set pieces, muddled social and political commentary, as well as some hilariously bad dialogue and tons of stock footage from nature documentaries to make the whole experience last a bit longer. You can laugh and you can mock Mattei's abilities as a director, but in a way this man's movies are the ultimate horror experience. Watch one of them and you'll learn more of the genre than by watching ten cleaner, tighter and more expensive chillers by artsier directors.

Now, let's see if the convoluted plot of *Hell* can be distilled to just one informative sentence. There's a problem at a mysterious, government factory in New Guinea, and instead of solving the problem of famine in the Third World countries, as is expected of them, the scientists unleash hordes of zombies on people living nearby; bites of the undead create more undead, and so the zombiefying virus spreads, soon to reach three groups of characters: the members of a New Guinean tribe, an unmatched modern couple (she is an adventurer-exhibitionist, he a cowardly journalist), and a tough little SWAT team ready to prove they can kill anybody, even the already dead.

However chaotically Mattei tangles the various plotlines and tries to weave an offbeat, inconclusive socio-political commentary around them (like in the subplot that has the SWAT guys wipe out a whole group of terrorists, so that we can hear several prophetic words of wisdom from one of the villains), he eventually creates a surprisingly vivid picture of the 1980s, with science, media and terrorism getting out of control, the poor being fed empty promises and the rich finding new depths to the word "hypocrisy." *Hell* is also a testimony to the "patchwork horror" style, so popular at that time, as opposed to the more straightforward recycling of already used ideas in remakes, so popular today. And whatever you feel about the idea of making horror movies that simply reshape what already exists and has been proved good, Mattei has made some of the weirdest, most confusing and yet decidedly fun horror medleys in the history of the genre, *Hell* being a perfect example of his method.

It's impossible to single out Mattei's best or worst movies, as they are all, with no exception, inherently bad. It's just a matter of how efficiently their badness translates into entertainment. *Hell of the Living Dead* no doubt belongs to the efforts with the best bad-means-fun ratio, together with *S.S. Extermination Love Camp* (1977), *The Other Hell* (1980) and *Rats: Night of Terror* (1984). Later Mattei became a king of sequels, as he infamously took over the director's duties from Lucio Fulci on *Zombie Flesh Eaters 2* (1988, aka *Zombi 3*), in effect giving us a movie much more similar to *Hell of the Living Dead* than to Fulci's original, and we can guess he didn't hesitate long when asked to helm *Terminator II* (1990, also shown under a less misleading title, *Alienators*), *Cruel Jaws* (1995, alternatively advertised as *Jaws 5*) or *Cannibal Ferox 3* (2003, aka *Land of Death*). Many of his later movies were tedious and unimaginative, but Mattei's eagerness to entertain his viewers was always there. It just didn't always work.

Mattei's infamous zombie movie recycles ideas from earlier works by Romero, Fulci, Deodato and Lenzi, and it struggles to form some kind of socio-political message, but it's also a blinding explosion of honest enthusiasm for the genre. Plus, it gives you a pretty good picture of the crazy era that spawned it.

Possession

DIRECTOR: Andrzej Żuławski
CAST: Sam Neill, Isabelle Adjani, Heinz Bennent, Johanna Hofer, Margit
Carstensen, Maximilian Ruethlein
France–Germany, 1981

Before Polish director Andrzej Żuławski started making intolerably boring and pretentious movies like *Szamanka* (1996) and *La Fidélité* (2001), he did manage to keep the balance between the unnerving and the unwatchable, and created two very good horror movies: *Diabeł* (1972; aka *The Devil*) and *Possession* (1981). Both have Żuławski's trademark documentary feel, and include scenes of uncomfortable violence and acting that borders on hysterical, but *Possession* turned out to be the more influential of the two: after all, one of its scenes was a direct inspiration for Clive Barker when he was shooting *Hellraiser* (to which Barker admits in his authorized biography *The Dark Fantastic*; but when you see the scene from Żuławski's movie — with a bloodied, vaguely human-shaped creature gradually coming to life — the *Hellraiser* legacy becomes quite obvious). Put on the list of Video Nasties in the UK, heavily cut in the U.S. (the American version was about 40 minutes shorter than the 127–minute original), and lovingly thrashed by critics, *Possession* certainly didn't have an easy start, but it did bring Isabelle Adjani a Best Actress award in Cannes, and today it is often recognized as an exceptionally challenging cinematic puzzle.

No one gets possessed like Isabelle Adjani: Andrzej Żuławski's shocking *Possession* (1981).

The first scenes seem to be a promise of a heartbreaking drama rather than one of the most enigmatic and uncompromising horror movies in the history of cinema. Mark (Sam Neill) returns to his apartment in West Berlin to find out that his wife, Anna (Isabelle Adjani), decided to leave him. Shattered by the news, Mark cannot make up his mind whether he should try to win Anna back, focus on the well-being of his young son, commit suicide or have an affair with his wife's look-alike, Helen (Adjani again). Eventually he pays a visit to Anna's lover, Heinrich (Heinz Bennent), and learns that the woman is spending most of her time elsewhere. To find out more about his wife's *other* lover, Mark hires a detective, but it turns out that Anna is ready to kill in order to guard her secret. And yes — that's the secret that involves the abominable creature Clive Barker took such a liking to.

It's not just wild plot ideas and frantic acting that make *Possession* so exception- ally intense. Of course, seeing Sam Neill in terrible spasms (in a scene just after Anna leaves Mark) or Isabelle Adjani going totally berserk (in a flashback that closes with Anna giving birth to a monster), is a shock, but it wouldn't have worked quite as well if it weren't for Żuławski's demented directing style. The camera seems to be either dangerously close to the characters (for example during the couple's fight in the kitchen) or unnaturally distant (the scene with Mark sitting on a rocking chair and talking on the phone); it's as if the director wanted to show us that the two main characters can- not solve their problems because they have been in the relationship for too long and they know each other all too well, and anyone from the outside cannot help them, either, as there is some kind of force field between the married couple and the rest of the world. This is also why there are not too many supporting characters or extras in the movie: the problem Mark and Anna have to deal with is their own, isolated from the world, and there is no one to turn for help to. In this respect, *Possession* is like a night- mare about a marriage falling apart — like in any dream, the less important characters are underdeveloped or caricatured (here: Heinrich, the detectives, the very occasional passersby), and there are no boundaries about how the story is to be told (hence the chaotic mixture of long tracking shots, unnatural camera angles and sudden bursts of onscreen madness).

The metaphors of a broken marriage led many critics to compare *Possession* with David Cronenberg's *The Brood* (a tale of an estranged woman who learned how to con- trol her anger and use it to produce bloodthirsty offspring ready to kill anyone who wronged her), which is fair enough as both directors confessed that their films were, in fact, reactions to painful divorces each of them experienced. Żuławski's take is, how- ever, more dimensional than Cronenberg's (which, to be perfectly clear, doesn't mean it's a better movie altogether), as the difficulty to communicate, the "isolation" of the married couple and the overall craziness depicted in *Possession* may just as well be metaphors for a disintegrating country. The very fact that the story takes place in Cold War–era West Berlin is quite significant for the metaphor of divorce — the wall that separates it from East Berlin being a symbol of disconnection of what once was united — but Żuławski's additional intention might have been for the Berlin wall to symbolize the Iron Curtain, and for Germany to symbolize Poland, a country he had to leave in order to keep making movies (he fled to France after the production of his sci-fi epic

Na Srebrnym Globie aka *Silver Globe* was halted; the movie was finished years later and eventually premiered in 1987). It is debatable whether *Possession* works better as a representation of a divided couple or a person disjoined from home country, but it's the movie's ambiguity that is one of its greatest assets. It's a huge pleasure to finally start noticing some hazy meaning behind this apparently incomprehensible piece of work.

To make an insane movie and have sane audiences applaud it, is not an easy task. It worked rather well in the case of *Possession* (though, obviously, it is hardly a film for all tastes), but it backfired badly 15 years later when the director returned to Poland and decided to apply a very similar approach in *Szamanka*, a controversial story of a woman who seems to have strange power over the men she meets. Young, inexperienced actress Iwona Petry was cast as the main heroine—virtually a clone of Isabelle Adjani's character in *Possession*—but since she lacked Adjani's skills, her efforts resulted in a highly annoying and unconvincing performance (not to mention the fact that she was allegedly deeply disturbed by the meditation techniques Żuławski imposed on her, so that she could get into her character).

An arthouse Video Nasty that is much more disturbing than most over-the-top shockers that made it to the infamous list. If you're looking for the best-ever performance of a woman being possessed, Żuławski's movie is a perfect choice. Watch Isabelle Adjani in the creepy flashback scene and tremble!

The Living Dead Girl (*La Morte Vivante*)

DIRECTOR: Jean Rollin
CAST: Françoise Blanchard, Marina Pierro, Mike Marshall,
Carina Barone, Fanny Magier
France, 1982

France needed an artist like Jean Rollin. With an eye for both the erotic and the terrifying, as well as a penchant for improvisation, Rollin dared make movies no other French filmmaker had attempted before. It's true that sometimes he's credited with more than he accounts for (for example, Rollin's 1967 feature debut, *The Rape of the Vampire*, is *not* "the first French vampire movie ever," as some critics would have it; after all, Carl Theodor Dreyer's *Vampyr* was made three decades earlier), but more often he is unfairly discredited as a talentless hack who never accomplished anything noteworthy. (Such opinions are usually voiced by critics unlucky enough to sit through nothing else but the undeniable "hackjobs" from Rollin, like the infamous *Zombie Lake* [1981], a movie he set out to direct without having read the script, after Jesus Franco, the production company's initial choice, didn't show up on set.) The movies of Jean Rollin are without doubt uneven, cheap, gratuitous and, more often than not, very badly acted, but some of them can also be presented as examples of European horror at its weirdest and wildest. Among the latter are: 1978's pioneering French gore fest *The Grapes of Death*, 1979's mind-boggling thing of beauty *Fascination*, and in the 1980s a successful revisioning of vampirism in *The Living Dead Girl*.

Since Rollin's creative peak came between the 1970s and 1980s and because he's been known for making horror movies of the perverse kind, he is often compared to Franco, another European director with a fondness for the eroticized horror. However, the styles of the two artists are hardly similar. Film historian David Kalat compared the two directors in the following way in his essay "Exoticism and Eroticism in French Horror Cinema": "Jess Franco's singular obsessions with erotic horror were exceeded by native Frenchman Jean Rollin's career-long fixation on deeply sexual, hideously gory vampire films, suffused with delicate, dreamy poetry. Equally as marginalized as Franco, Rollin also claims a niche audience of committed fans. His pictures are an odd, uncommercial blend of pornography and Gothic horror, entrancing and addictive to the select few." There is, however, a striking difference between the two filmmakers: while Franco's best movies are highly involving and irresistibly sexy, Rollin's finest works are bold, attractive and based on interesting concepts, but also awkward, difficult to get into, and with cold, wanton nudity in place of true eroticism. *The Living Dead Girl*, often cited as Rollin's most audience-friendly work, is not an exception to this rule.

The movie begins with a scene that has to puzzle the viewers—after all, Rollin admitted in one interview that he doesn't entirely get it, either, and that some portions of the plot were added to please the contemporary viewers (hence plenty of gore, the obligatory use of barrels with chemical waste and the difficulty to distinguish whether the main character is a vampire or a zombie). We see a young, pretty and long-dead Catherine Valmont (Françoise Blanchard) being suddenly brought back to life by a chemical spill in her coffin in the family vault. Although we learn that Catherine has been dead for two years, she looks as fresh as if her heart never stopped beating; next to Catherine's coffin there is her mother's coffin and she, too, looks surprisingly well-preserved, but for some reason she doesn't jump at the chance of resurrection when the chemical waste spills. Unanswered questions multiply as the plot unfolds, and the viewer's task is to resist counting them and focus on the upcoming events. Using her teeth and the overlong fingernails, the latter the only visible sign that she'd been dead for quite some time, Catherine kills the two men who brought the barrels to the vault, and then she similarly offs a woman who wanted to sell the chateau that belonged to Catherine's family; and she doesn't spare the woman's boyfriend, either. Though the two years spent in the coffin left her mute, Catherine finds a way to get in touch with her childhood friend Helene (Marina Pierro): she phones her and then plays a music box tune they both remember from their youth. Helene promptly packs her bags, gets in a car and rushes to Catherine's castle. She finds Catherine and her dead, drained-of-blood victims, and soon understands that to keep her friend walking she will have to get some more humans to visit the abandoned residence. One of the most obvious would-be victims is Barbara (Carina Barone), an annoying American woman who accidentally takes a snapshot of somnambulistic Catherine, and decides to track her down when everyone in the town keeps repeating that the girl in the picture is long dead.

The strength of Rollin's movie is neither gore (there's lots of it here, much more than in most other of his movies, but usually it doesn't look very convincing), nor better-than-usual acting (Blanchard is quite good in the main role but Pierro and Barone make their characters artificial and unlikable); the interesting thing is the atypical way of showing a zombie/vampire as an entity who doesn't rejoice in killing humans but suffers because of it and wants to put a stop to it. The whole zombie/vampire mystery works very well on its own, by the way, as it makes the viewer constantly redefine Catherine as one or the other: would she need the chemical spill to wake up if she were a vampire? Would she just drink blood if she were a zombie?

The early 1980s marked the beginning of the AIDS scare and the end of the sexual revolution, so it's understandable that some critics started seeing *The Living Dead Girl* as a metaphor for AIDS. This would make Rollin's movie the first horror ever to tackle the subject but it doesn't seem a very likely scenario: For a long time after the first reported cases of AIDS in June 1981, people didn't know much about the specifics of the disease, and the filmmakers, too, stayed away from the subject until as late as the mid–1980s. Therefore, Larry Cohen's *It's Alive III: Island of the Alive* (1985, an unknown blood disease being one of the themes it dealt with) still remains the earliest official metaphor for AIDS, while *The Living Dead Girl* may only be regarded as an unconscious foreshadowing of the future epidemic. In any way, the difficult subject appeared in horror movies much earlier than the mainstream cinema dared approach it in a more straightforward way: it wasn't until the early 1990s that we got Cyril Collard's *Savage Nights* (1992), Derek Jarman's *Blue* (1993) and Jonathan Demme's Oscar-winning *Philadelphia* (1993).

Just when he scored big with his special blend of horror-erotica, Rollin decided to abandon the bloody antics and return to two other genres he's been well acquainted with: the soft-core (1988's *Emmanuelle 6*, credited to Bruno Zincone who started shooting it) and hardcore porn (1994's *The Scent of Mathilde*, credited to co-director Marc Dorcel). He also tried his hand at low-budget crime thrillers (1984's *Sidewalks of Bangkok* and 1993's *Killing Car*), but most of the time he was struggling to get his projects made and ended up rewriting some of his movie scripts, turning them into novels. In the mid–1990s, when Rollin's most important horror films appeared on DVD and were cheered ecstatically by the fans, the director was encouraged to revisit the genre as well as to the themes of vampirism in the sexy but ultimately disappointing duo of *Two Orphan Vampires* (1997) and *Dracula's Fiancée* (2002).

While Jean Rollin's horror movies will never be regarded as the most complex or most satisfying works of the genre, they certainly are exceptionally daring and intriguing. *The Living Dead Girl*, one of the director's greatest achievements and a rare financial success, is a compromise between Rollin's tendency to improvise and his newfound ambition to meet the expectations of the '80s' gore-loving audiences. The result is curious: an original take on the vampire mythos, full of nudity, drenched in gore and blended with a zombie movie.

Basket Case

DIRECTOR: Frank Henenlotter
CAST: Kevin Van Hentenryck, Terri Susan Smith, Beverly Bonner, Robert Vogel,
Diana Browne, Lloyd Pace, Joe Clarke
USA, 1982

Basket Case is a movie that emerged from an idea for a single scene. The writer-director Frank Henenlotter imagined a young man walking down the street carrying a wicker basket. The rest of the plot simply grew out of this innocent picture and soon started taking weirder and weirder shapes. In the final version the young man was named Duane, and the basket a hiding place for Belial — Duane's mutated Siamese brother, once attached to his side. The siblings arrived in New York in order to look for the doctors responsible for the surgery that separated them, and the two boys sure don't mean to just say "Thank you" and leave. There's a psychic link between Duane and Belial, as well as true brotherly love, so they don't treat the separation as a favor but as the nastiest of all crimes — all the more so because after the surgery the doctors threw Belial in the trash hoping he'd just die. They were horribly wrong, of course. Now their odd-looking ex-patient — more or less just a deformed head with contorted arms — is ready for a bloody revenge. The only problem is that while visiting one of the doctors, the perfectly normal Duane falls for his receptionist, a girl as pretty as she is spooky (plus she's wearing an inexplicable blond wig). The possibility of an affair deconcentrates Duane, so far fanatically focused on exacting the revenge, and highly irritates Belial, who senses the transfer of pheromones via the psychic link.

When *Basket Case* was first shown theatrically, Analysis Releasing — a company that earlier delivered William Lustig's violent *Maniac* (1980) — saw fit to cut all the bloodiest scenes out of the movie and advertise it as a black comedy. Of course, *Basket Case* simply didn't work with all the most important horror elements trimmed down, so thanks to poor ticket sales as well as protests from critic Joe Bob Briggs, three months later the proper version of the movie was released. Its popularity started to grow steadily as more and more genre enthusiasts were citing the movie as providing an unusual cinematic experience, while some harsh opinions from mainstream reviewers turned out to be helpful rather than discouraging (like the declaration of *The New York Observer*'s Rex Reed that it was "the sickest movie" he had ever seen). But an even greater popularity awaited Henenlotter's debut in 1984: with the VHS tapes being a recent and rather expensive invention, the director insisted that *Basket Case* be sold at a budget price — and he hit a jackpot, as his movie soon turned out to be one of the year's best-selling video titles. Since then *Basket Case* seems to be gaining mostly positive reviews: according to Steven Puchalski in *Slimetime: A Guide to Sleazy, Mindless Movies* it is "one of the top ten horrors of the eighties"; *Blockbuster Entertainment Guide to Movies and Videos* calls it a "very low-budget but one-of-a-kind ... horror that mixes extreme gore with the blackest of humor"; it's "gruesomely entertaining," according to Mick Martin and Marsha Porter's *DVD & Video Guide*; and Leonard Maltin's *Movie and Video Guide* labels it as extremely self-conscious but intriguing and John Waters-ish.

However cheap and amateurish it may at times feel, there are many things to cherish about *Basket Case*. The special effects and makeup are by turns quite shocking (for example, in a scene where the female doctor has her face pierced with scalpels) and touchingly awkward (the scenes that see the stop-motion Belial going berserk in the hotel room); the acting ranges from the weird (Kevin Van Hentenryck as Duane or Terri Susan Smith as the blond-wigged receptionist), through the relatively natural (Beverly Bonner as a friendly hooker or Diana Browne as Dr. Kutter) to laugh-out-loud hilarious (Joe Clarke as a nosy hotel customer or Lloyd Pace as the obnoxious Dr. Needleman). The photography is as often too murky as it is overlit, but as a means of presentation of the seediest parts of New York this works surprisingly well, especially since most of the movie takes place on the 42nd Street that until the 1980s was famous for its many grindhouse theatres. Also important is the fact that together with Sam Raimi's *The Evil Dead* (1981), *Basket Case* started another horror subgenre: the splatter-comedy (or gore-comedy). It was a fusion of horrors-with-laughs in the vein of Roger Corman's *A Bucket of Blood* (1959) and serious (at least theoretically) splatter films like the ones directed by Herschell Gordon Lewis in the 1960s (Henenlotter openly referred to 1963's *Blood Feast* as his inspiration), that would continue developing throughout the decade with such titles as *Re-Animator* (1985), *Return of the Living Dead* (1985), *Evil Dead II* (1987), *Blood Diner* (1987), and *Bad Taste* (1987). But unlike many of these later splatter comedies, *Basket Case* wasn't just about putting the shocks and the laughs together. Through its wicked plot it also attempted to point out such issues as tolerance, family relationships and conforming to society.

The next decade spawned two more *Basket Case* movies, both directed by Henenlotter and with Hentenryck reprising his role of a likable psycho. *Basket Case 2* (1990) slightly re-staged the finale of the original in order to directly continue the story from that point on (if you watch the two parts back to back, the transition from one to the other is far from smooth: it didn't help that Hentenryck looked much less boyish in the sequel than eight years before), and instead of just one monster it boasted a full attic of them. It is often repeated that *Basket Case 2* includes "the most disgusting love scene ever committed to celluloid" (and it's hard to disagree with this when you see it), while *Basket Case 3* (1992) apparently tries to top it with the most excruciating and over-the-top birth scene ever. For both sequels Henenlotter joined forces with makeup and special effects artist Gabriel Bartalos who had previously worked on such films as *Jason Lives: Friday the 13th Part VI* (1986), *The Texas Chainsaw Massacre 2* (1986) and *Brain Damage* (1988, directed by Henenlotter and a bit similar to *Basket Case* plotwise), and then launched a successful career lending his talent to Sam Raimi's *Darkman* (1990), the *Leprechaun* and *Cremaster* movies, and more recently to Kevin Tenney's *Brain Dead* (2006), as well as Henenlotter's latest effort *Bad Biology* (2007). The creatures in *Basket Case 2* and *3* were yet meaner and slimier than what we could see in the original — watch out for the unexpected homage to *Alien* in the first sequel and the "cute" baby monsters in the second one — and these movies really pushed the boundaries of tolerable onscreen ugliness. Somehow, however, it's the cheap, character-driven 1982 effort that still remains the most impressive part of the trilogy.

While not as popular as Sam Raimi's *The Evil Dead*, *Basket Case*, too, marks the beginning of a new — gorier and sleazier — era in the history of American horror cinema. To this day, the whole *Basket Case* trilogy still belongs to a tight group of the most freakish, ugly and disturbing films ever made — something that undoubtedly has director Henenlotter blush with pride.

Escape 2000

aka *Turkey Shoot; Blood Camp Thatcher*
DIRECTOR: Brian Trenchard-Smith
CAST: Steve Railsback, Olivia Hussey, Lynda Stoner, Michael Craig, Roger Ward,
Carmen Duncan, Noel Ferrier, Michael Petrovitch
Australia, 1982

What better introduction to 1980s splatter horror than this little piece of nastiness? Especially since it's also a nod to the 1970s exploitation cinema, as well as to the *Mad Max* series — hugely popular at that time, with two entries already made by 1983; plus it was directed by Brian Trenchard-Smith, a man just as familiar to the fans of today's lightweight TV productions (like 2003's *DC 9/11: Time of Crisis* and 2006's *Long Lost Son*), as he is to die-hard fans of the horror genre (he also directed 1986's *Dead-End Drive-In*, 1994's *Night of the Demons 2*, 1995's *Leprechaun 3*, and 1997's *Leprechaun 4: In Space*), and those who love the freakiest genre hybrids (Quentin Tarantino is known to be an enthusiast of Trenchard-Smith's debut feature *The Man from Hongkong* made in 1975 — a wild spoof of the James Bond films and martial arts cinema, starring George Lazenby).

Escape 2000 was originally conceived as a gorier version of *1984*, but things quickly started getting out of Trenchard-Smith's control: there appeared to be not enough money to film the highly important introductory scenes (ones that would present the *1984*-esque oppression people suffer in this particular vision of the future), Steve Railsback insisted on sticking to his method acting (not exactly an easy thing in a hurried, low-budget production), Lynda Stoner, to the director's great surprise, refused to do the obligatory nude scenes (in the end, a compromise was reached and the actress agreed to bare her bottom), and Olivia Hussey was not only traumatized by the intensity of the shoot but also almost severed Roger Ward's hands (misinterpreting the director's "Cut!" in a scene where her character wields a machete). Trenchard-Smith did his best to overcome all the difficulties and though he had to tear over a dozen pages out of the script, angered some members of his crew and after the movie's premiere suffered a serious critical bashing, he succeeded in making one of the best guilty pleasure movies ever.

"Excess is what makes life worth living," says one of the movie's characters at one point, and excess is precisely what you are going to get when watching *Escape 2000*. We quickly learn about the trivial reasons for three likable characters to be thrown into a truck and transported to a remote prison (they were all disobeying certain rules that apparently make up good, futuristic society), and since this moment they are subject to all sorts of cruelty; if it doesn't happen to them personally, it either happens to their friends or they themselves inflict it on the bad guys. Rape, machine gun massacre, limbs chopped off, an eye taken out with a piece of wood, machete to the head or zipper to the penis — nothing's quite too much for Trenchard-Smith. And the plot? Well, the characters we met at the beginning — Paul (Steve Railsback), Chris (Olivia Hussey) and Rita (Lynda Stoner) — join two other prisoners in a cruel game organized by the camp's boss Thatcher (Michael Craig), and have to avoid being killed by their hunters for as long as possible. The unwritten rule is that if the victims are not caught within 48 hours, they become free men. But can a group of five bare-handed unfortunates really out-smart a bunch of rich psychos with all kinds of fancy guns?

If you think the above plot sounds a bit too much like that of *Punishment Park* (1970), or its older characters-run-for-their-lives sibling *The Most Dangerous Game* (1932), you are not mistaken. Trenchard-Smith admits to these two movies being an influence, but it's impossible to say that *Escape 2000* lacks the director's personal touch. Actually, here's where the movie's greatest value is to be found. Trenchard-Smith's trade-mark soft spot for letting his actors improvise pays off wonderfully (watch out for some delicious, clearly heat-of-the-moment lines from Railsback, Craig, and the two cari-caturally obnoxious bad guys played by Roger Ward and Gus Mercurio), while the director's urge to be political turns the whole effort into a satire on totalitarianism — all the more controversial for the fact that it's about a society ruled by a strict and hyp-ocritical guy named Thatcher. In the early 1980s, mentioning this particular name couldn't go unnoticed — after all, Margaret Thatcher became British prime minister mere months earlier and the violent conflict in the Falklands was not resolved until 1982; in fact, *Escape 2000* was later renamed *Blood Camp Thatcher* for the benefit of its VHS release in the United Kingdom. And whether you choose to call such politi-cal statement heavy-handed or not, it sure helped the sales, especially in the U.K. Tren-chard-Smith himself agreed in an interview that the controversy and the fact that the film had been reflecting the feelings of many young people (with the camp's motto "Free-dom is obedience, obedience is work, work is life" reflecting the youth's deepest fears) were the main reasons for its success.

But if you ask the director which of his movies you should watch, he most prob-ably won't mention *Escape 2000*; the similarly themed but milder *Dead-End Drive-In* has a much better chance of being given as an example. And, even more strikingly, if you ask actress Lynda Stoner about the movie, she'll tell you it's a "putrid, puerile bunch of crap" (her own words from the revealing documentary *Blood and Thunder Memo-ries*). That's because *Escape 2000* is a trademark, no-holds-barred example of 1980s trash cinema. There's no guarantee you'll end up loving it, but, at the very least, you will experience a thrilling journey to the edge of the genre.

Whether you see *Escape 2000* as a dark comedy, sci-fi–horror, splatter movie or an homage to exploitation cinema with a political subtext, it's certainly a hard-to-for-get, highly controversial effort and a very good lesson in selling a movie to angry young people.

Swamp Thing

DIRECTOR: Wes Craven
CAST: Adrienne Barbeau, Dick Durock, Louis Jourdan, Ray Wise,
David Hess, Reggie Ball, Nicholas Worth
USA, 1982

We join an extravagant party where all male guests seem to be already drunk or drugged, and all female guests are more than willing to show their breasts to anyone

Alice Cable (Adrienne Barbeau) seduces the monster (Dick Durock) in Wes Craven's *Swamp Thing* (1982).

who asks them nicely. At one table sits an enormous man who sips wine with a self-satisfied smile. Everyone admires him, as apparently he did something worthwhile and is now celebrating his success. But when the man's glass empties, a strange thing occurs: to everyone's shock he falls to the floor and beyond our vision, and then suddenly emerges eerily metamorphosed, no longer a threatening giant but a very odd-looking dwarf. And soon after this, we get another — even weirder — mutation scene: this time a seemingly respectable gentleman transforms, in a ludicrously messy way, into what looks like a monstrous piece of meat; then the creature tears the meat-like shell away and reveals its true self: a rather laughable wolf-man who will soon go on to battle the movie's hero, the eponymous Swamp Thing. Yes, Wes Craven's adaptation of Len Wein and Bernie Wrightson's comic book surely is an entirely different monster than anyone could have expected.

It starts casually enough, though: Alice Cable (Adrienne Barbeau) is a government agent sent to the swampland laboratory of Dr. Alec Holland (Ray Wise), and as soon as the woman meets the famed scientist, she is smitten by him, witnesses the effects of his latest discovery (plants growing in impossible conditions) — and has no time to wave goodbye to him as a group of thugs enters the laboratory and knocks her unconscious. Dr. Holland accidentally drops the precious formula and since it's "like nitroglycerine" he immediately changes into a ball of fire, escapes the laboratory and leaps into the swamps. Now he is the Swamp Thing (Dick Durock), a powerful half-man half-plant whose mission is to save the formula stolen by the attackers, to get revenge on Arcane (Louis Jourdan), the man who ordered the snatch, and to free the abducted Alice.

A perfect adaptation of a comic book is a blast both for hardcore fans of the original and for those who never had a graphic novel in their hands. *Swamp Thing* is not that. Craven decided to change the overall mood (from somber to campy) and even the sex of a major character (the book's Cable is a man), which is enough to make the fans of the good old monster mad. Neither does Craven's adaptation have the mainstream appeal of such movies as Richard Donner's *Superman* (1978), Tim Burton's *Batman* (1989) and Sam Raimi's *Spider-Man* (2002), as it relies too much on comic book conventions (the unnatural colors, the stylized scene transitions), and contains some truly odd scenes (the aforementioned messy transformation of a man into a wolf-like creature being a standout). This is, however, precisely why *Swamp Thing* is today regarded as a cult classic: it's weird, it's unpredictable, it's definitely not for all tastes. But it is also bucketloads of fun for the initiated, no doubt about that.

Craven is a director known for the uneven quality of his works. Just after the success of *A Nightmare on Elm Street* (1984) he made the unbelievably bad *The Hills Have Eyes 2* (1995), and he followed the inventive *Scream* trilogy (1996–2000) with the laughable werewolf tale *Cursed* (2005). *Swamp Thing* is also quite often regarded as one of Craven's lows, but unlike *Hills 2* and *Cursed*, this movie is not a mistake but an indulgence — and anyone whose taste for craziness is even a bit like Craven's own will enjoy the movie a lot. In fact, there may be yet another way of looking at *Swamp Thing*: in a way it is a bold declaration of Craven's moviemaking independence, as it reshaped his directorial route and was a clear sign that he refused to be labeled as a guy who's here just to shock us (let's not forget that he gained the status of a cult director with his very first feature *The Last House on the Left* [1972]). Most probably if it weren't for *Swamp Thing* we would never get *A Nightmare on Elm Street*— at least not in the scary/surreal/sarcastic form we know today.

However, *Swamp Thing*'s appeal lies not just in the vast amount of quirkiness and in the fact that it's a proof for Craven's artistic courage. It's also a nostalgia ride for everyone who used to adore the monster movies of the 1950s, Jack Arnold's *Creature from the Black Lagoon* (1954) being the most obvious source of inspiration for Craven. These two monsters are similar to one another in many ways: they look alike, they evoke the same "beauty and the beast" theme, and they are a step away from being human — Swamp Thing used to be a man, while the Creature was to become a man in the second sequel, *The Creature Walks Among Us* (1956). But while the beast-to-man transformation in *The Creature Walks Among Us* was a criticism of the scientists' urge to subordinate nature to their own purposes, the man-to-beast transformation in *Swamp Thing* ascertains the scientists' right to play with nature (Dr. Holland's formula could help overcome the famine in the Third World countries) but warns against the possibility of the abuse of certain inventions if they are intercepted by madmen. Still, Craven prevented the movie from playing like a boring lecture: the creature's ill-fitting costume constantly reminds us of the campy nature of the whole affair, and the performances — ranging from emotional (Barbeau, Wise, Durock) to pleasantly eerie (Jourdan, David Hess, Reggie Ball)— provide enough soul and variety to keep us interested in the onscreen events.

Unfortunately, the movie's sequel, *The Return of Swamp Thing* (1989), didn't manage to retain the charm of the original. Director Jim Wynorski — soon to become a bad sequel expert by adding *Sorority House Massacre II* (1990), *Ghoulies IV* (1994) and five *Bare Wench Project* movies (2000–2005) to his CV — somehow convinced Jourdan and Durock to return to their roles, but his movie became much sillier than Craven's and lacked its predecessor's many oddities and emotional depth.

Swamp Thing is one of those bold comic book adaptations that strays one step too far away from the source and causes rage among those who loved the original version of the story. But there's charm to Wes Craven's movie that should attract the fans of 1950s monster movies, and the finale contains enough freakishness to make David Lynch smile.

Q — The Winged Serpent

DIRECTOR: Larry Cohen
CAST: Michael Moriarty, David Carradine, Richard Roundtree, Candy Clark,
Bruce Carradine, James Dixon
USA, 1982

"The Chrysler Building needs its own movie, so that it is immortalized like the Empire State Building was in *King Kong*," was the thought that inspired director Larry Cohen to make *The Winged Serpent* (later renamed *Q*), the story of an Aztec monster terrorizing the people of New York City. Cohen had just been fired from the Armand

Assante–starring drama *I, the Jury* and was determined to show the producers that getting rid of him was not such a bright idea. He chose a script that called for an expensive movie, spent on it a fraction of the *I, the Jury* budget, and eventually managed to prove his point rather well: *Q* and *I, the Jury* (directed by Richard T. Heffron) opened at the same time and it was Cohen's movie that gained much more critical acclaim and snared more ticket-buyers.

Contrary to what one may think, the main character of *Q* is not the winged creature preying on New Yorkers but a poor, jobless chap named Jimmy Quinn (Michael Moriarty). When he fails to get a job as a jazz pianist in a bar, Jimmy decides to join a gang of thugs and earn some money robbing a jewelry store. Unsurprisingly, the robbery goes wrong and our man soon ends up hiding from the police at the very top of the Chrysler Building. There he discovers the nest of a monster bird and this discovery is the luckiest one he could have made. First of all, the hungry monster will free him of the thugs who were blaming him for the loss of the robbery loot and followed him to his hideaway; secondly, as soon the police get hold of Jimmy, he can offer them a fair deal: if they let him go and pay him "a lousy million dollars," he will be kind enough to tell them where the monster bird dwells ... oh, and he will also get the exclusive rights to then report on the horrors of the NYPD fighting the incredible flying serpent. And since the NYPD guys are played by David Carradine and Richard Roundtree, one can guess the police vs. monster showdown will not be an easy win for the creature.

In almost all reviews of the movie, whether positive or negative, the most emphasized thing is the praise for Moriarty's acting. And it really is that good; at the same time crazy and believable, improvised and controlled, mesmerizing and irritating. The character of Jimmy Quinn must have seemed bland on the pages of the screenplay but Moriarty "acted him into existence," to paraphrase one of the movie's lines, and he seemingly did that with astonishing ease. The success of *Q* is therefore as much Moriarty's as Cohen's: Moriarty shocked all the critics by injecting a healthy dose of genius acting into what was an unashamedly simple monster movie, and Cohen was clever enough to let his actor do whatever he fancied — improvising certain lines, adding a scene where he could sing a song he himself composed and, most importantly, overshadowing all the other actors and the monster itself. It is terrifying to even think what would become of *Q* if Moriarty was replaced by Eddie Murphy, a move the director actually considered.

Apparently, Eddie Murphy is not all. Cohen once confessed that *Q* could have been as well an Eddie Murphy-Bruce Willis pairing, with the then-unknown Willis playing David Carradine's character. To be completely honest, however, I think losing Carradine would be a shame, too. He may not be a great actor but the role in *Q* is one of the best ones in his long career, perhaps due to the fact that here he has Moriarty to play against. The first scene between them wonderfully contrasts these two characters and two different ways of acting: Moriarty's character is playing the piano and singing in a bar hoping to get a job there but the owner clearly doesn't like the performance and promptly switches on the jukebox to give the man a hint he should leave. When Jimmy is heading for the door, Carradine's cop turns to him and says that he actually liked his short jazz improvisation; Jimmy looks cynically at the cop's friendly smile and crushes him with the unexpected "Yeah? And what the fuck do you know?" Cohen admits that Carradine was very nervous on the set but it certainly does not show in the movie; he seems self-assured and easy-going, a nice contrast to Moriarty's volcano of all possible emotions.

Then there is Richard Roundtree, a great actor very often wasted in poor roles, here playing the bad cop to Carradine's good one. When the latter is doing his best to understand Jimmy Quinn's scheme and help him get the deal with the police, so that the city can be saved from the claws of the monster, Roundtree's cop clearly despises Quinn and would rather torture the information out of him than pay the million dollars. Incredible tension between these two characters can be sensed in a scene where Roundtree's cop explains his point of view to Moriarty's character, at the same time putting his palm on the man's head, as if he wanted to crack it open but eventually decided to settle for massaging Moriarty's bald spot. The scene looks as if it was improvised by Roundtree; notice the surprise in Moriarty's eyes when Roundtree's huge hand lands on his head.

Moriarty has several impressive solo scenes here, too. A good example would be the one in which his character is trying to silence his conscience after he let the creature dine on his ex-partners in crime: the man is nervously talking to himself, explaining how he had no other choice but to sacrifice the thugs, and the viewer can actually feel for him here, no matter how annoying or deceitful he was just before that. Cohen is famous for having a way with actors, and this undoubtedly pays off here. He encouraged them to improvise, was constantly rewriting the script so that the roles fit them better, made them work at the heights of the real Chrysler Tower rather than in the studio, and he even got rid of the trailers and the production assistants in order to make the movie set more homey. One of Cohen's rules of good filmmaking is to never let an actor get bored on the set, and he achieved this by making all the actors an important part of the creative process. That is why, no matter how over-the-top *Q*'s plot summary may sound, the movie emanates realism untypical of Hollywood fare.

But even if acting is *Q*'s major strength, there are portions of the movie that electrify the viewer with the sheer beauty of Robert Levi and Fred Murphy's photography. The shot of the Chrysler Tower mirrored in the windows of the skyscraper opposite it; the shadow of the flying monster reflected on the buildings below; the moment when Jimmy Quinn suddenly faces a giant egg at the top of the tower — these are all unforgettable pieces that make *Q* one of the most handsome-looking monster movies ever, even if the monster itself is a rather disappointing tribute to the works of the great Ray Harryhausen.

Q is not, however, a cop movie with the monster in the background. It is without doubt a horror movie, one with effective jump scenes (for example, when the main character is startled by a pigeon in the tower) and some gore that was quite shocking at the time of the movie's original release; at one point, for instance, we see a man whose skin is being carefully removed from the body. (Cohen himself actually thinks he needn't have filled the film with so much violence — which is a surprising confession to be heard from a man who also gave us movies about cannibal babies and yogurts that eat you from the inside.) If, however, there is any important message hidden within this enjoyable little monster movie, it has much less impact than these from the director's other classics, like *It's Alive* (a metaphor for the fears of parenthood) or *The Stuff* (a critique of consumerism).

A rare monster movie in which the monster is not quite as important as the characters who keep trying to take it down. It's also one of the first movies to prove the acting genius of Michael Moriarty.

Sleepaway Camp

DIRECTOR: Robert Hiltzik
CAST: Felissa Rose, Jonathan Tiersten, Karen Fields, Christopher Collet,
Katherine Kamhi, Mike Kellin, Loris Sallahian, Tom Van Dell
USA, 1983

Whoever says that a good slasher movie has to be serious — they're terribly wrong. And there's more to the magic of this peculiar subgenre: a good slasher movie doesn't even have to be well-acted, believable or suspenseful. It's quite enough that it keeps you entertained, includes several good, violent set pieces, and leaves you shocked. Robert Hiltzik's *Sleepaway Camp* is a perfect example of such an effort. It's an exceptionally bad movie but a very good slasher.

While making the movie, Hiltzik was aiming to shock us out of our genre expectations and to create a portrayal of teenagers that would be more convincing than what usually ends up on screen in the case of pictures with a camp setting. He succeeded in both regards, even though at first all the main plot ideas seem to be by the numbers. The main character is Angela (Felissa Rose), a pretty, wide-eyed and extremely shy teenager who has problems making friends with her peers (and, to use a line of the film's dialogue as an additional description of the girl, she is also "a carpenter's dream: flat as a board and needs a screw"). Several years earlier Angela lost her father and brother in a strange accident on a lake and now Aunt Martha (Desiree Gould, playing the weirdest role of her life) is taking care of her. Spending some time at Camp Arawak could be a much needed escape from the tragic memories — and from the spooky aunt — but it appears that Angela is one ill-fated girl, as she winds up in one place with the most spiteful kids and adults who are either stupid, ignorant or perverted. Fortunately, there's gutsy cousin Ricky (Jonathan Tiersten) to keep Angela's company and defend her whenever possible, but it doesn't seem likely he could also deal with the brutal and inventive killer who starts stalking and slashing the campers.

Despite some bad acting, Hiltzik's teenagers are surprisingly realistic as they curse their way through the movie and display all the cruelty, malice and recklessness that only kids of that age are capable of. (Tiersten said in an interview that during the audition, the director was particularly interested in whether his child actors could improvise rude behavior.) This is the key to the movie's success, especially since Hiltzik is much more concerned with his teenage characters than most other directors of 1980s slasher flicks. While in *Friday the 13th* (1980), *Prom Night* (1980) and *The Burning* (1981) the kids were mostly bland victims who only needed to die nasty deaths for the story of an intriguing killer to be told, *Sleepaway Camp* elevates the kids to the position of the movie's mass protagonist and becomes a tricky metaphor of the unspeakable pains and anxieties of growing up. (Note that in an attempt at showing the true evils that await a teenager, the director didn't hesitate to bring up molestation in one of the film's most painful scenes; the acceptance of one's sexual identity is also a major theme here.) Even if Hiltzik also uses the well-worn idea of "mystery from the past" as the core of his plot, he makes an inventive use of it and doesn't let the movie turn into a simple tale of wrongdoing and revenge; after all, he has the blood-curdling final scene up his sleeve. The epiphanous ending brings *Sleepaway Camp* further away from the likes of *Friday the 13th* and closer to such 1980s "slashers with a twist" as *Happy Birthday to Me* (1981) and *April Fool's Day* (1986); but Hiltzik's movie goes even further than that: in this case the denouement doesn't just add a new dimension to everything we saw up to this point, but it pushes its way deep into our minds and stays there forever. Regardless of how enjoyable or clever the endings of *Happy Birthday to Me* and *April Fool's Day* were, they certainly weren't as powerful and overwhelming as the single wicked image that culminates *Sleepaway Camp*.

After the movie's relative success, Hiltzik allegedly wanted to prepare a worthy sequel, but after experiencing problems trying to get the movie made, he ended up selling his rights to it. In consequence, *Sleepaway Camp II: The Unhappy Campers* (1988) was helmed by Michael A. Simpson, and it went far off the original course: it did not tease the viewer to guess who is butchering all the campers (the identity of the killer is revealed at the very beginning of the movie), and it couldn't boast a similar shock-factor, but it sported several genuinely funny scenes and it cleverly reversed the message of the first film (this time each murder is accompanied by the villain's explanation of why the victims deserved their fate, which makes it almost a travesty of *Halloween* and *Friday the 13th*— movies which were said, not always rightly so, to employ killers as "a punishing hand of morality"). Another strength of the sequel was that it had the cheek to laugh at the clichés and icons of the genre — in one scene, Freddy Krueger, Jason Voorhees and Leatherface are jokingly brought together — even though it was often just as guilty of repetitiveness and predictability as the movies it mocked. Simpson made one more movie in the series (the 1989 *Sleepaway Camp III: Teenage Wasteland*, for the most part a copy of the first sequel; it is usually considered the weakest of all entries), and recently wrote a script for *Sleepaway Camp: Berserk*, which is promising an odder and more realistic movie than the previous two parts. Hiltzik also eventually decided to continue the story of his original characters in *Return to Sleepaway Camp* (2008; just as trashy, but not quite as enjoyable as the original) and *Sleepaway Camp Reunion* (scheduled for release in 2010). The completists may want to know that Jim Markowic's *Sleepaway Camp IV: The Survivor* (2002) is actually not a proper third sequel but a 30-minute collection of scenes from an unfinished movie.

This amateurish and seemingly innocuous slasher movie has such a wonderfully disturbing ending that there's a good chance you simply won't believe your eyes. Best watched back-to-back with the first sequel which doesn't care so much about shocking the viewer with the final twist but instead gives us a playful continuation of the original plot.

The Toxic Avenger

DIRECTORS: Lloyd Kaufman, Michael Herz
CAST: Mitch Cohen, Andree Maranda, Mark Torgl, Jennifer Prichard,
Robert Prichard, Pat Ryan, Dan Snow, Cindy Manion
USA, 1985

Starting around 1980, videotapes and video cassette recorders rapidly gained in popularity, and by the mid–1980s they were no longer just a novelty and a supplementary form of entertainment, but for many people, especially teenagers, they became a substitute for cinema-going. By 1985 it was also clear that the decade would belong to muscular heroes (Rambo, Conan and Superman all kept returning in successful sequels and didn't seem willing to stop anytime soon), as well as to meaty villains (Michael Myers of *Halloween* [1978], Jason Voorhees of *Friday the 13th* [1980] and Freddy Krueger of *A Nightmare on Elm Street* [1984] were all hugely popular and had a similar tendency to regularly return to the screens). Lloyd Kaufman and Michael Herz cleverly combined all the above box office-friendly features in *The Toxic Avenger*, a breakthrough movie for their independent studio Troma: it had a muscled, super-strong superhero who looked, and often behaved, too, like a most degenerate villain, plus the whole enterprise was targeted at the young, VCR-loving audiences.

One of the definitive movies to re-watch with a finger always near the PAUSE and REWIND buttons (without which the invention of home video wouldn't have been

The super-violent superhero is born: Mark Torgl in Troma's breakthrough movie, *The Toxic Avenger* (1985).

quite as revolutionary), *The Toxic Avenger* contains everything the rebellious 1980s youth could dream of: scenes of Rambo-inspired violence pushed to extremes, splatter moments prolonged to grotesque, laugh-inducing lengths, nudity to rival the immensely popular *Porky's* (1982), and bucketloads of bad taste jokes — enough of them to make sure that some would hit the mark. There is, however, something about the movie that makes it memorable even on the surface level: one can feel that the stupidity of the script is clearly intended and that it must have taken pretty intelligent people to come up with it, *and* many of the dumb lines are addictively quotable (starting with the opening narration, spoken in a very serious manner: "Every year, millions of gallons of poisonous wastes, garbage, and radioactive chemicals are disposed of in ... Tromaville, the toxic-waste-dumping capital of the world"). The plot is unexceptional but some fans of the genre may applaud its handy recycling of several themes popular at that time: Melvin (Mark Torgl) is a naïve, helpless kid humiliated by his peers (much like the main character in 1975's *Carrie*), which leads to a terrible accident (like in 1980's *Prom Night*). Melvin doesn't die but is now the disfigured, super-strong and obsessively vengeful Toxie (Mitch Cohen) (quite similar to *Friday the 13th*'s Jason). What follows boils down to extremely bloody carnage as Toxie fights crime on the streets of Tromaville, and there's just the right amount of weird love story added to the mix when the good monster falls for blind and beautiful Sara (Andree Maranda).

The presence of a unique hero/villain, the wild plot and the readiness to offend quickly made *The Toxic Avenger* a must-see title among teenagers, but underneath it all there was another reason for the movie's lasting success; *yes*, I do remember we are talking about a Troma movie here, and —*yes* again — what I mean here is that there is some kind of a *message* here. It is not, however, the tongue-in-cheek ecological subtext ("Be *extra careful* when storing the toxic waste!"), nor is it the well-worn metaphor of teenage angst allegedly embodied in the character of Toxie (it's highly improbable that many teenagers would truly empathize with such an extraordinary loser as Melvin, Toxie's human alter ego). The message behind *The Toxic Avenger* is simple but persuasive: forget about all the soulless blockbusters and start looking for movies that are labors of love and don't surrender to political correctness. The very fact that an anti-blockbuster like *The Toxic Avenger* could be made and could then grow to become a success were good credentials to support the message; Kaufman then backed it further with his two books: *All I Needed to Know About Filmmaking I Learned from The Toxic Avenger* (written with James Gunn in 1998) and *Make Your Own Damn Movie: Secrets of a Renegade Director* (written with Adam Jahnke and Trent Haaga in 2003) in which he praises independent cinema and encourages his fans to follow his example. For anyone acquainted with Kaufman's books, it will be hard to perceive his movies simply as vehicles for controversy and cheap laughs — and *The Toxic Avenger*, scorning human dependency on religion or the compulsion to meet the expectations of others, is a very honest suggestion that we break from the many chains of everyday life. And the film happens to be clever in pointing out the hypocrisy and inconsistency of people who try to do everything "just right"; for example, there's an amusing scene with two bad guys doing sit-ups and sharing a cigarette at the same time; apparently, that's what you end up with when trying to be both healthy and cool.

"Then, two rotten sequels were made. Sorry about that..." says the narrator at the beginning of *Citizen Toxie: Toxic Avenger IV* (2000), before proclaiming the new movie "the real sequel." And, truth be told, Part IV actually *is* the best *Toxic Avenger* sequel to date. It's also the bloodiest, craziest and most offensive of all four films, plus it is based on the most complex concept the Troma people have ever come up with (Philip K. Dick–style, Toxie accidentally enters a parallel universe, and has to battle the Evil Toxie from Amortville). Superficially, it's all just unpretentious fun, but somewhere inside there are shreds of a surprisingly poignant message scattered. To find a good example of it, please pay attention to the hilarious media coverage of the Tromaville massacre, with two doppelganger presenters doing their best to put the blame for it on everyone but their own TV people who unashamedly relish and exploit the tragedy.

The two other sequels, *The Toxic Avenger II* (1989) and *The Toxic Avenger III: The Last Temptation of Toxie* (1989), are not quite as "rotten" as described in the intro to *Citizen Toxie*, either. They are, however, a clear departure from the horror genre. The traces of suspense and dark atmosphere from the original are gone, and even Toxie's makeup became here more obviously rubbery and much less scary and revolting than in Part I or Part IV. Still, if you just look for another dose of Troma trademark weirdness and/or want to see a movie that has nothing to do with political correctness for a change, you can't say these two sequels don't deliver.

This cheap, outrageous, disgusting, violent and offensive little film is not just great fun (or at least a bona fide guilty pleasure), it's also a political statement: Kaufman and Herz insist we stop listening to others and start watching — or perhaps even making — movies shaped to our own damn liking.

Bad Taste

DIRECTOR: Peter Jackson
CAST: Peter Jackson, Craig Smith, Terry Potter, Pete O'Herne,
Doug Wren, Mike Minett
New Zealand, 1987

Peter Jackson's feature debut *Bad Taste* is often given as an example of a successful independent quickie that stands in contrast to his later, elaborate, big-budget movies. But while the budget on *Bad Taste* was admittedly very low, the whole thing certainly wasn't a quick and easy exercise in amateur filmmaking. The shooting lasted for about four years and throughout the whole period Jackson was busy preparing the special effects, gory makeup, latex prosthetics and all kinds of props, as well as designing camera rigs that would let him film the story in a more energetic way. (This worked very well here and later became the director's trademark: because of the way he learned to handle the camera, all his subsequent movies feel so impressively alive.) Apart from all this, Jackson also had to be ready to perform schizophrenic acting duties whenever there was enough money to shoot the scenes. He appears here as two distinct characters, clean-shaven Derek and bearded Robert.

Derek, an employee of Astro Investigation and Defense Service ("Wish we'd change that name," complains another character, unhappy about the acronym of the name being AIDS), was sent to Kaihoro, New Zealand, to investigate the mysterious disappearance of the town residents. "The Boys," Barry (Pete O'Herne), Ozzy (Terry Potter) and Frank (Mike Minett), are there to help him. The group soon encounters some unfriendly, human-shaped aliens. Initially, the humans do surprisingly well fighting the visitors from space, and Derek even manages to capture an alien prisoner — the bearded Robert — and torture him a little; however, the counter-attack is fierce and in the end Derek falls from a cliff to scatter his brains all over a seagull's nest. Obviously, this won't stop him from doing his job: he stuffs the brains back, wears a hat to hold them in place and is promptly back in the game. Now the plan is to get to the aliens' main quarters, infiltrate them, save a kidnapped charity collector (Craig Smith) and, well, kill as many aliens as possible, be it with the machine guns or a chainsaw. Things get violent and the creatures shed their human masks to show their true, grotesque rubber faces.

The movie owes as much to Sam Raimi's *The Evil Dead* (1982) as it does to the skits and comedies of Monty Python, but all in all there was no movie similar to *Bad Taste* before it. Jackson puts all the '80s favorite themes — commandos, ninjas, crazy action set pieces and offbeat humor — in a horror–sci-fi blender and then shapes the outcome according to his own theories on what makes cinema entertaining. The desolate New Zealand setting adds to the experience, too, giving *Bad Taste* a distinguished feel and helping create the atmosphere of otherworldliness and abandonment. And, of course, Jackson turns out to be a talented makeup and special effects man: the movie would certainly *not* have become famous if it weren't for the grisly and convincing scenes of brains falling out, human heads being severed in half and the like; all this done by the director himself, with a little help from makeup assistant Cameron Chittock and Jackson's mother who hardened all the latex masks in her oven.

Bad Taste's assets as a genre curio aside, the movie seems to have also put New Zealand, Jackson's home country, on the filmmaking map. Laurence Simmons notices in *The Cinema of Australia and New Zealand* that *Bad Taste* is "peppered with sideglances to such New Zealand icons and institutions as sheep, chainsaws, charity collectors and 'mateship,'" while Harmony H. Wu argues in *Defining Cult Movies: The Cultural Politics of Oppositional* that *Bad Taste* and Jackson's two later movies not only promoted New Zealand's landscapes and peculiar customs, but completely changed the country's image in the eyes of the world. "When the squarely Hollywood-centric trade paper *Variety* explicitly labels Jackson 'kiwi,'" writes Wu, "the rhetorical gesture brands not only the director but also New Zealand itself as 'gore-meisters' in the imaginations of industry insiders, critics and consumers." The author then states that the "inscription of Jackson and New Zealand as purveyors of horror, splatter, bad taste and gore develops out of and reinforces an international perception of New Zealand as an off-kilter land with strange and dark obsessions," an image to be perpetuated in Sam Neill and Judy Rymer's informative documentary *Cinema of Unease* (1995). In effect, argues Wu, the cultism of *Bad Taste* (and Jackson's other movies) turns out to be contagious and spreads throughout the whole country that produced it, which is itself "genrified" and "figured as cult object, a site where kooky perspectives and horrific bad taste can be reliably found."

In his next two films, Jackson was apparently trying to improve his *Bad Taste* formula. It didn't quite work in case of *Meet the Feebles* (1989), which was, in essence, *The Muppet Show* with sex, violence and swearing. Funny, but neither crazier nor more shocking than his debut. The zombie extravaganza *Braindead* (1992; aka *Dead Alive*), on the other hand, became Jackson's goriest calling card and introduced him to the pantheon of horror directors. It was a shock, therefore, to find out that his next effort was *Heavenly Creatures* (1994), a dramatic tale of friendship between two teenage girls; even there Jackson squeezed in some great special effects and the two lead actresses (Kate Winslet and Melanie Lynskey) were very good, but a trademark Jackson piece of cinema this wasn't. His return to horror with *The Frighteners* (1996) was another disappointment; sure, the effects were fine and it was a treat to see Michael J. Fox in an atypical role, but the meanness and weirdness of the director's early films was mostly gone and what the audience got was no more than an enjoyable mainstream horror. Even though *The Frighteners* was no box office scorcher, someone somewhere decided that Jackson would be the right person to adapt J.R.R. Tolkien's *The Lord of the Rings*, invested several hundred million dollars in the project — and since then the director has been stuck in the high-budget cinema. Which is, on one hand, a good thing — after all, *The Lord of the Rings* trilogy (2001–2003) was an unforgettable experience and the *King Kong* remake (2005) was pure fun — while on the other hand, it doesn't leave much hope for Jackson descending back to the gory underground any time soon. (Although he occasionally does mention his willingness to do this in interviews, and allegedly has some ideas for *Bad Taste 2* and *3*.)

Peter Jackson didn't just jump to blockbusting success with the *Lord of the Rings* trilogy and the *King Kong* remake from out of nowhere. *Bad Taste* was his first step towards a filmmaking career and — sick and noncommercial as the movie is — it shows that Jackson surely had *some* kind of directorial talent in him.

Killer Klowns from Outer Space

DIRECTOR: Stephen Chiodo
CAST: Suzanne Snyder, Grant Cramer, John Allen Nelson, John Vernon,
Peter Licassi, Michael Siegel
USA, 1988

Don't ever underestimate the power of a killer clown. Residents of a small American town did and look what happened to them: they were promptly paralyzed with toy laser guns and changed into cotton candy cocoons to satisfy the hunger of the cosmic intruders. The Earth's only hope are blonde cutie Debbie (Suzanne Snyder), her boyfriend Mike (Grant Cramer) and a police officer — coincidentally, Debbie's ex-boyfriend — Dave (John Allen Nelson). The three are hardly heroes (Mike doesn't seem to have a three-digit IQ, Dave takes his time before he starts believing something is wrong, and Debbie spends a large portion of the movie relaxing in a shower), but they are certainly better defenders of the planet than the tough-looking officer Mooney (John Vernon), who honestly thinks that all calls about the invasion of killer clowns are part of an unfunny joke being played on him. The clowns act quickly, though, and soon the majority of the townfolk end up in pink cocoons. The viewer is observing the main characters' panicky attempts at doing something to resist the attack and wonders, with some seriousness, "What would *I* do in a similar situation?"

Or perhaps not. Stephen Chiodo's movie is an unashamed guilty pleasure, one that doesn't try to pretend it was in fact done by Ingmar Bergman and that it requires a lot of thinking. It does, however, require some cinematic knowledge. And it is not enough to be a horror expert to fully enjoy *Killer Klowns from Outer Space*. Stephen Chiodo (together with his brothers, Edward and Charles, who co-wrote and co-produced the movie) is as happy to pay tribute to *The Blob* or the *Godzilla* movies, as he is to riff on *The Wizard of Oz* and the comedy of *Looney Tunes* and Laurel and Hardy.

But anyone who expects *Killer Klowns* to be a simple parody — whether a parody of horror or a multi-genre parody — will most probably be disappointed. The Chiodo brothers don't aim here at imitating as many cinematic set pieces and techniques as possible, but they rather try to squeeze a record number of laughs and thrills out of their very own, very weird concept — the idea of oversized clowns annihilating the human race. The fact that the plot occasionally reminds us of classic horror movies and the laughs bring to mind classic comedies is no more than a pleasant side effect. Some critics are perhaps too trustful of the Chiodo brothers' not-so-serious comments on their own work, and this leads to labeling the movie a parody. But is it really possible to believe the Chiodos when they deadpan that in a scene with mini-clowns bursting out of the toilet, they "wanted to do for toilets what Alfred Hitchcock did for showers"? Certainly not. The scene is nothing like Hitchcock's famous scene from *Psycho* and the Chiodo brothers are hardly the horror-oriented Zucker brothers (of *Airplane!* and *The Naked Gun* fame), which is a good thing, in fact: if *Killer Klowns* was a straightforward horror parody, it would never have made it onto so many lists of Best Cult Horror Movies.

Another often overlooked fact is that the movie includes several genuinely scary moments, the best one being the scene where a major character is killed and then used by a clown as a creepy ventriloquist dummy. The victim's makeup (that likens him to a clown), the overall atmosphere of the scene (the uncertainty about the clown's intentions) and the horror sound effects (when the clown takes his hand out of the man's body and shakes the blood off it) all authenticate the Chiodo brothers' intentions to give us something more than a forgettable horror-comedy. The characterization of the clowns (crooked yellow teeth, insane look, their monstrous size) and the surprisingly elaborate set design (great, otherworldly matte paintings, and dreamlike, candy-colored interiors of the clowns' space-tent) are yet another sign that no matter how frivolous the movie they were making, the brothers certainly approached the whole project with astonishing seriousness. The budget for *Killer Klowns* was by no means gargantuan — just look at cartoonish laser gun effects here and there — but whatever money there was, was spent cleverly. Also, it's quite unusual for a movie with such a far-out title to be, for the most part, acted in a poker-faced manner, with no winking and no tongue-in-cheek. Okay, so John Vernon clearly enjoys his caricatural role of a grouchy police officer, but the trio of Snyder, Cramer and Nelson play it straight, as if they were really in a most austere remake of *Invasion of the Body Snatchers*.

That the Chiodo brothers have talent, determination and love for cinema could already be glimpsed in *The Beast from the Egg*—an amusing, Ray Harryhausen–influenced short that the siblings shot in their teens to a bewilderment of their unsuspecting parents. *Killer Klowns from Outer Space* was the finest cult moment of the Chiodos, but it wasn't their only foray into the genres of horror, sci-fi and comedy: throughout the years, they were helping to create the furry little monsters in *Critters* (1986), took care of the stop-motion sequences in the Philip K. Dick adaptation *Screamers* (1995), and gave us the love-making and vomiting puppets in Trey Parker's crazy *Team America: World Police* (2004).

Known for being one of the funniest Ed Wood–style movies ever, *Killer Klowns from Outer Space* is not as inherently bad as could be expected (the laughs are all intentional and the sets look surprisingly good), but it's yet another proof that best horror-comedies are made by people who love the genre and don't have too much money.

Night of the Demons

DIRECTOR: Kevin S. Tenney
CAST: Cathy Podewell, Amelia Kinkade, Billy Gallo, Linnea Quigley,
Lance Fenton, Hal Havins, Jill Terashita, Don Jeffcoat
USA, 1988

"Angela is having a party, Jason and Freddy are too scared to come. But you'll have a hell of a time." In the late 1980s, the tagline for *Night of the Demons* sounded bold and enthralling but the idea might have backfired had the movie been a weaker offering. Just four years had passed since the premiere of the original *A Nightmare on Elm Street* (1984), and the *Friday the 13th* franchise had already grown to impressive proportions (with *Part VII: The New Blood* coming out in 1988), so most fans of the genre perhaps weren't glad to hear that their two favorite villains were, in fact, pathetic cowards. But director Kevin S. Tenney delivered the horror goods aplenty, and soon *Night of the Demons* gained a group of followers as ardent — though not as numerous — as those who were supporting the movies with Freddy and Jason.

The tone of Tenney's movie is set when the director introduces us to one of the characters — the seductive, dressed-in-pink Suzanne (Linnea Quigley) — via an indecent close-up of her bottom as she is stooping to reach a low shelf in a store, and then has her ask the two clerks still mesmerized by what they saw, if they have "sour balls." And before you say "That's gratuitous!" and "Bad taste!," let me add that, in fact, Tenney has a rather good excuse for setting the scene like that: Suzanne's sexy pose was, it turns out, just a distraction, so that her friend Angela (Amelia Kinkade) can steal some provisions for a Halloween party the two girls are about to host. The party takes place in an allegedly possessed — not *haunted*, mind you — Hull House, somewhere on the outskirts of the town. Among the invited youths are kind-hearted blonde Judy (Cathy Podewell), her handsome but not overly faithful boyfriend Jay (Lance Fenton), and wild and irritating Stooge (Hal Havins). As soon as the gates of Hull House close behind the last visitor, the demons that own the place get ready to take over all the young bodies within the premises.

Without trying to hide the obvious *Evil Dead* influences, *Night of the Demons* forces us to guess who's got the best chances of surviving the party and what's going to happen to the unlucky ones. Owing to the combined talent of Tenney and his crew, the movie's derivativeness soon ceases to be a problem. The energetic synth soundtrack by Dennis Michael Tenney (Kevin's brother) grabs us immediately and perfectly fits the animated opening credits, David Lewis' photography makes the most of the creepy house sequences (Tenney even claims that *Night of the Demons* is his best-looking film to date), and the makeup and special effects supervised by Steve Johnson are still a treat. The movie is filled with censor-baiting scenes, the most infamous being the lipstick vs. nipple, razors ripping through the throat, the lesbian kiss, the tongue being bitten off, and Angela's demonic dance to Bauhaus' "Stigmata Martyr." The acting is far from perfect but for

Linnea Quigley in the infamous breast scene from Kevin Tenney's *Night of the Demons* (1988) (photograph by Edwin Santiago).

some reason it doesn't spoil the magic of the movie and, to the contrary, often increases the movie's anti-mainstream appeal. Plus, believe it or not, this gory and frantic effort is deep inside a reassuring tale of the power of friendship: apparently, the only effective weapon against demons.

Night of the Demons established Tenney's position in the horrormaking world, and also kicked several careers into gear, most notably those of Linnea Quigley and Steve Johnson. Quigley had already been quite noticeable in Dan O'Bannon's *The Return of the Living Dead* (1985), but after Tenney's film she became one of the genre's most wanted actresses, playing in such "guilty pleasure" horror movies as *Witchtrap* (1989, directed by Tenney), *Blood Nasty* (1989) and — an acquired taste, this — *Mari-Cookie and the Killer Tarantula in 8 Legs to Love You* (1998). Johnson, on the other hand, made several B-grade horrors but ended up in the mainstream and worked on such films as *Species* (1995), *Eraser* (1996), *Blade II* (2002) and *War of the Worlds* (2005).

Tenney's demons didn't return until the 1990s. Brian Trenchard-Smith directed

Here be the demons: the fiery finale of *Night of the Demons* (photograph by Edwin Santiago).

the first sequel in 1994 ("Angela's throwing another party ... Trick or Treat, Suckers," the tagline read this time), and even though for the most part he simply reused the original storyline, he did manage to resurrect the spirit of the first movie. Tenney himself wrote the script for Jim Kaufman's 1996 *Night of the Demons III* but the movie wasn't received as well as the previous two, perhaps because it added too many then-modern computer effects that changed the overall mood a bit. (It should be said that ultimately Kaufman's effort was not a bad continuation of the Hull House saga: the script was more twist-oriented than before, the young actors were quite convincing in their often tricky roles, and Amelia Kinkade was at her most alluring there. Unfortunately, the once cheeky tagline degenerated into the bland "You Can Check In Anytime You Like, But You Can Never Leave...") But even if for most viewers the third part was a letdown, the *Night of the Demons* trilogy remains the most recognizable horror series with a female creature at the center. Tenney's pre–*Night of the Demons* horror movie, *The Witchboard* (1986), also turned into a franchise, albeit not one quite as cherished: *Witchboard 2: The Devil's Doorway* (1993), scripted and directed by Tenney, was a disappointment, and *Witchboard III: The Possession* (1995), directed by Peter Svatek from the script that Tenney helped write, was a bomb (though certain portions of each sequel are quite attractive and engaging).

With *Night of the Demons*, director Kevin S. Tenney reminded us that the 1980s horror movies should be crazy, perverse and inventive. Topping more popular horror franchises in those respects — especially in being perverse — was one of Tenney's greatest achievements, and another one was bringing to life the world's most famous horror series centered on a female villain.

Society

DIRECTOR: Brian Yuzna
CAST: Billy Warlock, Devin DeVasquez, Ben Slack, Connie Danese,
Patrice Jennings, Evan Richards, Tim Bartell, Charles Lucia, Pamela Matheson
USA, 1989

"Money and power-driven Hollywood, frequently but quite erroneously characterized as a hot-bed of liberalism, contributed to the nation's mood swing to a new conservatism, with mainstream commercial cinema of the 1980s elaborating on many of the ideas and ideals being expounded from the White House," wrote Angie Errigo in her essay depicting the decade ("The Reagan Years" in *Cinema Year by Year*). "Family-oriented spectacles, gung-ho action and escapism became the staples of the screen. Social comment, and themes dealing with that which was ugly, threatening or cautionary were, for the most part, left to independent filmmakers or the impressively emerging Third World cinema." Among these independent filmmakers were also ones working within the horror genre, like John Carpenter (*The Thing*, 1982), Tobe Hooper (*Poltergeist*, 1982), Frank Henenlotter (*Basket Case*, 1982), David Cronenberg (*Videodrome*, 1983), Wes Craven (*Invitation to Hell*, 1984), George A. Romero (*Day of the Dead*, 1985), and Larry Cohen (*The Stuff*, 1985); they all contributed movies that touched upon poignant contemporary issues or were at least depicting the 1980s in the typical-for-the-genre, no-holds-barred style. Near the end of the decade, the group was joined by Brian Yuzna in whose shocking debut feature *Society*, the critique of the American dream of becoming ever richer and aspiring to a higher status is hidden beneath layers of gross makeup and special effects.

Reality turns into a nightmare for teenage Billy Whitney (Billy Warlock) when he discovers the rotten truth about his family. It appears that his beautiful sister Jenny (Patrice Jennings) is having an incestuous threesome with their parents (Connie Danese and Charles Lucia) and, to make matters even worse, they are all shape-shifting creatures who plan to do something *weird* to Billy. The problem is, no one wants to believe the boy — neither his psychologist (Ben Slack), nor the police. And it's hard to blame them, too, as there's no hard evidence to prove that Billy is not imagining the whole thing: a revealing tape, for example, miraculously changes its content when Billy wants to use it to prove his point. Amidst the confusion and multiplying conspiracy theories, the teenager meets Clarissa (Devin DeVasquez), the girl of his dreams ("How do you like your tea?" she asks on their first date, "Cream, sugar — or do you want me to pee in it?"), but it's not easy to focus on his love life in such circumstances. And even less so when people around him start turning up dead, and it is revealed that the boy's parents belong to some sort of a snobbish "society" and are preparing for a mysterious ritual. This spells trouble for Billy, who's been told before that he would "make a wonderful contribution to society"— but clearly not as its member.

It is telling that *Society* takes place in Beverly Hills among super-rich kids who don't want anything from life but to be as successful as their parents; the parents, on the other hand, are constantly looking for more perverse ways of entertaining themselves and for new ways to exploit the poor. Billy feels that he is different from his family and other people around him because, unlike them, he cares for friendship and loyalty more than he does for money or status. This makes the message of Yuzna's movie very similar to the anti-consumerism of Cohen's earlier *The Stuff*, in which a young boy discovers that he is different from the rest of his family as their bodies have been taken over by an alien life-form disguised as a popular dessert. Of course, the problem with *Society*, especially in the United States, was that too many viewers identified with Billy's parents rather than with Billy himself (allegedly, even the studio that released the movie was disgusted with it). This is how Yuzna evaluates his movie's success in Europe that stood in contrast to the reception in America, where — to quote the director — it was thought to be "a big joke," and was not released until 1992: "I think Europeans are more willing to accept the ideas that are in a movie.... I was totally having fun with them, but they are there nonetheless." The ideas in question concerned not just the critique of a success-oriented society, but apparently also the application of Jean Baudrillard's concept of simulacra — "the most extreme example of how we all look at things differently," according to Yuzna; in the movie, Billy slowly arrives at a Baudrillardian conclusion that the reality he's been living in is just an artificial façade: in the end, he will have to choose whether he should conform to the newly discovered rules of the "real society" (which would involve no effort on Billy's part — just sacrificing his old self), or whether he should put up a fight and keep on living in the "dream society," the rules of which he had learned to accept.

Before debuting as a director with *Society*, Yuzna became known in horror circles as a producer of three films helmed by Stuart Gordon: *Re-Animator* (1985; still one of the best adaptations of H.P. Lovecraft's prose, even if it's not very faithful), *From Beyond* (1986; also based on Lovecraft's short story) and *Dolls* (1989). Yuzna's later directorial efforts were always characteristically grotesque, but his fondness for multiplying shocks and gruesome special effects was often obscuring the content, like in *The Dentist 2* (1998), *Rottweiler* (2004) and *Beneath Still Waters* (2005). *Society* remains his best work, but *Bride of Re-Animator* (1990), *Silent Night, Deadly Night 4: Initiation* (1990), *The Dentist* (1996) and *Beyond Re-Animator* (2003) are all worthwhile and appropriately nasty pieces of horror. Special effects man Screaming Mad George, who prior to *Society* worked on such movies as *Big Trouble in Little China* (1986) and *A Nightmare on Elm Street* parts 3 (1987) and 4 (1988), became Yuzna's regular collaborator and provided some ghoulish makeup and visual tricks for *Bride of Re-Animator, Silent Night, Deadly Night 4: Initiation, Necronomicon* (1993; a hit-and-miss anthology based on stories by Lovecraft that Yuzna directed with Christophe Gans and Shusuke Kaneko), *Faust: Love of the Damned* (2001) and *Beyond Re-Animator*.

A reckless gore-comedy? A brutal attack on the *nouveau riche* society? Or perhaps the weirdest-ever utilization of Baudrillardian concepts for horror purposes? That Brian Yuzna's directorial debut raises such questions already speaks in its favor, plus it has one of the craziest and most disgusting endings in movie history.

PART V:
THE NEW WEIRDNESS

Begotten

DIRECTOR: E. Elias Merhige
CAST: Brian Salzberg, Donna Dempsey, Stephen Charles Barry
USA, 1991

Begotten, E. Elias Merhige's puzzling black-and-white feature debut, is often called "the weirdest movie ever" or at the very least "the strangest thing since David Lynch's *Eraserhead*." But while it certainly is a very peculiar piece of work, *Begotten* lacks the power, shock value and depth of Lynch's mesmerizing first feature.

"Whatever happened to Search and Discovery in the arts of today? Artists must behave like archaeologists if the guts of visionary filmmaking can happen. They will have to return to the depths of the collective unknown to find out what we're all about. From that universal dream our most individual and forceful voices can emerge." This mission statement from Merhige, voiced on the occasion of the movie's much-anticipated DVD release is no doubt praiseworthy, except it is impossible to agree that *Begotten* adheres to much of it.

The movie is a succession of sequences that make us *suspect* that we see that something very unpleasant is happening to a strange trio of characters. Merhige went to great lengths to ensure that whatever is happening onscreen is hardly recognizable (apparently, the postproduction took over eight hours for one minute of the film to achieve that effect), but still there are several fairly clear images left and they add up to what substitutes for a conventional plot. First we see a man in white bandages madly slashing at his belly with a razor; all we hear is his muffled panting, drops of liquid hitting the floor and, most nauseously, the sound of the razor cutting through flesh. As the minutes pass, we see the same character digging deeper and deeper into his body; the pool of blood under his feet widens, then the innards come splashing down, one grisly piece after another, and then, when the slashing finally stops, chunks of black goo join the pile of guts, and we guess the man has died. Merhige's visual poem on the gruesomeness of death and bodily functions continues as a woman is born out of the bloodied carcass, gets pregnant, gives birth to a sorry, humanlike creature, and then.... But this perhaps would be giving the ending away — whether it matters in the case of a movie of this type or not. A small epiphany is hidden within the final credits; only then do we learn that the razor-wielding man was "God Killing Himself," the woman was "Mother Earth" and her son was, naturally, "Son of Earth — Flesh on Bone."

Seeing his movie being referred to as "the weirdest ever" in a string of reviews, Merhige must have felt extremely proud; after all, this was exactly what he was aiming at: to make a movie that's different than anything cinema experienced so far, and to get the attention of the critics and the audience alike. Even he must have been surprised, though, at writer Susan Sontag's prompt endorsement of *Begotten* as "one of the ten most important films of modern times" or *Time* magazine's decision to put it on the esteemed list of 10 Best Pictures of 1991. Richard Corliss, a staff reviewer at *Time*, explained that when watching the movie, one feels "as if a druidical cult had re-enacted, for real, three Bible stories — creation, the Nativity and Jesus' torture and death on Golgotha — and some demented genius was there to film it."

Corliss' statement might sound "spot on" to those viewers who have just watched the movie's spellbinding trailer or perhaps to those who didn't yet have time to get past the five-minute mark in the movie. The beginning of *Begotten* really promises a gutsy and unconventional spectacle, but the promise fades away around the time when God successfully kills Himself, and we are left with an arrhythmic parade of unsettling images, occasionally interrupted with equally unclear scenes of violence. If only Merhige had taken better care of the editing and pacing of his movie, he might have come up with a very creepy short; as it is, *Begotten* is a nightmare that lasts much too long, so that when we wake up, our major concern is not the memory of how frightening it was, but rather that we wasted too much time dreaming it.

Many comparisons have also been made between the aesthetics of *Begotten* and that of the experimental rock–heavy metal videos so popular in the late 1980s and early 1990s (mostly because of the rise of MTV at that time), but this analogy doesn't sound like much of a compliment for what Merhige prearranged as mysterious and poignant. Whoever honestly thinks that a music video should last around 80 minutes and feature no music whatsoever, may consider *Begotten* their kind of movie.

The controversy of the movie's depth and quality aside, *Begotten* no doubt opened for Merhige several doors to serious filmmaking business. Demonic musician Marilyn Manson was so overwhelmed with the movie, after he had rented it by accident, that he quickly found Mehrige and asked him to direct one of his videos (for the song "Anti-Christ Superstar" in 1996). Then along came Nicolas Cage, also highly impressed with *Begotten*, and handed to Merhige a screenplay for a fictionalized documentary on the shooting of F.W. Murnau's *Nosferatu*, called *Shadow of the Vampire*. Overall, the movie was not very convincing and, like *Begotten*, suffered from serious pacing problems, while the depiction of actor Max Schreck as a real vampire was rather naïve; but it sported some extraordinary cinematography, makeup and acting (it received Oscar nominations for Best Supporting Actor, Willem Dafoe starring as Schreck, and for Best Makeup). This allowed Merhige to take on an even more expensive project: a dark, twisted thriller, *Suspect Zero* (2004; starring Aaron Eckhart, Ben Kingsley and Carrie-Anne Moss), that was a bit too weird for wide audiences and much too conventional for the die-hard fans of *Begotten*. It seems, though, as if the director's drive towards filmmaking hasn't changed much since his bewildering debut. In one of the interviews after the premiere of *Suspect Zero*, he said: "I want to bring people to a higher ground, I don't want to just take people to dark places and leave them there, because CNN can do that." He's still ambitious then, and still can deliver movies with a healthy amount of eccentricity, but the greatest challenge in his career would be trying to find a balance between the surface beauty of *Shadow of the Vampire* and the raw magnetism of the otherwise incomprehensible and self-indulgent *Begotten*.

At first, *Begotten* is compellingly weird and genuinely frightening, but after some time it becomes overlong, repetitive and uninvolving. Watch the trailer for a much better effect.

Benny's Video

DIRECTOR: Michael Haneke
CAST: Arno Frisch, Angela Winkler, Ulrich Müche, Ingrid Stassner,
Hanspeter Müller, Paulus Manker, Wolfgang Böck
Austria-Switzerland, 1992

Just like Merhige's *Begotten*, Haneke's *Benny's Video* is designed to shock and it, too, prolongs certain tough-to-watch scenes to the point of unbearableness. The difference between Merhige and Haneke is, however, that the latter knows how to use violence without making it gratuitous, his playing with the viewers' patience is always very carefully measured out, and he adorns his movies with a suspenseful, mesmerizing rhythm.

Benny's Video opens with a scene of a pig being shot. The animal doesn't die right away, it goes on squeaking and wriggling on the ground, with the unrelenting camera zooming in on it, as if trying to capture all its pain and suffering. And if this scene was hard for you to take in, you will have to be prepared for some more of it, as the movie's main character, Benny (Arno Frisch), rewinds the tape and treats himself to another closely scrutinized viewing. Benny is a young boy, very proud of the expensive TV-VCR set his parents (Angela Winkler, Ulrich Müche) bought him, and immersing himself in video violence is his daily ritual. The pig-slaughtering, excerpts from *The Toxic Avenger* and other movies from his collection flicker on the TV screen from the moment he wakes up until he goes to sleep. Benny also owns a video camera, and when one day he invites a girl (Ingrid Stassner) to his house, we expect he might be tempted to make his own violent movie, with the unsuspecting girl in the leading role.

Haneke takes this simple premise and stretches it masterfully, so that it brings forth events and emotions we would have never anticipated. Benny's relationship with the parents turns out to be much more complex than it was initially suggested; the parents themselves aren't quite as predictable as they might have seemed at first; and the conclusion is another eye-opener, after we've been misled that it may all end in a relatively traditional and logical way. Haneke clearly dislikes logic and predictability in cinema, and that's why his own movies are always anarchistic and intriguing. At the same time, he always fills them with difficult questions (in case of *Benny's Video*, it is the question of what exactly spawns violence), and then refuses to provide us with clear or agreeable answers.

Contrary to what has been implied in many reviews, *Benny's Video* does *not* put the blame for bestiality among the youth solely on video-watching; what really pushes Benny to violence is the constant craving for novelty, the need to break away from the mind-numbing routines everyone seems to be following without trying to question them. To the huge surprise of his parents, Benny doesn't want to follow the safe path of their own lives; he is afraid that obeying the rules of society will turn him into a boring, emotionless creature like everyone around him. There is a significant scene in the movie: Benny is going down the street past an ice rink crowded with people who don't seem to be enjoying their skating very much; the rink is separated from the street with a heavy fence, so when the boy moves on after having peeked at the sad skaters, we are left with the image of people locked in a cage — and Benny is gone, breaking free.

It is difficult to answer the question of what pushed Benny to commit the crime (Haneke suggests it might have even been an accident), but it is just as tough to recognize the movie's true villain. The most obvious choice — Benny — seems to be the least fair of all. After all, the boy *is* sympathetic throughout most of the movie, and we feel the accusing finger should be rather pointed at somebody else — perhaps at his father, so concerned with himself all the time; or perhaps at his mother, who never cared too much about being there for Benny; or maybe at the whole money-oriented society? The latter view is favored by filmmaker Maximilian Le Cain, who in his essay "Do the Right Thing: The Films of Michael Haneke" recollects a scene that shows Benny filming people participating in a pyramid investment scheme; Le Cain then concludes: "Nothing is more telling of this society's and this class's crass materialism, its egotism, its exploitative acquisitiveness, and its complete and total disconnection from any commitment to one's fellow citizens and a wider society. We view these scenes as shot by Benny himself, where the rushed, shaky, hand-held nature of the video emphasizes the frantic and unthinking self-centeredness of the people involved."

However challenging the search for the complete message encoded in *Benny's Video*, one thing is certain: it is a captivating and mystifying take on the phenomenon of the video culture that was born a decade before the movie was made, and was still developing in the early 1990s. But apart from this, *Benny's Video* is also the essence of Haneke's filmmaking method that eventually reached much wider audiences with films like *Funny Games* (1997; with another chilling performance from Arno Frisch, here playing a grown-up incarnation of Benny), *The Piano Teacher* (2001) and *Hidden* (2005); the motifs of a disturbing videotape, the blurred sense of reality, the difficulty in communicating with others, the dysfunctional family, locked-up emotions, and even details like the childhood memory of an animal getting killed, would all keep on haunting Haneke's subsequent movies. While in some cases they were to be later applied even more effectively than in *Benny's Video* (for example, the rewinding of a videotape reused to a stupefying effect in *Funny Games*), nothing can be compared to the experience of being exposed to such a hazardous concentration of Haneke's fears and obsessions for the first time ever while watching this second feature of his. Also the director's big screen debut, *The Seventh Continent* (1989; including a subplot about a teenage girl who wants to get her parents' attention by pretending that she went blind), introduces some of Haneke's trademark themes and doesn't shy away from unexpected unpleasantness. Together with *The Seventh Continent* and *71 Fragments of a Chronology of Chance* (1994), *Benny's Video* constitutes a loosely connected "bourgeois trilogy" (or the "trilogy of emotional glaciation," as Haneke likes to call it) and is, arguably, its nastiest component.

Michael Haneke had learned how to make shocking movies long before he brought us *Funny Games*. *Benny's Video*, the director's second feature, is a cold horror that attempts to define the nature of evil, but in the end, after scattering too many clues and false trails along the way, leaves the impossible task to the viewers. A chilling and challenging picture.

Schramm

DIRECTOR: Jörg Buttgereit
CAST: Florian Koerner von Gustorf, Monika M., Carolina Harnisch,
Micha Brendel, Xaver Schwarzenberger, Gerd Horvath
Germany, 1993

Some genre filmmakers become famous because even their earliest features show that they have a way with the camera and the actors, and are a promise of thrilling future spectacles; that would be the case of John Carpenter, Sam Raimi and M. Night Shyamalan, to mention just a few of them. Other horror directors gain their fame simply because they are willing to go to any lengths to shock the viewers, despite lacking filmmaking talent; that would be the case of the "godfather of gore" Herschell Gordon Lewis and modern German director Jörg Buttgereit.

Buttgereit's first widely recognizable exercise in nastiness was *Nekromantik* (1987), a cheap and amateurish movie about all the darkest imaginable secrets of necrophilia. The acting in *Nekromantik* was laughable and the cinematography terrible, but the accumulation of disgusting, taboo-breaking scenes was so huge that the movie became a must-see for all the toughest horror fans, and it delivered more filthiness than they might have expected (a character ejaculating while committing suicide is just a sample of what *Nekromantik* has to offer). Cult guru John Waters famously called the movie "the first ever erotic film for necrophiliacs," which must have been quite a compliment for Buttgereit, and the director didn't disappoint his fans, Waters among them, with his next feature, *The Death King* (1990). This time we were treated to seven episodes depicting suicides and violent deaths that took place on different days of the week. The episodes are only linked by the gruesome theme and the sight of a dead body decaying day by day. *The Death King* was another success and another controversy, while it also marked Buttgereit's big step towards an art horror. *Nekromantik 2* (1991), though generally a better acted and bigger-budgeted rehash of the first movie, again set new standards for onscreen impurity with its excessive finale. In *Nekromantik 2* the director discovered a talented and undaunted actress, Monika M., who would later get a major part in his dark serial killer drama, *Schramm*. This movie, so far Buttgereit's last, is his most successful fusion of shocking antics and art movie ambitions.

The plot of the movie is almost as unsophisticated as that of both parts of *Nekromantik*, but this time, except for some ridiculous special effects, Buttgereit did his best to keep the mood serious and down-to-earth. Florian Koerner von Gustorf (who also appeared in a small role in *Nekromantik 2*) plays the title character, Lothar Schramm, a cab driver who lives alone in a bland apartment, occasionally escorts to work his neighbor Marianne (Monika M.), a prostitute he fell for ... and in his free time he kills a person or two. He's sexually frustrated, haunted by visions of his body falling apart and, most importantly, he's already dead when we meet him. What we see on screen are shreds of the man's memory, swirling back and forth, informing us about the extent of piteousness of his life.

Schramm opens with a foreboding quote from serial killer Carl Panzram: "Today I am dirty, but tomorrow I'll be just dirt." Does this make the main character of the movie, Lothar Schramm, an incarnation of the real-life murderer? Perhaps not, since Panzram, who lived from 1891 to 1930, had a very different personality; having himself been tortured as a young man, he became the essence of evil, a man who feared nothing and was ready to rape, injure or kill anyone crossing his path on a wrong day. Schramm, on the other hand, is quite the opposite of evil in his everyday life; to most of his passengers he must look like an average, sweet, shy guy.

We learn that Schramm's nickname (invented by journalists to make good headlines) is "Lipstick Killer." Does this, perhaps, make him a fictitious double for another serial killer, William George Heirens (born in 1928, currently in jail), also called "The Lipstick Killer" by the press? Most probably it doesn't, as Heirens used lipstick for an entirely different purpose than Schramm: instead of applying it to the victims, he used it to scrawl a message for the police (part of which read "Catch me before I kill more").

In David Kerekes's book *Sex, Murder, Art: The Films of Jörg Buttgereit*, Schramm's co-scriptwriter, Franz Rodenkirchen, admits that a partial inspiration for the main character was Ted Bundy (1946–1989). But the *modus operandi* of this violent maniac who claims to have killed 30 people, often kidnapping and brutally raping them, is again nothing like Schramm's, who didn't plan any elaborate schemes for his crimes, and preferred taking post-mortem photos of the victims rather than defiling them. If anything, Schramm is a "civilized" breed of a serial killer; he might have been a representation of Panzram, Heirens, or Bundy in an alternate reality where they actually make an effort to try and hold on to nine-to-five jobs.

Serial killers were like the plague in the 1980s and at the beginning of the following decade. The papers were busy describing gruesome details of the murders, the killers were being caught, put on trial, waiting to be executed or breaking free again, and—more often than not—becoming celebrities (cases in point are necrophiliac and cannibal Jeffrey Dahmer; and the "Killer Clown" John Wayne Gacy, who was given a record-breaking 21 consecutive life sentences and 12 death sentences). No wonder then, that so many serial killer–themed films were made at the time: two *Psycho* sequels (1983 and 1986), *Confessions of a Serial Killer* (1985), *Henry: Portrait of a Serial Killer* (1986), *Manhunter* (1986), two *Texas Chain Saw Massacre* sequels (1986 and 1990), *The Silence of the Lambs* (1991), *To Catch a Killer* (1992), and *Man Bites Dog* (1992), to mention just a few. Most of them were to some degree based on real events, were quite depressing (especially *Henry: Portrait of a Serial Killer*), and included many scenes of realistic violence, but none was quite as bizarre and at the same time as sympathetic towards its main character as *Schramm*. The killer played by von Gustorf doesn't only seem less threatening than most onscreen psychos and murderers—it is also emphasized that he is useful to society in more than one way (he drives a cab, and acts as his neighbor's "bodyguard," so to speak). We can also see how much he tries to cope with his wild visions and obsessions; at one point, he even punishes himself for being unable to control his desire by nailing his member to a chair. If Schramm doesn't ultimately succeed in conforming to the world around him, it's not because he wasn't trying, or because the society kept rejecting him; it's because in his head he was experiencing never-ending nightmares that wouldn't let him function normally, no matter how calm and kind he seemed on the outside. Buttgereit's greatest achievement is such a convincing depiction of Schramm's inner hell — where a vagina full of teeth is continually trying to bite him, he's now and again losing his leg, and an imagined dentist is taking out his eyeballs — that despite knowing he is a killer, we can't start properly hating him.

Instead of taking the easy path of endlessly cloning his necrophiliac breakthrough piece *Nekromantik*, director Buttgereit chose to search for an artist deep inside him and made an ambitious — though still customarily freaky — movie about the obsessions and dilemmas of a serial killer. It works surprisingly well, and the title character is unlike any other onscreen psycho.

Dark Waters

aka *Dead Waters*
DIRECTOR: Mariano Baino
CAST: Louise Salter, Venera Simmons, Maria Kapnist, Anna Rose Phipps,
Alvina Skarga, Lubov Snegur
Russia-Italy-UK, 1994

Contrary to what you may hear and read, the 1980s were not the end of great Italian horror cinema. It's true that Lucio Fulci's last efforts were but a flickering shadow of his classic genre output (like 1991's *Voices from Beyond*) or were hardly watchable at all (1989's *The Sweet House of Horrors*), Dario Argento has been semi-successfully struggling to make another worthy movie since *Deep Red* (2001's *Sleepless* is more than decent but hardly a classic), the films of Lamberto Bava have been gradually becoming duller and duller (even "his 'shocking comeback,'" 2005's *The Torturer*, is a disappointment), and Ruggero Deodato has been relegated to appearing in occasional documentaries or playing cameos in popular American horror movies (last seen as a cannibal in Eli Roth's *Hostel II*, made in 2007). Should we make an effort and try look for a new talent, though, we may be in for a huge surprise, especially if one of our discoveries is Mariano Baino's debut feature *Dark Waters*, a thrilling and unforgettable journey to the heart of Italian horror.

It is one of those movies that immediately grabs you and screams for your full attention. The opening sequence of a furious flood destroying a mysterious cliffside chapel is a proper introduction to Baino's style. It's very well executed but you don't look at it and say: "Ah, that's a very nice special effect here"; you look at it and are drawn right into the movie, as if the waters of the flood took you in. When the story begins, you already feel like you're a part of it — a castaway on an unknown, highly depressing island. You feel, in fact, as if you were an alter ego of Elizabeth (Louise Salter) who visits a suspicious convent on the once flooded island. She wants to meet Theresa (Anna Rose Phipps) who is studying there, and she also wants to learn why her deceased father decided to make regular payments to the convent. Not an easy task this, since Elizabeth's interlocutors are the old, always-whispering Mother Superior (Maria Kapnist) and her equally enigmatic interpreter, sister Sarah (Venera Simmons). Also, she is told that Theresa has already left the convent. Staying on the island in order to get to the bottom of the whole mystery, Elizabeth unknowingly steps into the blackest, most

Cross against the wall: Anna Rose Phipps in Mariano Baino's *Dark Waters* (1994) (photograph by Steve Brooke Smith, courtesy of Mariano Baino).

Say hello to the demonic Mother Superior (Maria Kapnist) from *Dark Waters* (photograph by Steve Brooke Smith, courtesy of Mariano Baino).

unnerving nightmare imaginable. If she only knew what lurks behind these convent walls, she would have never left the safe, comfortable confines of her London apartment.

Fulci didn't need a coherent plot to make the genre masterpiece *The Beyond* (1981), and most of Argento's early movies thrived on chaotic, dreamlike plotlines, so it would be unfair to criticize Baino for not making *Dark Waters* Hollywood-clear. Scrawny dialogue and the lack of an eventful story increase the movie's aura of mystery, and are the reasons why it's so often referred as being Lovercraftian: just like the creator of the Cthulhu Mythos, Baino is more interested in showing us an unknown reality, than focusing on a group of characters encountering a set of nicely measured, suspenseful adventures. What sticks in our minds after getting through one of Lovecraft's stories is usually the picture of a place he brought us to. Analogically, what we remember after watching *Dark Waters* is the sad, windy, God-forsaken shore the main character arrives at; the events that follow are vague at best, but we are already mesmerized by the atmosphere of the place, and want to find out as much as possible about it, even if we realize we can never fully understand most of the things happening there.

The troubled shoot of the movie (of which Baino and his crew talk passionately in a documentary called *Deep into Dark Waters*) appeared to be partly responsible for the greatness of the final outcome. The unplanned setting near Chernobyl looks so foreboding that you will feel you've just stepped into the saddest circle of hell, and some scenes that had to be improvised turned out much creepier than planned. (If you wonder why

Mother Superior only communicates in inaudible whispers, it's because Maria Kapnist who played the role spoke no English.) *Dark Waters* is, indeed, made of nice little touches like this, some of them intended, some accidental, but it's one of those cases where the sum of all the minute particulars is much bigger than anyone would have expected, almost overwhelming. Most importantly, Baino manages to save the movie from falling apart, even though at times it does seem to be on the brink of it. Baino's method for keeping things under control is quite similar to the methods once successfully used by Fulci, Argento and Mario Bava: even though *Dark Waters* doesn't have the tightest of all plots, it's so masterfully choreographed and edited that it feels like a powerful trance; you don't need much of a story, it appears, if you have a bag of good set pieces and know how to sew them together, so that they can do their job. You may have noted that the less talking there is in an Italian horror movie, the more impressive it usually is — and this rule works fine to show you the quality of the mostly mute *Dark Waters*.

Had the cult factor of a movie been easily translated into a financial success, Baino would have had a string of weird horror movies under his belt by now. Alas, it often works the opposite way, so it's not a huge surprise that since *Dark Waters* the director has been struggling to get another project made. The long-promised adaptation of Graham Masterton's *Ritual* still escapes him (though he vows he won't stop trying to finally make it, as he is a huge fan of the writer and this particular novel), and his second effort as a director —*Hidden*— is still to be seen. The only pieces of evidence that Baino is still around and still in love with horror are the great, grim short movie *Never Ever After* (2004), and the script he wrote for *Thy Kingdom Come* (2007). As a scriptwriter, however, Baino aims to cover many genres: drama (*Flower of Shame*), thriller (his adaptation of Chris Niles' *Hell's Kitchen*) and noir (his adaptation of Jean-Patrick Manchette's *3 to Kill*).

Despite being labeled as a British production and shot in the Ukraine, deep at heart *Dark Waters* is a very Italian horror movie. If you like the 1970s–1980s pieces from Bava, Fulci and Argento, you won't ask questions about the sketchy plot but will embrace the movie as a hypnotizing, atmospheric whole.

The Day of the Beast (El Día de la Bestia)

DIRECTOR: Álex de la Iglesia
CAST: Alex Angulo, Santiago Segura, Armando De Razza, Nathalie Sesena, Maria Grazia Cucinotta, Terele Pavez
Spain-Italy, 1995

Spanish director Álex de la Iglesia predicted the worldwide end-of-the-century panic and made a movie about it five years before the unholy 1999 switched to the yet scarier, panic-inducing 2000. De la Iglesia either didn't have patience to wait for the magic dates to pop up, or he didn't think he needed them (after all, the trick of releasing the movie at the end of 1999 and putting the date upside down to find 666 in it, wasn't of much help in the case of Peter Hyams's *End of Days*, one of the proper horrors prophesizing the coming of the new, killer century). In de la Iglesia's version of the Apocalypse, the Antichrist is set to arrive in Madrid on December 25, 1995 — and there are just a couple of days left until this blackest Christmas ever when we start watching the movie.

Only one person in the whole world knows the exact date of the Antichrist's visit. That's Father Angel (Alex Angulo), who carefully studied the Book of Revelations, then did some crazy math and came up with the foreboding date. He also came up with the idea to commit as many evil deeds as he can in order to draw Satan's attention. Therefore, on his way to Madrid, Father Angel does his best to act evil (he steals money whenever possible, snatches somebody's suitcase, shoves a mime off a railing), and to be yet better prepared to summon the Devil, he enters a music store and asks for a heavy metal tape with a hidden Satanist message. But he finds more than that, as the store's owner — a metalhead with his heart still in the 1980s (Santiago Segura) — is fascinated with Father Angel's peculiar quest and soon becomes his accomplice. Now they just have to kidnap Professor Cavan (Armando De Razza), an occult guru whose popular program they glimpsed on TV, and they can start calling the Antichrist forth.

The Day of the Beast is a horror *tour de force* with lip-smackingly sinister mood and wicked twists on a number of genre clichés, but it's also a very effective satire on media (it turns out, for example, that outside the TV studio, Professor Cavan is not that much of an expert), family relationships (the metalhead's permanently stoned grandpa and bossy mother are a source of some of the movie's best jokes), and obsession with the occult (the three main characters are supposed to summon the Devil, yet it turns out their knowledge of the occult is based on silly misconceptions). Jaume Martí-Olivella sums up the movie in *Basque Cinema: An Introduction* as "a Satanic action comedy that reworks parodically several recurrent narrative elements in Basque and Spanish cinema: the (Oedipal) family metaphor as national allegory, the spectral presence of ghostly enemies and the foreign (bad) influence."

De la Iglesia's directorial style is breathtaking. From the opening shock death in a church he easily blends several film genres into what appears to be one of the most eclectic and original horror movies in history. He's greatly helped by cinematographer Flavio Martínez Labiano who perfectly captures the grotesqueness of the proceedings, special effects supervisor Rafa Solorzano who treats us to an unforgettable climax, and a group of talented actors (the performances of Angulo and Segura are both hilarious and perfectly convincing). The director's other works are also worth seeing, especially his crazy feature-length debut *Acción mutante* (1993), the multi-genre hybrid *Perdita Durango* (1997), the unpredictable thriller *Common Wealth* (2000) and the rollicking comedy *Ferpect Crime* (2004).

In 2006, de la Iglesia made his most traditional horror movie, part of Spanish TV series, *Films to Keep You Awake*. Titled *The Baby's Room*, the episode is an effective mixture of classic themes (ghosts, doppelgangers, descent into madness), and a piece of evidence that a movie by de la Iglesia can be quite extraordinary even without the usual amount of weirdness and oddball comedy. The aforementioned horror series is all the more interesting for the fact that each part was directed by a different director working in Spain. *To Let*, a tale of a young couple whose life turns to a nightmare when they move to their new flat, was helmed by Jaume Balagueró, who made his name with *The Nameless* (1999) and recently scared the whole world with the excellent *[REC]* (2007). *The Christmas Tale*, an '80s-style horror about a woman trapped in a well, was made by *[REC]*'s co-director, Paco Plaza, who had earlier brought us a decent mystery about family secrets based on Ramsey Campbell's novel *Second Name* (2002) and a flashy horror about a serial killer–werewolf, *Romasanta* (2004). Enrique Urbizu, director of the gritty cop thriller *Anything for Bread* (1991) and the engaging revenge tale *Box 507* (2002), here contributed an episode called *A Real Friend* that sees a young girl's imaginary companion, a vampire, unexpectedly entering the real world. Another part of the series, *Blame*, was made by Narciso Ibáñez Serrador, one of the most important genre directors working in Spain (born in Uruguay), author of the shocking classic *Who Can Kill a Child?* (1976), about a likable couple stranded on an island with a group of murderous kids; in *Blame*, arguably the most depressing of all *Films to Keep You Awake*, Ibáñez Serrador depicts hidden horrors of a certain gynecology clinic. The last installment, *Spectro*, about an elderly writer returning to his childhood town and discovering that his old flame is still young, was signed by Mateo Gil, so far best known for scripting Alejandro Amenábar's drama *The Sea Within*, as well as being an assistant director–writer on two other films by Amenábar: the tense, underrated *Thesis* (1996) and the creepy *Abre los Ojos* (1997; remade in 2001 as *Vanilla Sky*). All in all, *Films to Keep You Awake* is a great, concise introduction to contemporary Spanish horror, with its eccentric characters, odd sense of humor and the inimitable mood.

De la Iglesia's talent to handle the horror, the grotesque and the slapstick of the story told in *The Day of the Beast* is simply astonishing. Oh, all right — so it's not a typical genre piece peppered with jump scenes and suspenseful set pieces, but another movie that so perfectly captures all these different moods is yet to be made.

The Lost Skeleton of Cadavra

Director: Larry Blamire
Cast: Fay Masterson, Larry Blamire, Andrew Parks, Susan McConnell, Jennifer Blaire, Brian Howe, Dan Conroy, Robert Deveau, Darren Reed
USA, 2001

"Never a Motion Picture Like This!"
"Supreme Shock Sensation of Our Time!"
"Do You Dare See ... *The Lost Skeleton of Cadavra*"

Many movies have tried to resurrect the charm, simplicity and shoddy quality of vintage horrors and sci-fis — most of them failed, some were surprisingly effective (in this book: 1988's *Killer Klowns from Outer Space*), but none of them went to such lengths at mimicking the vices and virtues of these B-cinema classics as *The Lost Skeleton of Cadavra* does. Director Larry Blamire took his crew to the legendary Bronson Canyon (where the cheapest sci-fi–horrors used to be shot decades ago), instructed the actors to play as if these were their first, not very smooth attempts at performing in front of the camera, and was determined to resort to the worst special effects one could think of (watch for the shockingly explicit miniature of a spaceship as it lands on Earth; the laughable chemistry set being reused in two different locations; or the stock footage of "forest animals" bluntly edited into the movie). The effect is, at least for those viewers who always dreamt of discovering a lost movie of Ed Wood, a "supreme shock sensation of our time" indeed.

The plot of *The Lost Skeleton of Cadavra* may be utterly ridiculous, but everyone in the movie treats it with such seriousness that it wouldn't seem fair to simply brush it off. Larry Blamire plays Dr. Paul Armstrong ("He was the man — of science!" we are informed in the old-fashioned trailer) who travels with his wife, Betty (Fay Masterson), to a cabin in the wilderness and intends to search for a meteorite filled with atmospherium — apparently a very rare and much needed element ("It could mean actual advances in the field of science!" quips the doctor at one point). Dr. Armstrong discovers atmospherium without much difficulty, but it may not be easy to keep the treasured find, as there's another, *meaner* scientist around: Dr. Roger Fleming ("He was a man — of evil!" according to the trailer). Dr. Fleming, played with a truly villainous enthusiasm by Brian Howe, needs the element to bring back to life the lost skeleton of the title ("The most horrifying fiend mankind has ever known!"), a mind-controlling creature that can help him rule the world. Then there are two aliens ("from Outer Space!"), Kro-Bar (Andrew Parks) and Lattis (Susan McConnell), who could use some atmospherium to repair their ship. The aliens are a likable and friendly couple but as

The best combination of four different forest animals ever: lovely Animala (Jennifer Blaire) in *The Lost Skeleton of Cadavra* (2001).

they crashland, their flesh-eating pet (Darren Reed) escapes from the cage and becomes a threat to everyone around ("It was a mutant — that killed for kicks!"). The wicked Dr. Fleming is clever enough to use a handy transmutatron the aliens left behind, in order to create a female companion for himself; with a girlfriend, he reasons, he will pass for a good guy when he visits the cabin where Dr. Armstrong keeps atmospherium. Thus, Animala (Jennifer Blaire) is born: a lovely creature made of "four different forest animals." Now, as soon as the newly found Skeleton of Cadavra starts doing what brought him fame — controlling the minds — the "titanic battle for world supremacy" begins.

Understandably, not all film critics adored the quirkiness and retro charm of Blamire's movie. Robert K. Elder of the *Chicago Tribune* famously wrote that "*The Lost Skeleton of Cadavra*, in retrospect, should have stayed lost"; Dave Kehr of *The New York Times* called it "a gray, unfunny parody of 1950's science fiction films." More favorable was the review written by Mark Holcomb of *The Village Voice*, as he labeled *The Lost Skeleton* "100 percent cult-in-a-can" that should satisfy the "aficionados"; and Glenn Kenny of *Premiere* followed Holcomb's trail when writing "*Cadavra* is largely a hoot, although if you haven't seen, say, *The Atomic Brain* in a while you might not be attuned to its frequency." But it was a review from *Variety*, written by Dennis Harvey, that will most closely reflect the feelings of everyone attuned to the movie's frequency: "It takes true trash cinema devotion to satirize the clunky visuals, banal dialogue, logic gaps and pseudoscientific silliness of a bygone era's schlockiest obscurities quite so accurately, complete with one-beat-tardy editorial rhythms." Just think of all the hilarious lines with which Blamire stuffed *The Lost Skeleton* ("If I wanted to live a safe life, well, then I guess I wouldn't have married a man who studies rocks" being the motto of a scientist wife, and "That atmospherium can do some mighty powerful things" being a sufficient explanation of why the world needs the rare element, to mention just two of them), and you'll realize that the man was *chosen* to bring us a movie like this.

The Lost Skeleton of Cadavra closes with the announcement of another tribute to retro cinema from Blamire, *The Trail of the Screaming Forehead*. Fortunately, this was not a hoax, and in 2007 *The Trail* finally hit the screens. This time, Blamire infused the movie with bright, comic book colors, and chose to bring back the magic of Ray Harryhausen's early movies, but overall the new concept turned out to be very similar to the one *The Lost Skeleton* was based on, and again the movie's success depended on the delightfully corny acting from Masterson, Parks, Blaire, McConnell and Blamire himself (though the cameos by Dick Miller and Kevin McCarthy are a treat, too). The greatest surprise is that what seemed to be a one-off twist, works here just as well as it did the first time around.

Larry Blamire's deadpan "re-envisioning" of cheap horror–sci-fi movies from the 1950s and 1960s is hilarious — unless you think that *Plan 9 from Outer Space* wouldn't be funny if its trashiness and lunacy were intended. Whatever critics may think of the final outcome, there's no denying that *The Lost Skeleton of Cadavra* features some of the best bad acting and the most inventively awful special effects in the history of cinema. Ed Wood would have certainly applauded this.

No Such Thing

DIRECTOR: Hal Hartley
CAST: Sarah Polley, Robert John Burke, Julie Christie, Helen Mirren,
Baltasar Kormákur, Erica Gimpel
USA-Iceland, 2001

For some, the very idea of Hal Hartley, director of such thought-provoking, independent works as *Surviving Desire* (1991) and *Simple Men* (1992), tackling horror themes must have come as a shock. In reality, though, with *No Such Thing*, a tale of an indestructible monster who wishes he could finally die, Hartley came full circle as a filmmaker. At the beginning of his career he wrote a script for a cheap horror movie that aimed at meeting all possible expectations of the genre-loving audience (i.e., it included the necessary amount of nudity and gore). The movie was never made but after hearing some good opinions on the script, Hartley decided to give horror another chance, and set out to write a script for a vampire movie. Again — some encouraging praise followed but no movie was made. More than a decade had to pass for Hartley to finally finish something that would echo those early ideas. This time, however, there was no gore to speak of, no nudity and not a vampire in sight.

In *No Such Thing* the vampire is replaced by a nameless creature (Robert John Burke) that lives in a sad, decrepit shack near the sea, somewhere in Iceland. An American TV station bossed by a heartless ratings-freak (Helen Mirren) sends a crew of journalists to the monster's lair in order to get a good, controversial documentary, but they soon vanish, most likely killed by the beast. Beatrice (Sarah Polley), who also works at the TV station and is the fiancée of one of the lost men, decides to travel to Iceland and discover the truth about the disappearance. But in a movie by Hartley, things cannot go too smoothly and predictably, so after a wonderfully suspenseful shot of Beatrice looking straight at the camera, deciding whether to board the plane or not, we are informed that all the passengers on the plane died when it crashed in the sea ... all, that is, except for Beatrice, who was saved by Icelandic fishermen and brought to a hospital. Seriously injured, the girl has to undergo a painful experimental surgery, and after some time, with the help of Dr. Anna (Julie Christie), she leaves the hospital and continues her journey. When she finally arrives at the creature's doorstep, she learns two important things. Firstly, the monster did tear her fiancé to shreds, yes. Secondly, she cannot do much to avenge her loved one as the monster is not only supernaturally strong but also immortal. And that's where the proper movie starts: Beatrice will have to find a way to destroy the indestructible, and not because she hates the beast — in fact, she becomes more and more fond of it — but because the beast asks her to do that. Life is dreadfully boring, it turns out, when you cannot die.

In a movie so lovingly dubbed incomprehensible, illogical and chaotic, this message sounds suspiciously clear: since human life does end, we should make the most of it, never allow it to be devoured by boredom and routine, not waste it on trivialities. Beatrice is our guide here. She escapes from the dazzling but ultimately useless world of media, and through personal suffering finds the compulsion to live a full life. Cleverly, the monster is not shown as either purely evil or entirely sympathetic. It drinks, swears, spits fire and kills people *but* it's got good reasons for doing all this; after all, it's been witnessing the evolution of mankind since Year Zero (as we learn later in the movie), and it lost its patience with the stupidity of our race. Beatrice attracts the beast because she's different — purer and truer — than most other people. This is why the monster decides to let her live and agrees to stop killing humans. But let's just stop and think about this for a moment... Why exactly did Beatrice forget about her dead fiancé so easily? Why did she make a deal with the murderous monster rather than at least give it a try and claw its eyes out?

These questions will seriously bother anyone who expects to find logic and realism here. *No Such Thing* cannot be approached as a logical movie, and perhaps that's exactly why so many people rejected it, and labeled it Hartley's first true misfire. Undeservedly so, as there's always sense in Hartley's choices, it's just that in the case of *No Such Thing* one needs to dig for it a bit deeper than usual. If Beatrice chose not to claw the monster's eyes out when she found out that it killed the man she loved, it's because at that time, when she faced the monster at last, she entered an entirely new dimension; she was disjoined from the realm of her old self and understood how shallow her life was up to that moment. And as she experienced this sudden clarity of the mind, she might have also glimpsed God in the eyes of the monster (it's not a coincidence that in another scene the monster speculates, however jokingly, that the odds are it actually *is* God). Which justifies the act of forgiving for all the deaths; after all, what's the use of holding grudges against God? Instead Beatrice will try to understand the monster, give it a helping hand, and make better use of everything in her that so impressed it in the first place — understandably, not without a misstep or two.

At the beginning, the movie may seem tougher to get into than Hartley's earlier works, but in the end it emerges as an effort that deals with all the subjects that always fascinated the director (the difference between the Americans and people of other nationalities, the fear of consumerism, the quest for spirituality and the exquisiteness of love). Plus there's the impressive, ugly-but-distinguished, dangerous-but-not-really-scary monster: a masterful invention of Hartley, several makeup artists and actor Robert John Burke who breathes life and individuality into this odd character. If *No Such Thing* were a simple B-grade horror movie, I bet we would already have a whole new franchise devoted to the beast's bloodiest adventures.

No Such Thing is in many respects more challenging than Hartley's other films. Not only does it throw a scaly, fire-spitting creature into the director's typical romantic tale, but it also shows affinity for sudden jumps in narration and for characters behaving against human nature. Then again, if you manage to get into this offbeat story, there's lots of beauty and cleverness to be found in it, and Robert John Burke's Monster is beyond doubt one of the genre's finest creations.

Bubba Ho-tep

DIRECTOR: Don Coscarelli
CAST: Bruce Campbell, Ossie Davis, Ella Joyce, Heidi Marnhout, Bob Ivy, Larry
Pennell, Reggie Bannister, Edith Jefferson, Daniel Roebuck
USA, 2002

"How cult movie is that? We'll tell you: it's cult to the power of cult. Squared."
So wrote Jon Brown of *Total Film* in his review of *Bubba Ho-tep*. And he was right, of
course, but apart from being "cult to the power of cult," *Bubba Ho-tep* is also surprisingly thoughtful, and even though it is hilarious, its laughs are infused with bitterness.
It certainly is not as reckless a movie as might have been expected upon finding out
that its premise is, more or less, "an impotent Elvis Presley and a black JFK battle a
soul-sucking mummy in a nursing home."

There are three main reasons for the cult status of *Bubba Ho-tep*: it was directed
by Don Coscarelli, a favorite among fans of weird horror since *Phantasm* (1979); the
script was based on a novella by Joe R. Lansdale, author of many great, twisty tales of
horror and mystery; and the role of old Elvis Presley was given to Bruce Campbell, the
eponymous Ash in Sam Raimi's *The Evil Dead* (1980). Of course, there was no guarantee it would all add up as nicely as it eventually did, but since the first announcement about the movie actually being made, anyone who cared about Coscarelli, Lansdale
and Campbell had been keeping the fingers firmly crossed. And when *Bubba Ho-tep*

The mummy (Bob Ivy) is out to get Elvis and JFK in Don Coscarelli's *Bubba Ho-tep* (2002).

premiered, most viewers were mildly surprised that it was not the constant laugh riot or the horror feast they had expected, but they embraced it nevertheless and agreed that it was one of the greatest accomplishments of both Coscarelli and Campbell (plus, there was hope that its success would result in more adaptations of Lansdale's prose, this being the first one). Mark Wheaton of *Fangoria* expressed the feelings of the vast majority of fans when he concluded his review with: "Bruce Campbell in a lead role fighting a mummy directed by Don Coscarelli based on a short story by Joe Lansdale: it just sounds like one of those rumored projects that will never get made." It sure did.

The story of *Bubba Ho-tep* should perhaps not be revealed in detail before those who haven't yet seen it, but for the sake of arguments to follow, let's just say that Elvis (Campbell) and President John Fitzgerald Kennedy (Ossie Davis), now old men with serious health issues, meet in a nursing home in Texas and share the secrets of their lives, proving that even the wildest conspiracy theories formed throughout the years since their disappearance, were not as outlandish as the truth. But while Elvis sounds reasonable enough (telling a story of how he switched places with an impersonator back in the 1970s), "Kennedy" is depicted as most probably delusional (and his tale of how after the assassination a portion of his brain had to be replaced with a sandbag, and how he was then "dyed black" so that nobody could recognize him, is a bit too much to believe in, even in a movie like this). After having chit-chatted about their illnesses, regrets and fantasies, the two men have to face a monster that has recently started feeding upon the residents of their home. The monster is the frail-looking mummy Bubba Ho-tep (Bob Ivy), that wears an inexplicable cowboy hat, but it is also quite deadly and very mean, so Elvis and JFK will have to fight hard to prove that they are still heroes and not just useless VIPs patiently waiting for death.

Before the mummy appears in the movie, it is made clear that Elvis is much more annoyed with the burden of old age than he is with the loss of fame and fortune. His reflections on being old and sick are at the same time funny and sad. When a young woman accidentally allows him to peek under her skirt, the King is doubly depressed: first of all, he couldn't get an erection even though he appreciated the view, and secondly, he suspects the girl wouldn't let something like that happen if she hadn't seen him as "physically and sexually non-threatening." And when a nurse laughs instead of being offended by Elvis' "Fuck you!" he ponders that when you get old, "you can't even cuss someone and have it bother 'em. Everything you do is either worthless or sadly amusing." It may sound suspicious that a film as kinky as *Bubba Ho-tep* should be interpreted as musings on old age (and especially on being an old man in the United States, where the tradition of sending elderly family members to rest homes is especially strong, and unconditionally isolates them from their loved ones), but it really is the dominant and most heartfelt theme here. For those who know Coscarelli's filmography and are not afraid to analyze it, this shouldn't be too much of a shock, though: after all, his equally kinky *Phantasm* was a concealed statement on how Americans cannot cope with death.

Equally as interesting as the movie's depiction of the fears and misery of getting old, are the questions it asks about identity. Elvis first habitually complains about how people disregard him because they don't believe he is who he is, but then stops to think about it and realizes his life wouldn't change all that much if he was still recognized as the King — he wouldn't be able to win back his family, and he would still be suffering from what appears to be cancer. Perhaps this is why Elvis so easily accepts JFK's claim of having been dyed black for the purpose of disguise and so on: he no longer cares whether his buddy is who he claims to be or not; the important thing is that he's a great companion and will help him take care of the mummy-slaying business.

In the fashion of the James Bond movies, the ending credits of *Bubba Ho-tep* announce the return of some of its characters in *Bubba Nosferatu: Curse of the She-Vampires*. Coscarelli later admitted that it was intended as a joke, but the unexpected success of the movie and constant inquiries about the sequel from the fans, encouraged the director to give *Bubba Nosferatu* a go. Unfortunately, it seems Bruce Campbell won't be returning as the King (explaining that he "couldn't reconcile a few points" concerning the plot with the director), but Paul Giamatti expressed interest in one of the roles, and Lansdale is again helping with the script.

In 2005 Coscarelli directed another Lansdale adaptation, this time a short story made into one of the better Season One episodes of the TV series *Masters of Horror*, called "Incident On and Off a Mountain Road." Apart from *Bubba Nosferatu*, there's also an adaptation of Lansdale's 2002 novel *A Fine Dark Line* in the works (to be helmed by Adam Friedman, so far mostly known for Playboy videos and biographies of Hollywood stars).

Of the many Joe R. Lansdale's stories available for adaptation, Don Coscarelli chose the bitter and off-the-wall novella *Bubba Ho-tep*, one that seemed to have little movie potential, and turned it into an unforgettable and highly unconventional mixture of horror, comedy and drama. The deadpan turns from Bruce Campbell and Ossie Davis demand that the viewers treat the weird plot with respect, examine it carefully, and look for the sad truth about aging and fame somewhere beneath the genre disguise.

The Stink of Flesh

DIRECTOR: Scott Phillips
CAST: Kurly Tlapoyawa, Ross Kelly, Diva, Kristin Hansen, Billy Garberina,
Andrew Vellenoweth, Devin O'Leary, Bryan Gallegos
USA, 2004

Watch the crazy opening of *The Stink of Flesh* and there's a good chance you won't be able to leave your seat for the next 80 minutes. Unlike many modern zombie movies, this one is so briskly paced and packed with so many weird ideas that it just takes you right in, and refuses to let go, even though it's not exactly flawless.

Within the first several minutes we meet the three most important characters: handsome Nathan (Ross Kelly) and his insatiable wife Dexy (Diva), whose greatest concern in the zombie-infested world is to be able to continue having kinky sex with perfect strangers. Before we learn too much about these two, the camera rushes to a place nearby Nathan and Dexy's house, and we are introduced to Matool (Kurly Tlapoyawa), a short but impressively fit Mexican who takes great pleasure in battling zombies and killing them off with the use of a hammer and awfully long nails. Matool may at first look like a violence-addicted psycho but it all changes when, after an energetic and nicely choreographed fight scene, he reaches for his glasses and carefully puts them on to see more clearly all the bloody mess he caused. Matool is, we find out, both a fighter and an intellectual. And he also loves kinky sex, so when he meets Nathan and Dexy they don't have to force him to participate in their evening rituals. But cool and brave as he is, even Matool screams his lungs out when Dexy's sister Sassy (Gunnar Hansen's niece, Kristin Hansen) sneaks into the room and tries to join in the sexual eccentricities. What especially startles Matool is the sight of a rather awful "parasite sister" growing out of Sassy's side. And there's so much more to come: a sexy zombie-girl (Stephanie Leighs) hidden in the shed, a spooky kid (Bryan Gallegos) who stares at everything and everyone around, and never says a word, and a group of military men who nearly got eaten by zombies — and who are now more than eager to have sex with Dexy.

Director Scott Phillips loves European zombie films as much as George Romero's classics or weird horror movies of the 1980s, and he makes no attempts at concealing his cinematic taste; the name Matool is a nod to Lucio Fulci's legendary *Zombi 2* (1979), the blue-tinted living dead are taken straight out of Romero's *Dawn of the Dead* (1978), and the idea of a "parasite sister" is clearly inspired by Frank Henenlotter's *Basket Case* (1982). But it seems that Phillips thought it fair to reflect both advantages and disadvantages of all these films, so *The Stink of Flesh* is, on one hand, as bold and crazy as anything the abovementioned directors would have done, but on the other hand it tends to be as gratuitously violent as the movies by Romero occasionally are, it includes scenes as badly acted as those with kids in Fulci's films, and sports some special effects that are as dodgy as Henenlotter's worst works.

The question is then, "Can you cope with the bad stuff to get to the good parts?" The most off-putting thing for an average viewer will be bad acting. Fortunately, the major actors (Tlapoyawa, Kelly and Diva) don't have serious problems with their roles for most of the time, but whenever the screen fills with supporting actors, all hell breaks loose. The moment of utter acting horror comes near the very beginning, when Matool enters the house of Mr. Rainville (Bob Vardeman) and has to interact with the movie's worst actor, Chris Vardeman, who plays Mr. Rainville's teenage loverboy. Chris Vardeman visibly struggles not to look in the camera, so he doesn't even have to open his mouth to prove he cannot act, but as soon as Bob himself has a longer line to deliver ("That's what happens when you go for a Sunday drive in a world full of flesh-eating corpses," he says with no emotion whatsoever) it turns out that he isn't much better than his co-star. And to make things worse, there's also this poor Bryan Gallegos (in the same scene) as a puzzling mute kid who will stay with us for the rest of the movie. The director claims that the young actor did a "great job" but perhaps he is just being nice. The boy's constant "looking around thoughtfully" is, in fact, one of the most annoying things about *The Stink of Flesh*.

But when the movie is good, it's a horror fan's heaven. The fight scenes are all great (Tlapoyawa is much more convincing as a fighter than as an actor), and I don't think there's another movie that puts together action sequences and gore as seamlessly as *The Stink of Flesh* does. There are also plenty of good lines ("We've made a choice to live an alternative lifestyle," says Nathan to Matool, "it's just a lot harder now that everybody's dead"), several intentionally cheesy flashbacks (the best one showing the armed military men being unable to deal with hungry zombies that jump at them literally out of nowhere), and effective gross-out moments (one of the cinema's most disgusting kissing scenes among them). Also the New Mexico locations look suitably eerie as photographed by Richard Griffin. Made for just $3,000, *The Stink of Flesh* really is a movie to be loved and loathed at the same time, and let's just hope Phillips' next effort doesn't lose the anti-mainstream edge and the ability to surprise us every several minutes.

   If you like twisted horror movies and don't mind some bad acting, *The Stink of Flesh* may be your thing. Certain disadvantages aside, it's a bold, energetic and unpredictable exercise in craziness.

Calvaire

aka *The Ordeal*
DIRECTOR: Fabrice Du Welz
CAST: Laurent Lucas, Jackie Berroyer, Jean-Luc Couchard,
Philippe Nahon, Jo Prestia, Brigitte Lahaie
Belgium-France-Luxembourg, 2004

   In an interview, Belgian director Fabrice Du Welz said that his home country is a "dark, surreal, schizophrenic, absurd place to live" and therefore *Calvaire*, his feature debut, is a "very Belgian film." Also, like many of Du Welz's favorite horror movies (notably, Tobe Hooper's 1974 classic *The Texas Chain Saw Massacre*), *Calvaire* was inspired by real crimes. In this case, ones that occurred in Belgium in recent years, the most infamous of which was the string of kidnappings, sexual abuse, tortures and murders committed by Marc Dutroux, Michelle Martin, Michel Lelièvre and Michel Fourniret ("the Ogre of the Ardennes"). It ran from the 1980s through the late 1990s and early 2000s when they were all finally imprisoned.

   The outburst of violence and disturbing surrealism that marks *Calvaire* was foreshadowed in Du Welz's short movie *A Wonderful Love* (1999), an odd and captivating story of a lonely, aging woman going mad. In *Calvaire*, the woman is replaced with a lonely, aging man, Bartel (Jackie Berroyer), who lives in a defunct inn in a very primitive part of Belgium, and mourns over the loss of his wife, Gloria. When a young and handsome singer, Marc (Laurent Lucas), visits the inn because his van broke down in the nearby woods, Bartel starts showing signs of madness, too; since Gloria, like Marc, was a singer, reasons Bartel, the visitor could perhaps stay in the inn and, well, simply become a substitute for Gloria — sing him an occasional song, listen to his jokes, share his bed ... Marc, however, won't stop talking about how he has to leave, and how he has to get to his Christmas gig, which finally makes Bartel furious enough to demolish Marc's van with a sledgehammer, set it on fire, and then knock out the singer with a car battery. Tied and wearing Gloria's dress, Marc has to be prepared for the worst —

and not just from puppy-eyed Bartel, but from other love-depraved villagers led by Robert Orton (Philippe Nahon) as well.

Calvaire is filled with many grotesque scenes that set the tone and then effectively build up the suspense (an old woman putting Marc's hand on her crotch in a pathetic attempt at seducing him; Marc walking through the countryside to spot the villagers having sex with a pig; a group of silent, crazy-looking men doing a monstrous dance routine in a pub), but the movie's main asset stems from Du Welz's determination to avoid certain horror clichés. Here, unlike in *Deliverance* (1972) and *The Texas Chain Saw Massacre*, to which movies *Calvaire* is often compared, the villain is sympathetic (at least initially), the hero is quite unpleasant, and at one point you can even suspect that the victim enjoys all the tortures. Also, there's no typical horror ending here, and instead of grabbing us by the throat, the final scene illuminates the purpose of the

In *Calvaire* (2004), Marc (Laurent Lucas) learns to say "I love you" the hard way.

whole ordeal: apparently, it was all about learning how to acknowledge love. Since the first scene that has Marc performing dispassionate love songs in front of elderly ladies, we can see that he has serious issues with expressing emotions. He treats everyone in a strictly businesslike manner, avoids making bonds, and refuses to spend his time with people if it can't bring him any profits — as is the way of the modern, money-oriented world. Therefore, learning how to express emotions will have to involve a clash with a bygone world where everything, including love, used to be taken by brute force. The Biblical symbols Marc encounters along the way (the crucifixion is being pointed out in several scenes, and the movie is set just before Christmas) are just another reminder that the main character, just like Jesus, needs to walk through hell in order to be born again.

Most of Du Welz's influences rooted in American cinema are clear (complete with an homage to early horror movies in a recurring scene of a demented character Boris looking for his dog Bella, as well as Bartel's name bringing to mind the cult director Paul Bartel). But esthetically *Calvaire* is much more similar to European shockers from the last decade, most importantly these made by Gaspar Noé. This doesn't come as a surprise since *Calvaire*'s director of photography, Benoît Debie, also worked on Noé's

Irreversible (2002) and Dario Argento's *The Card Player* (2002), and yet earlier on *A Wonderful Love*, the already mentioned short by Du Welz — and here he practices his coldly realistic style to perfection. It is, therefore, as much to Du Welz's credit as it is to Debie's that *Calvaire* is not just a detached surreal nightmare, but also a painfully realistic indication at real-life crimes that recently plagued Belgium, one that depicts the country in a much darker tone than usual.

Vynyan, Du Welz's next project, is — in the director's own words — "about the confrontation of the Western world and the Oriental world"; more precisely, it is about how the inhabitants of the Western world are "sick" because they "refuse to accept death." It appears then, that after having come to terms with *love* in *Calvaire*, Du Welz in now to embrace *death*, which sounds all the more promising that despite hitting it big with his debut, he is unwilling to join the mainstream: *Vynyan* is going to be an independent, low-budget project, so that there is no studio pressure over what the movie is going to look like and how happily it should end. And based on the director's output so far, we guess he hasn't planned too many happy moments for the characters of his upcoming feature.

It's an intense and unpredictable offering for those who loved each excruciating second of Gaspar Noé's *Irreversible*. Except that Fabrice Du Welz, unlike Noé, finds some very black comedy in the bleak subject matter, and even concocts some painful Biblical metaphors on the way. Most importantly, however, *Calvaire* is a desperate cry for love in a world that deems emotions expendable.

Lunacy (Sílení)

DIRECTOR: Jan Svankmajer
CAST: Pavel Liska, Jan Triska, Anna Geislerová, Pavel Nový, Jaroslav Dusek,
Martin Huba, Jiří Krytinař, Stano Danciak, Jan Svankmajer
Czech Republic–Slovakia, 2005

Two great directors were born in Czechoslovakia on September 4, 1934: Juraj Herz and Jan Svankmajer. They both started their careers as specialists in puppetry and animation, but later became interested in horror — a genre that wasn't particularly popular in a country where censors make sure that nothing remotely controversial ever gets to the screens. Herz managed to make one horror masterpiece (1968's *The Cremator*), and after seeing his subsequent films being continually butchered by the censors, he decided to emigrate to Germany. Svankmajer had similar problems: his depiction of life in Czechoslovakia in *Leonardo's Diary* (1972) got him banned from directing for several years, and when the ban was removed he was only allowed to adapt literary texts. This brought him to the stories of Horace Walpole (the short movie adaptation *The Castle of Otranto*, made in 1977) and Edgar Allan Poe (another short, *The Fall of the House of Usher*, in 1981). Then he made *Dimensions of Dialogue* (1982), a surreal short showing, among other things, two human-shaped figures first being passionate and then tearing each other apart; this was Svankmajer's early critique of consumerism, but the censors didn't like it and promptly banned the movie. At the same time, however, it was being shown in other countries and became very successful (it was awarded the Golden Berlin Bear for Best Short Film in 1983), in consequence making Svankmajer better known abroad than he was in his own country. Around this time he also had an artistic affair with MTV, directing two surreal shorts for the station (*Darkness/Light/Darkness* and *Meat Love*, both 1989), as well as shooting a rather spooky music video for Hugh Cornwell's "Another Kind of Love."

Alice (1988), a claymation take on Lewis Carroll's *Alice in Wonderland*, was the director's first feature-length movie. In 1994, after the communist Czechoslovakia turned into a federal democracy (divided into the Czech Republic and the Slovak Republic) and the obsessive censorship was gone, Svankmajer made another feature: *Faust*, based on folk legends as well as the Goethe and Christopher Marlowe versions of the tale. This was another extraordinary accomplishment that blended live action with puppetry and claymation, and only after having made it the director realized how his obsession with food and consumerism sneaked into the movie. "It's funny," recollects Svankmajer in a recent interview, "but when I showed *Faust* to my surrealist group one of them exclaimed, 'For crying out loud, food again,' and I replied 'Where?' as I had not even realized that food was so evident in the film." The themes of food/meat/eating/consumerism were to return in all his later films: *Conspirators of Pleasure* (1996), often regarded as the director's best work, was a story of a group of people looking for

Anna Geislerová (left) and Pavel Liska in Jan Svankmajer's *Lunacy* (2005).

the weirdest ways to satisfy themselves; *Little Otik* (2000; aka *Greedy Guts*) combined live acting and stop-motion techniques to tell a creepy tale of a tree stump coming to life and developing an insatiable appetite. And then there was *Lunacy*, a loose adaptation of the writings of Edgar Allan Poe (*The Premature Burial* and *The System of Dr. Tarr and Dr. Fether*) and the Marquis De Sade.

Lunacy is an ambitious and rewarding piece of work, but it doesn't try to seduce the viewer with laugh-out-loud humor or gratuitous shocks. It's often vague, difficult to watch, repetitive and rather slow-paced. But as soon as you get to the poignant final image, you'll know these two hours of your life were by no means wasted. The choppy plot sees young Jean Berlot (Pavel Liska) returning home after the funeral of his mother. On the way he meets the strange Marquis (Jan Triska), who invites him to his mansion. Since the weather is awful, Jean doesn't feel like going home on foot and accepts. There he is a witness to a blasphemous orgy in which Marquis and his men ridicule God and abuse the innocent Charlotte (Anna Geislerová). Jean lacks the courage to do anything about it, but in the morning decides he's not going to stay at the place a minute longer. Marquis has some tricks up his sleeve and uses them to keep the naïve young man around. Most importantly, he promises Jean to cure his fear of ending up in an insane asylum like his mother did. However, Marquis's cure means facing the fear, and Jean finds himself locked in a very special asylum — one that is being run by the patients.

The movie is regularly interrupted by animated sequences in which tongues, eyeballs, trotters and raw meat perform their own puppet theatre and seem to provide commentary for the live action scenes (in which some characters have lost or are going to lose eyes, tongues or other organs). Marina Warner mentions in her essay "Dream Works" that the severed-but-alive organs play in *Lunacy* "the part of a chorus, appearing to punctuate the unfolding of the plot in a kind of hilarious and horrible variety show"; on the other hand, they also bring additional meaning to the story. "[T]he tongues are wagging with libertine hedonism and excess," writes Warner, "but they are also cut off at the root, and condemned to ineffectual gabbling or vicious mischief-making." Svankmajer vents his obsession with food again and makes *Lunacy* as much a political allegory (the laissez-faire management of the asylum is replaced by an even worse, fanatically authoritarian one) as a critique of consumerism. "I believe that the consumer society is the final stage in civilization," says Svankmajer. "I am not saying that mankind will die out, but we are now watching the consequences of the end of the civilization that we have. Terrorism is nothing more than a consequence of the absolute inequality that we have in this cycle of civilization." And why does he so often resort to gallows humor while depicting serious issues? "Black humor is important," replies the director, "and must remain one of the essences of the civilization. I mean, the Americans are currently dropping bombs on Afghanistan and then immediately afterwards they are dropping food parcels."

This is Svankmajer's most complex film to date, combining all the major themes he's been obsessively dealing with since the 1960s: Poe's projection of the subconscious, de Sade's disrespect for rules and moral boundaries, the abuse of political power, visions of inanimate objects coming to life and of food acting as if it didn't want to be eaten.

Convoluted and with lots of unpleasantness on display, *Lunacy* doesn't lend itself to a smooth viewing, but is a rewarding experience, and is one of cinema's most convincing critiques of the consumer society.

William Winckler's Frankenstein vs. the Creature from Blood Cove

DIRECTOR: William Winckler
CAST: Larry Butler, William Winckler, Corey Marshall, Alison Lees-Taylor,
Gary Canavello, Lawrence Furbish, Dezzirae Ascalon, Rich Knight
USA, 2005

It is enough to look at the title of this film to get a good picture of what you are in for. Not only is the title handsomely long but it immediately triggers our minds to project an odd image of a Boris Karloff–type Monster wrestling a fish-man monster similar to the one we remember from the classic *Creature from the Black Lagoon*. And the idea of these two particular creatures having a fight is surely not an obvious one — an average fan of the Universal horror classics could perhaps think of the Frankenstein Monster wrestling Dracula or knocking-out the Wolf Man, but why would he bother getting his hands on a monster that spends most of its time deep in the water? Well, William Winckler, the mind behind the concept, has the answer for you, right there within the fun 90-minute flick that combines the charm of the aforementioned mon-

Frankenstein's monster (Lawrence Furbish) is brought to life to fight terrorism in *William Winckler's Frankenstein vs. the Creature from Blood Cove* (2005) (© 2005 — William Winckler Prods., Inc. All Rights Reserved).

ster movies, a touch of humor straight out of a Troma production, the lovely awkward-
ness of the first Godzilla films and some gratuitous nudity that has the cheek to pretend it is actually essential to the plot. Doesn't all this sound like something you might
love?

The Frankenstein Monster and the half-fish half-man are brought together by a
genius-madman, Dr. Lazaroff, who is fed up with the never-ending wars all over the
world and the latest acts of terrorism. The solution to this, Dr. Lazaroff thinks, would
be to capture or create an invincible monster and then program it to serve the world
peace. The result of his first experiment turns out to be an uncommonly strong amphibious creature but the doctor fails to program its mind into obedience and the creature
soon escapes from his laboratory. Undeterred by the lack of success with the fish-man,
the scientist decides the easiest way to continue his experiments would be to, well, find
the grave of Frankenstein's Monster, dig it out, bring it to life and then let it battle
both world terrorism and the hungry amphibious creature. Dr. Lazaroff leaves for mysterious Shellvania together with his assistants Dr. Ula Foranti, whose scientific obsession equals Lazaroff's own, and a fisherman named Salisbury, a poor sod who sports
extensive facial scars and a blind eye — reminders of an unfortunate meeting with the
fish-man. The three characters find Frankenstein Monster's grave without much
difficulty but while digging they are attacked by a Wolf Man who resides within the
woods surrounding the cemetery. The beast's cameo appearance ends when Dr. Lazaroff,
clearly a man prepared for anything to happen, fires some silver bullets at the Wolf
Man's hairy chest.

Frankenstein's monster faces the creature (Corey Marshall) in *William Winckler's Frankenstein vs. the Creature from Blood Cove* (© 2005 — William Winckler Prods. Inc. All Rights
Reserved).

After being exhumed, Frankenstein's Monster is transported to the doctor's laboratory, quickly kicked into life (with the movie wasting no time for complex scientific explanations), and finally "brainwashed" into cooperation with the U.S. army. However, as soon as the Monster sees a woman who reminds him of his long-lost Bride, the brainwash ceases to work; now the monster's only aim is to win back the Bride, even if this means killing off everyone else around. And that's not all! Let's not forget that the amphibious creature is still spreading terror on a nearby beach and waiting anxiously for a violent *mano a mano* with the resurrected Frankenstein's Monster.

One thing you obviously cannot accuse the scriptwriter of is a lack of ideas and plot twists. Every several minutes there is something new and unexpected happening. The plot refuses to settle on simply spoofing well-worn horror set pieces and the viewers cannot even start guessing how the warped mind of William Winckler is going to end this enjoyable mess. And he does have a clear idea what to do with the ending, you can be sure about that.

The movie's links to the uncertainties of life at the beginning of the 21st century are fairly obvious even if the director repeats in interviews that his "whole concept of entertainment is escapism"; most importantly, the war with terrorism is mentioned as the reason for bringing the monsters to life, but then there is also the panicky decision to make a "better monster" in order to destroy the previous one, and a rather unambiguous depiction of how difficult it is to have a powerful weapon and always use it in the right way.

If *William Winckler's Frankenstein vs. the Creature from Blood Cove* is not an immaculate homage to horror films of the old days, it is only because some common faults of independent cinema are visible here and there. The quality of acting varies from very good (the inspired performances of Larry Butler and Alison Lees-Taylor as the two obsessed scientists) to highly annoying (Gary Canavello pushes the boundaries of overacting in the role of a super-gay makeup man held hostage by Dr. Lazaroff). The creature costumes look very impressive most of the time, partly because they were well designed and made, and partly because Matthias Schubert's great black-and-white photography makes them truly alive and reminiscent of all the classic monster suits we love so much. A pity then that the scenes of showdowns between Frankenstein's Monster and the fish-like creature look like a slo-mo wrestling match where no one even pretends to be hurt. However, with the help of Mel Lewis' distinguished score and Schubert's photography, these scenes always emanate the atmosphere of the old Godzilla films, so even here the viewers cannot feel they were totally let down.

The nudity seems to be the most controversial element of the film. First of all, it is something that does not belong to any type of films William Winckler aims to honor here; even in the Hammer horror films, the nudity was milder and better rooted in the plot. Secondly, each nude scene is clearly gratuitous, no matter how much the makers were trying to conceal it; after all, what we get in these scenes are not just glimpses of the girls taking their clothes off, with the rest of the story being developed in the background, but always a full strip-tease with the plot paused, waiting for the last piece of lingerie to fall to the ground. Whether this is the movie's vice or not is, of course, up to each single viewer, and it must be said that the three girls who get the nude scenes — Selena Silver, Tera Cooley and Carla Harvey — are definitely not unpleasant to look at.

Though *William Winckler's Frankenstein vs. The Creature from Blood Cove* is hardly a flawless picture, it boasts enough energy, good ideas and old-fashioned charm to win the hearts of all those already in love with retro-horror. And most probably it will leave them wanting more of this type of fun, too — *William Winckler's Transparent Man vs. the Undead Mummy*, perhaps?

It's an unforgettable mixture of elements from the *Godzilla* films, Universal monster movies and crazy horror-comedies from Troma. The superb photography and fine costumes make this much more than just an average homage, but the viewers who can't stand gratuitous nudity are advised to stay away.

BIBLIOGRAPHY

Alexander, John. *Films of David Lynch*. London: New Holland, 1993.

Ashbrook, John. *Brian De Palma*. Harpenden: Pocket Essentials, 2005.

Assayas, Olivier, and Stig Björkman. *Conversation avec Bergman*. Paris: Cahiers du Cinéma, 2006.

Austin, Bruce A. *Immediate Seating: A Look at Movie Audiences*. Belmont: Wadsworth, 1988.

Bradley, Doug. *Sacred Monsters: Behind the Mask of the Horror Actor*. London: Titan Books, 1996.

Brenez, Nicole. *Abel Ferrara*. Champaign: University of Illinois Press, 2006.

Campbell, Bruce. *If Chins Could Kill: Confessions of a B Movie Actor*. New York: LA Weekly Books, 2002.

Carroll, Noël. *The Philosophy of Horror*. London: Routledge, 1990.

Chibnall, Steve. *Making Mischief: The Cult Films of Pete Walker*. Guildford: FAB Press, 1998.

_____, and Julian Petley, eds. *British Horror Cinema*. London: Routledge, 2007.

Clover, Carol J. *Men, Women and Chainsaws: Gender in the Modern Horror Film*. London: BFI, 1992.

Creed, Barbara. *The Monstrous-Feminine: Film, Feminism, Psychoanalysis*. London: Routledge, 1993.

Curry, Christopher Wayne. *A Taste of Blood: The Films of Herschell Gordon Lewis*. Washington, D.C.: Creation Books, 1999.

Davies, Steven Paul. *A–Z of Cult Films and Film-Makers*. London: Batsford, 2001.

Dendle, Peter. *The Zombie Movie Encyclopedia*. Jefferson: McFarland, 2000.

Durys, Elżbieta, and Konrad Klejsa. *Kino Amerykańskie: Twórcy*. Kraków: Rabid, 2006.

Dworkin, Susan. *Double De Palma*. New York: Newmarket Press, 1984.

Eco, Umberto. *Travels in Hyperreality*. London: Picador, 1986.

Fenton, Harry, and David Flint, eds. *Ten Years of Terror: British Films of the 1970s*. London: FAB Press, 2001.

Grant, Barry Keith, ed. *Planks of Reason: Essays on the Horror Film*. Metuchen: Scarecrow, 1984.

Grant, Michael. *The Modern Fantastic: The Films of David Cronenberg*. Trowbridge: Flicks Books, 2000.

Harper, Graeme. *Unruly Pleasures: The Cult Film and Its Critics*. London: FAB Press, 2000.

Hawkins, Joan. *Cutting Edge: Art-Horror and the Horrific Avant-Garde*. Minneapolis: University of Minnesota Press, 2000.

Hoberman, J., and Jonathan Rosenbaum. *Midnight Movies*. New York: Da Capo, 1991.

Humphries, Reynold. *American Horror: An Introduction*. Edinburgh: Edinburgh University Press, 2002.

Hutchings, Peter. *Hammer and Beyond: The British Horror Film*. Manchester: Manchester University Press, 1993.

_____. *The Horror Film*. Harlow: Pearson Longman, 2004.

_____. *Terence Fisher*. Manchester: Manchester University Press, 2002.

Jancovich, Mark. *Rational Fears: American Horror in the 1950s*. Manchester: Manchester University Press, 1996.

_____, and Antonio Lazaro Reboll, Julian Stringer, Andrew Willis, eds. *Defining Cult Movies: The Cultural Politics of Oppositional Taste*. Manchester: Manchester University Press, 2003.

Johnson, Jeff. *Pervert in the Pulpit: Morality in the Works of David Lynch.* Jefferson: McFarland, 2004.

Johnstone, Nick. *Abel Ferrara: The King of New York.* New York: Omnibus Press, 2000.

Kael, Pauline. *I Lost It at the Movies: Film Writings, 1954–65.* New York: Marion Boyars, 1994.

Kaleta, Kenneth. *Hal Hartley: Kino Prawdziwej Fikcji i Filmy Potencjalne.* Gdańsk: Słowo/obraz Terytoria, 2007.

Karney, Robyn, ed. *Cinema Year By Year.* London: DK, 2006.

Kerekes, David. *Sex, Murder, Art: The Films of Jörg Buttgereit.* Manchester: Headpress, 1998.

_____, ed. *Creeping Flesh: The Horror Fantasy Film Book.* Manchester: Headpress, 2003.

King, Stephen. *Danse Macabre.* London: Warner Books, 2000.

Kołodyński, Andrzej. *Dziedzictwo wyobraźni.* Warszawa: Alfa, 1989.

_____. *Film Grozy.* Warszawa: Wydawnictwa Artystyczne i Filmowe, 1970.

Krogh, Daniel. *The Amazing Herschell Gordon Lewis and His World of Exploitation Films.* Albany: Fantaco Enterprises, 1983.

Loska, Krzysztof, and Andrzej Pitrus. *David Cronenberg: Rozpad ciała, rozpad gatunku.* Kraków: Rabid, 2003.

Lowenstein, Adam. *Shocking Representation: Historical Trauma, National Cinema, and the Modern Horror Film.* New York: Columbia University Press, 2005.

Mathijs, Ernest, and Xavier Mendik. *Alternative Europe: Eurotrash and Exploitation Cinema Since 1945.* London: Wallflower Press, 2004.

_____, and _____, eds. *The Cult Film Reader.* Open University Press, 2007.

McDonagh, Maitland. *Broken Mirrors, Broken Minds: The Dark Dreams of Dario Argento.* London: Sun Tavern Fieds, 1991.

Morrison, James. *Passport to Hollywood: Hollywood Films, European Directors.* Albany: SUNY Press, 1998

Newman, Kim. *Nightmare Movies.* London: Bloomsbury, 1988.

Paszylk, Bartłomiej. *Leksykon Filmowego Horroru.* Michałów-Grabina: Latarnik, 2006.

Polański, Roman. *Roman.* Warszawa: Wydawnictwo Polonia, 1989.

Puchalski, Stephen. *Slimetime: A Guide to Sleazy, Mindless Movies.* London: Headpress, 2002.

Rhodes, Gary Don. *White Zombie: Anatomy of a Horror Film.* Jefferson: McFarland, 2001.

Russell, Jamie. *Book of the Dead: The Complete History of Zombie Cinema.* London: FAB Press, 2005.

Schaefer, Eric. *Bold! Daring! Shocking! True! A History of Exploitation Films, 1919–59.* Durham: Duke University Press, 1999.

Skal, David J. *Hollywood Gothic: The Tangled Web of Dracula from Novel to Stage to Screen.* New York: Faber and Faber, 2004.

_____. *The Monster Show: A Cultural History of Horror.* New York: Penguin, 1993.

Slade, Michael. *Ghoul.* London: Star, 1988.

Slater, Jay. *Eaten Alive! Italian Cannibal and Zombie Movies.* London: Plexus, 2005.

Telotte, J.P. ed. *The Cult Film Experience: Beyond All Reason.* Austin: University of Texas Press, 1991.

Thrower, Stephen Edward. *Beyond Terror: Films of Lucio Fulci.* London: FAB Press, 2001.

Tombs, Pete. *Mondo Macabro.* New York: St. Martin's Griffin, 1998.

Tudor, Andrew. *Monsters and Mad Scientists: A Cultural History of the Horror Film.* Oxford: Blackwell, 1989.

Weaver, Tom. *Attack of the Monster Movie Makers: Interviews with 20 Genre Giants.* Jefferson: McFarland, 1994.

Weinstock, Jeffrey. *Cultographies: The Rocky Horror Picture Show.* London: Wallflower Press, 2007.

Winter, Douglas E. *The Dark Fantastic. Clive Barker: The Authorized Biography.* London: Harper-Collins, 2001.

INDEX